Audie —

Never grew up!

Growing Up Simple

AN IRREVERENT LOOK AT KIDS IN THE 1950s

George Arnold

George Arnold

www. CIAcats. com

WITH FOREWORD BY
Liz Carpenter

EAKIN PRESS ⱹ Austin, Texas

Dedication

—To my wife, Mary, and my brother, Jim. Neither of whom is as strange as I am.

—To the principal *In-Betweeners* whose creativity made these stories worth telling—Don, Jack, Kenny, Lee. If any of you is not real, let me know right away.

—To Andy. We miss you, Bud.

—To *In-Betweeners* everywhere. Strange, yet quality, to a person. The smallest and best generation of the 20th century.

Contents

The Way We Were

An Introduction by LIZ CARPENTER

George Arnold invited me to write an introduction to this book—*Growing Up Simple*. He felt I would understand simple living because I grew up in small-town Texas—Salado and Belton. As a child, I experienced simple delights—feeding the baby goats with a bottle, riding a tame mare from my grandmother's house to the post office for the mail, feeling the wind blow through my hair in our Model T Ford as we drove from Salado to Belton. I have written about that now and then.

This author pretested his text on twenty-four readers from across the U.S. and received twenty-one answers with positive reactions.

One of the values of George's story of his days living the simple life is that he sets you reflecting on your own, remembering a world that has become overpowered by meetings, conferences, cell telephones, and e-mail—all those time-taking events which we add to our lives to fill every minute and crowd out all else.

I wasn't far into his chapters of hitchhiking, fixing broken cars, attending summer revival services when preachers could cure your ailments on the spot, when suddenly the words to a song—"The Way We Were"—kept running through my mind.

> "...*Can it be that it was all so simple then* ...
> *or has time rewritten every line?*"

Our lives are frequently being rewritten by events, most recently by the twin-tower explosion of September 11, 2001. We are told, and we are convinced, because we hear its staccato message on the media, that life will be forever changed for us—we who are lucky enough to live in an America of freedom and liberty.

To me, that is why George Arnold's book is significant. He turns our thoughts back to growing up in an uncluttered time and place that we ourselves have complicated or permitted to be complicated by others. Must we let September 11 forever plague us with its ugly images and thrust of fear? We need to come out of it, and maybe we can.

Arnold's style is a conversational method of carrying you along with occasional "you sees" and "we figureds"—inclusive expressions you haven't heard since you went back home. They set me thinking of the way I was and missing that slower pace.

What it also did for me and what it will do for you, I believe, is to make you pause and wonder if some of the "busyness" of life can't be dropped. It made me re-read some of my Christmas letters with their tedious and tiny details and see them in a new light:

> *"We took the baby to visit her grandma and grandpa who are celebrating 60 years of marriage. She dipped her toes into Lake Michigan with her 86 year old great grandpa and more than a coupla' times napped on her grandmother's lap. Watching the love and interaction across four generations was special."*

Before George's manuscript came, I would have trashed that letter... but somehow I saved it all these months to read again to myself and others.

It brings back the refrain of that song:

> *"... If we had the chance to do it all again,*
> *tell me, would we, could we?"*

I think not. And yet, there is a calming to the frenzy of life today in remembering those "misty watercolor memories." I thank George Arnold's book for suggesting we can.

Author's Notes

The characters in this book are *really* characters. So much so, in fact, that I have a lot of trouble remembering who are the real people and who I just made up. The real people, whoever they may be, are weird enough to be among the fictional, anyhow. Truth is, after all, stranger than fiction.

Right?

Both Harry Truman and General MacArthur are real, I think. And F-86s, too. So am I. Sometimes, anyway. So if you think you see yourself in here somewhere, great! But you might be somebody else. Thankfully, though, I'm likely not you. And you never are me. Be grateful. Not that it matters. I mean, who cares, anyway?

Most of the stories in the book are somewhat true. Some of the stories are mostly made up. One (or two, maybe) is a complete and outrageous lie. Totally the product of my own strangely firing neurons.

For the *Bean Counters* among you, look at it this way: Eighty-five percent of the book is at least half true. Ten percent, or thereabouts, is a total pack of lies. And the other five percent came to me in a dream while driving a school bus somewhere between East Jesus and West Overshoe.

Go figure. That's what *Bean Counters* do.

Isn't it?

Prologue

My 30-plus years' experience with consumer research led me to become intrigued with a demographic group that consistently displayed irreverent, if not outlandish, tendencies in study after study of attitudes and usage.

This group, a half generation born between 1939 and 1947, has isolated itself so thoroughly with U.S. market researchers that it has been given a name and identity by psychologists, sociologists, and researchers.

It is called the *In-Betweeners*.

The name derives from the fact that members of the group were born between the Great Depression and the pig-in-a-python known as *Baby Boomers*. The group is considered contrarian. Its members tend to display, in market research studies, remarkably similar tendencies, but tendencies unlike any other demographic group of the 20th century.

We, the *In-Betweeners*, being the contrarians that we are, have a name for the above-mentioned psychologists, sociologists, and researchers. We call them *Bean Counters*.

While the phenomenon is real (and perhaps exciting to the *Bean Counters*), the subject, to the rest of the world, is a big yawn. Boring, boring, boring.

Undaunted, in *Growing Up Simple*, we have found a fun (and funny) way to isolate this group of contrarians and report them to the world. Our premise, which will stand unchallenged until some boring *Bean Counter* decides he or she has nothing better to do than challenge it, is simple: *In-Betweeners* are what they are because they all grew up in the placid 1950s, a decade totally different from any other in the 20th century. In a laid-back, happy-go-lucky, black-and-white world of Donna Reed, Loretta Young, and Beaver Cleaver. The only real thing we had to fear while growing up was the ever-present danger of contracting polio.

In-Betweeners will be ready, if the day of the *Bean Counter* ever comes. Because this book prepares them, with one hilarious escapade after another, to defeat the likes of these green-visored and garter-sleeved *Bean Counters*, dratted Church Ladies, pompous politicians, sanctimonious executives, racist bigots, mean and hateful rich people, and even the radar guns of our uniformed protectors of the peace and tranquility.

In-Betweeners, you see, don't believe in any of these types.

And now they are ready for almost anyone to try to make them color within the lines.

Fat chance!

Growing Up Simple is a tongue-in-cheek voyage from kindergarten through high school—a trip made by a small group of innocent pranksters determined to save the world from itself. It is their story, the story of five young overachievers with the time and freedom to be hellishly creative while learning life's important lessons. A story told with humor and sensitivity through a series of sixteen chronological vignettes, each a virtual stand-alone short story.

It is the story of five young *In-Betweeners* whose sometimes almost unbelievable hijinks give the reader an unfiltered glimpse of life in the 1950s, a simpler time—a time when it was still possible to *Grow Up Simple*.

—GEORGE ARNOLD

CHAPTER 1

It Was a Dark and Stormy Night

AUSTIN, 1947

Life's first indelible lesson came upon me at the age of four and a half one cold, rainy, foggy January night in the parking lot of a Safeway store at West Sixth Street and Lamar Boulevard in Austin, Texas.

I suppose Freud might have called it "a cathartic impression with lifelong implications." I wouldn't argue with that diagnosis. I can still remember it today, fifty-five years later, as if it occurred last night. I've thought of it often and been influenced by it mightily over these five decades.

Our family—my father, mother, older brother, Jim, and myself—had just recently moved to Austin from Missouri, where Mom, my brother and I were all born. Younger sister Mary would not come along until early 1948. She and my father, who was born in Dallas, always claimed to be the only real Texans in the family.

After the war, my father had decided to give up dual careers teaching school and farming a piece of the old family homestead outside Smithville, just north of Kansas City. We had stuffed everything we could either into, or tied atop, our old black 1933 Plymouth coupe. Like the Okies a generation earlier

YOU CRANK IT. NO, YOU CRANK IT!

George and Jim take one last ride on the family's Farmall Cub before giving up farming for good and heading south to Texas.

trekking to California, we headed south to Texas and Austin, where my dad would take a temporary job teaching sixth grade at Pleasant Hill Elementary School while he waited to be called to begin training as a State Trooper, called Highway Patrolmen in those days.

My Uncle George, who was named for my Grandfather George on my father's side, and for whom I was named (naming wasn't an art in our family), had already graduated from his training and was wearing a badge and gun and driving around in a new black-and-white Ford in the little hamlet of Boerne, a German community northwest of San Antonio.

Austin, like most places after four years of World War II, was painfully short on places to live. When we first arrived, we had to settle, for a few months, in a converted tourist cabin, an early-day roadside motel. I remember it had but one hanging light bulb into which we had screwed a double socket so we could have light and still be able to listen to John Cameron Swayze deliver the news and to *The Shadow* cloud men's minds (so they could not see him) on our little Philco radio.

It was a spooky place, and I missed our old farm and all the snow we would have had to play in back home in Missouri. Listening to *Gangbusters* and *The Shadow*, I always situated myself so I could see both doors—just in case one of the bad guys, or even Lamont Cranston, *The Shadow* himself, was lurking around outside.

But by this January night, we had just moved from the old tourist cabin into a little rock house on South Congress Avenue, otherwise known as U.S. 81, the old San Antonio Highway. It was less than a mile south of Pleasant Hill Elementary School, so my dad could walk to work every morning. The site's in the middle of a sprawling city today, but back then it was out in the country. There was but one building of any sort between our new home and the school—a tiny little store where I regularly traded in ten soft drink bottles I had picked up along the highway for a fresh Grapette.

Grapette was one of the few things I had found that I really liked about this new place. It was sweet and syrupy, and if you worked it just right, you could make that small bottle last a couple of hours until you had picked up another ten bottles. I was the first local recycler, for sure.

My new home was lonely. There was nobody to play with all day long. My brother went off to school on a big, yellow bus every morning, so I didn't even have him to pester. To satisfy a four-year-old's natural inclination to socialize, I had to invent imaginary playmates. That is, they were imaginary to everybody but me. I could see them. I could touch them. Heck, I could even smell them.

As four-year-olds are naturally curious, I remember noticing that almost all the boys here in this new land of Texas were called by two names—Joe Bob, Billy James, Sam Boy. So I named one imaginary playmate John Joe. The other was Lady Archibald, an

OLD, BEAT UP, AND UGLY!
The car, not various members of the family. We piled into this overloaded 1933 Plymouth coupe for the drive to Austin in 1946. It would be more than a year before the new Ford we had ordered, back in Missouri, could be delivered.

idea I had picked up from the radio drama *Our Gal Sunday*. We talked, we played games, we demolished red ant mounds together, my invisible playmates and I, and we had us some fun.

Our fun, though, was often at the expense of other members of the family. My mother was mortified when one of the "Church Ladies" would drop by and I would be wandering about, alone, carrying on a three-way conversation. Word was getting out that Mrs. Arnold had a little boy who wasn't quite "all there," if you know what I mean.

I found that "Church Ladies" most often wore gloves and hats with little veils that covered their foreheads. I thought maybe they were covering up pimples along their hairlines. They puckered up their mouths like they'd been eating persimmons all day, and they clucked their tongues a lot and talked real slow. If they thought I was simple, I had my own four-year-old's blasphemous thoughts about them. I've noticed that, to this day, "Church Ladies" haven't changed much. Still puckering. Still clucking. Still messing with kids' minds.

Sometimes I would even dress up like one of my invisible friends. John Joe was easy. Since he was a boy, like me, he had plenty of wardrobe from which to choose when I became him. His odd quirk was that he always wore all his clothes inside-out. So when I was John Joe's persona, I needed help with that last tough step, closing an inside-out zipper. Try it sometime. It's not easy.

Of course, I invariably wanted to be John Joe when my mother was entertaining another of those dratted "Church Ladies." I would pop in to interrupt their coffee sipping and cookie munching long enough to ask my mother, "Would you please help John Joe zip up his pants?" Sometimes if I really wanted to startle a "Church Lady," I would add, "Lady Archibald doesn't like him going around with his pee-pee hanging out, you know."

I could always count on seeing the "Church Lady" of the day roll her eyes up into her veil, slowly shake her head, pucker up her little mouth, and let forth two or three clucks. Mom just turned red. She had given up telling people about my make-believe playmates for fear they would think her own genes the reason for her little boy's unfortunate and multiple afflictions.

The business of family embarrassment at the antics of me and my invisible playmates came to a head one day when I, cross-dressed as Lady Archibald in one of my mother's old dresses and hats, complete with "Church Lady" veil, met my brother's school bus in the afternoon and proceeded to board and entertain about thirty of his best friends in Lady Archibald's peculiar falsetto voice. I was Tiny Tim before Tiny Tim was cool.

That day was the first time my brother tried to kill me.

He demanded of my mother and father that they put a stop to my little play group. Or just send me off to some institution. He railed on about how hard it is to make new friends in a new place, and how this appearance by Lady Archibald had ruined his chances and set him up to be the laughingstock of his school.

I allowed as how he didn't need any help being a laughingstock, although I hadn't a clue what a laughingstock might be; I thought of the laughing cow jumping over the moon in one of my storybooks.

In my own defense, I said I was doing nothing more than any "Church Lady" might naturally do on any given day, and, further, I was disappointed that he hadn't introduced Lady Archibald to his friends on the bus. He had been thoughtless and impolite, in my estimation.

Even at four years old, I was capable of holding my own in an adult-level verbal disagreement. My motto was, "Always seize the initiative."

Well, as you might imagine, my mother took my side of the brouhaha, and my father took my brother's side. Dad and Jim had some funny, mysterious notions about cross-dressing that meant nothing to me. And, so the war was on. It lasted until a Solomon-like compromise could be reached. To wit: John Joe and Lady Archibald were allowed to remain in the family. However, in the future, John Joe was to wear his clothes right-side-out, and Lady Archibald was never to go outside.

I protested that it would be impossible to identify John Joe if he wore his clothes properly and that Lady Archibald was the best red ant hill destroyer, ever. "If she can't blow up red ant hills," I pleaded, "she will be very, very sad."

My protest was a complete sham, however, since I secretly considered not having to kill off my invisible friends, *in toto,* a diplomatic victory. And I vowed two things: that I would seek vengeance on my brother for messing in my social life; and that Lady Archibald, if not permitted to go outside, would concoct an indoor plan so diabolical as to cause all "Church Ladies" on the face of the earth to cease and desist drinking up our supply of coffee, eating my cookies, and otherwise puckering and clucking indoors at our house.

Bring on the "Church Ladies." Lady Archibald was ready to attack!

I wanted to tell you about the time I dropped the chocolate pies, utterly destroying a half day of work by my mother, and how I managed to blame it all on John Joe, so real had my imaginary friends become. Or about the time my mother locked Lady Archibald in a linen closet upon the sudden and unexpected appearance of yet another blasted "Church Lady," and why my mother severely regretted that lock-up later.

But these stories and more will have to wait for another time and venue, since I promised you, some pages back, the story of the Freudian cathartic impression with lifelong implications, experienced in a Safeway parking lot at West Sixth Street and Lamar Boulevard.

With apologies to decent writers, everywhere, I must start off by telling you it was, in fact, *a dark and stormy night* that January in 1947. We were experiencing what we called "ground fog." That is, the fog was so thick you couldn't see a horsefly if it landed on the tip of your nose. And it was raining, the kind of a cold rain that always caused the windows inside our funny-looking old Plymouth to fog up from our breath.

It must have been payday for teachers since my parents always seemed to go to the grocery store on payday. My brother had decided to stay home; trips to the grocery store weren't exactly exciting for ten-year-olds. But for me, trapped as I was all day, every day, with just John Joe and Lady Archibald and the occasional "Church Lady" for entertainment, any chance to escape the small compound between our rock house on South Congress Avenue and the little store where I traded my empty bottles for a full and cold Grapette was an adventure.

So I had opted to go.

There were always interesting people at the Safeway. Since we didn't have a lot of money, my parents were careful shoppers, taking their time to complete the family provisioning. That gave me the leisure to watch people and try to imagine where they would go when they, too, finished their shopping. It was not unlike having imaginary friends, except I never told anyone about this particular game. I had suffered too much grief over the other.

My parents had finished their shopping, and I had dispatched at least a dozen anonymous shoppers to new, and far better, lives. We loaded the groceries into the trunk of the old Plymouth, and my father started slowly to back out of our parking space.

On my knees, looking backward, I peered out the oval back window into the dense fog just in time to see the taillights of a car exactly opposite us, backing out of its space, too.

Before I could sound the alarm, there was a crunch and a jolt as the two cars met, rear bumper to rear bumper, in no man's land—the middle of the parking lot.

It was just a love tap, really, and even a four-year-old, given the sturdiness of bumpers made of real steel in those days, knew not much damage, if any, had been done.

The driver of the other car began to honk frantically. Angrily, it seemed to me, as if we had encroached, somehow, on private territory.

My dad pulled the old Plymouth forward to let the other driver back on out. But the frantic honking persisted. We waited. The honking continued. We waited some more, speculating that the other driver might not be a very nice person, making a federal case out of a non-incident.

Finally, when the other car's horn continued its frantic blasts, my dad hopped out, and I hopped out right behind him.

Then I saw it. The other car was a shiny new Cadillac. Black it was, and half a city block long. It was not even scratched, and it was beautiful.

Still thinking to help in some way, my father approached the driver's door. As he got close, the door swung open and a well-dressed woman considerably older than my father stepped out and began shouting. She was furious. And she was way out of line.

"You trailer trash ran into my car! I was backing out first, and that old piece of junk comes barreling out and runs into me! I wish they wouldn't let trash like you even come to this store!"

Then came the telling, and chilling, exclamation: "Decent people, people who have money, aren't safe from you riff-raff!"

That was it! This woman was a "Church Lady" on steroids. She had to be silenced! And then punished, severely!

Equating decency with being well-to-do was unacceptable to me, even at four years of age.

I charged toward her, head down and eyes shooting flames.

My dad intercepted me, turned me around, and led me back to our Plymouth, which I saw as old and beat-up and ugly for the very first time. He never said a word to the raving "Church Lady-Rich Woman."

Still furious, I asked, "Why didn't you let me hit her? She was mean."

My dad said two things that stuck with me. "First," he said, "a man never hits a woman. That is absolutely wrong. And, second, remember this, son: it is not possible to humiliate a person who has pride. And we are proud. We're not poor. And we're certainly not rich. But that woman, for all her money and her new Cadillac, has a lot more problems than we do, believe me."

Strangely enough, one of us—either John Joe, Lady Archibald, or me—got it. We understood. And I remember it to this day.

But I was still righteously angry. I said one more thing, and that was the end of this first cathartic impression with lifelong implications. I said, "When I get big, I'm going to be rich and have two Cadillacs. And I'm going to be nice to people."

That ridiculous experience of being unfairly tongue-lashed on a cold, rainy, foggy night in a Safeway parking lot by a self-righteous, monied, hate-filled old woman drove me to succeed. To make more money. To actually own two Cadillacs (both of which were among the worst of the twenty-five or so new cars I have had). To share my money with others less fortunate. And never to talk down to another human being.

I often think of that poor, rich, old woman, and I wish I could thank her. That chance encounter had more impact on my life, for the good, than she could ever have imagined.

Even today, I would just like to stick my tongue out at her, and utter, "Nyah, nyah, nyah-nyah-nyah! Ninny-ninny, boo-boo!"

Life's Lessons Learned:

- *A man never hits a woman.*
- *You cannot humiliate a person who has pride. You will surely only humiliate yourself.*
- *Having money or a new Cadillac doesn't automatically make one a decent human being. In fact, decency and riches are completely unrelated, best I can tell.*
- *It's better to have a lot of money than to have not enough money, just as long as you're willing to share some of it.*
- *When it comes to parking lot duels, a Cadillac ain't shucks to a long-bed, extended-cab, Ford F-250 4X4 with a big, black brush guard in the front and a massive trailer hitch in the back.*

CHAPTER 2

You're Too Little

UVALDE, 1948

My troubles with rebellious, incorrigible behavior began the afternoon of January 22, 1948. About 3:48 P.M., as I remember. It was cold and snowing. Not real snow, three feet deep, like we used to get back on our farm in Missouri, but a couple of inches of wet stuff that thrilled the Central Texans who rarely saw any snow at all.

That was when my younger sister was born at Seton Hospital in Austin.

She wasn't really the cause of my two-year reign of terror. In fact, I liked her. She was small. She smelled like Johnson's baby powder all the time. She was cute, and I had fun playing with her, along with John Joe and Lady Archibald. They liked her, too. She was funny from day one. In fact, she still is one of the funniest people I know.

No, it was not her fault that I suddenly became, to quote Red Skelton, who came to us out of that same little Philco radio, the "mean widdle kid." But I did become that "mean widdle kid" the instant she was born.

Already I have told you that naming was not an art in my family. We were woefully lacking in creativity when it came to names. My older brother was a "Junior," named precisely for my father. I was named for my grandfather and uncle. And, so, it seemed quite natural that the new baby would be named for somebody I knew. Sure enough, my parents named her Mary. That was my mother's name.

The real reason I immediately went from being Mrs. Arnold's "not-quite-all-there" little son (in the eyes of every Church Lady I had ever encountered) to "that little monster" (to every Church Lady I would encounter over the next couple of years) was that I was no longer the baby of the family. All the attention that used to go to me now shifted immediately to that cute little baby girl. I was left, alone, in her dust.

Not only was it impossible to compete with her, but even trying turned into a lost cause that led to five or six spankings a day and the promise of reform school if I didn't straighten up.

I knew what school was, but of reform school I knew nothing. Jim explained it all to me in terms so grotesque that, to this day, I believe his explanation was his second attempt to kill me.

Almost at once after little Mary was born, I began to seek my lost attention in evil ways. My thinking was, "Push, push, push. Get ever more radical in your shenanigans until your parents start to pay attention to you once again."

As you might expect, my plan initially had the opposite effect. Of course, my parents were not too bright to not see my problem, but they had themselves a little girl. After two scruffy boys, she was the household novelty. And I felt like dog poop.

A month or so after the baby was born, my father finished Highway Patrol training, and we packed up and moved to his first assignment—Uvalde, in southwest Texas. It was a long drive west of San Antonio, which was the closest big city. It was close to the Mexican border. John Joe and Lady Archibald did not move with us. They stayed in Austin, and I gradually lost contact with them.

We moved into a duplex in town, the other side of which was inhabited by the structure's owner, Mrs. Martin. I immediately feared she might be a Church Lady because her favorite phrase was, "Praise the Lord, and pass the potatoes." She must have said that twenty-five times a day. For a while I thought that was all she could say, as if she were some kind of underachieving parrot.

Not everybody had telephones in those days, especially in little out-of-the-way places like Uvalde. Because of my father's occupation as protector of the peace, we had to have a phone twenty-four hours a day. So the phone company promptly installed an eight-party line. Our ring was two-longs and a short. Really.

Mrs. Martin was a lummox of a woman who, because of her girth and general slovenliness, wore muumuus before anyone ever heard of a muumuu. That challenged me, in my new little-monster mode, to try to see what she had on under that tent, kind of like you would wonder what was under a hula skirt or a kilt. There was nothing lascivious about it. I was just curious what such a huge butt might look like.

She didn't have a telephone. When she saw the phone repairman string a wire to our side of the hovel, she came rushing over to congratulate us on having it. Of course, the first words out of her mouth were "Praise the Lord, and pass the potatoes. You've got a telephone!" as she stared at the black thing hanging on the wall with a hand crank on one side.

Thereafter, she frequented our side, always with some lame excuse that eventually led to her use of our phone to call one of her equally obnoxious girlfriends and chat for an hour or so until Sadie, the local operator, would shoo her off the line so one of the other seven who shared it could receive, or make, a call.

Her uninvited cohabitation and frequent use of our phone led to having her around way too much. Although she was far too sloppy to be a classic Church Lady, I found her equally objectionable, and I did nothing to hide my lack of enthusiasm for her presence. And, still, I wondered what such an enormous butt looked like.

One day, while she was talking, "Yada, yada, yada," to one of her cronies, she caught me looking up her dress. "Just a second, hold on, Mabel. What're you lookin' at, boy?" she quizzed me directly.

Having just been punished for the tenth time that week for making up big lies, I answered quite honestly. "I just am wondering what such an enormous butt looks like," I said to her.

"Mabel, I'm going to have to hang off now." She always said "hang off" instead of hang up.

"You're a very mean little boy," she said to me. "I think you're going to be a prevert."

With that, she stomped off in search of my mother to report

my disgusting behavior. That conversation ended with her demand that we would have to move, as she would not live in such close proximity to such a devious, little "prevert."

"Praise the Lord and pass the potatoes, that little hellion may be peeping in my windows at night." She went home and never again set foot in our side of the house.

We did move very soon thereafter. My parents had already been looking for another place to live because of Mrs. Martin's frequent uninvited intrusions, constant use of our telephone, and her propensity to wake up the baby twice a day. My mother's fear of a confrontation made moving a better option than simply telling Mrs. Martin not to come over so much. I didn't get it.

For once, though, I was not punished for my actions. Rather, I even got a smidgen of positive attention when my parents actually laughed at my prank and my older brother congratulated me for chasing off "that old sow," as he called her.

In April of that year, it snowed in Uvalde. Now, snow in that part of Texas is as rare as teats on a boar hog, as we used to say. Not only did it snow, it *really* snowed. More than a foot of light, dry powdery snow. We broke out the sled we had brought from Missouri, and we were the kings of the hill. Nobody in Uvalde had a sled. Nobody in Uvalde had ever seen a sled, except maybe in the moving pictures.

Of course, Uvalde, like much of West Texas, was mostly flat as a pancake. There were no serious hills on which to properly exercise a *bona fide*, big-time sled. We even made snow ice cream and taught some of the luckier local boys how to write their names in yellow in the snow. It only lasted two days, and then we were back to being the new kids in town, but with a little more respect from the others.

That summer, when five-year-olds around the world were learning to swim, we were in the midst of a total drought. The Frio River stopped flowing. Dried up and turned to just another rocky gash on the landscape. The one local municipal pool was not filled for the summer season. What water we had was for drinking and bathing, period. I didn't mind so much because I could usually talk my mother into letting me go two or three days with just a swipe of a washcloth to get the dust off my feet before getting into bed. Although there was no place around Uvalde where a June bug could drown, let alone a five-year-old kid, I was, for several years, afraid to go near a large body of water.

The crescendo of my rebellious reign of horror following little Mary's birth came that September when it was time for me to start to school for the first time. First grade. Whoopee! At least some of the kids I played with actually looked forward to the first day of school. I prayed it wouldn't come.

There were many reasons for my recalcitrance.

Most important, my older brother had told me that while I was at school one day, the family would move to another town and just leave me there. That was not encouraging.

Then there was the matter of keeping tabs on the attention the baby would get all day long while I was not there. Who better than me could do that job?

Finally, the big kids down the street told me that school was conducted in Spanish, and if I could not speak it real well I would have to sit in a corner with a pointy dunce cap on my head. Now, my playmates were mostly of Mexican heritage, and I had picked up a healthy dose of street lingo—Tex-Mex, it was called. But I knew for sure I would not be able to keep up in Spanish, and I was *not ever* going to be put in a corner with a funny hat on my head so the other kids could make fun of me.

No, sir. I had an alternative plan. It was called "Go in the school's front door each morning, walk casually down the long hall, and go out the back door that led to the playground." By the time I got back outside, whoever brought me to school would be blocks away. I could then saunter downtown to the Hall & Schawe Gulf station and get me a Grapette with a nickel of my lunch money. Then I could go to the dime store and check things out there. I might even take a nap. Who knew? But I would be back to school in time to be picked up at the end of the day, which was 2:30 P.M. for first graders.

That plan actually worked for three whole days. Then the fact that we had to have a blasted telephone caught up with me. The school called my mother to ask if I were sick. "No, he's at school. I dropped him off myself."

The local Barney Fife, one of Uvalde's finest two, found me at the Gulf station, sipping on my Grapette and chewing the fat with Happy Schawe, one of the proprietors.

Getting caught did not end my truancy. Not by a long shot. I would escape and hide in the park the first time the teacher's eyes were not glued on me. Some days, I lasted an hour at school. Others, ten minutes.

After a month of this (and getting a licking every day for it), the kindly old principal called my parents in and advised them that I was, after all, too young to be in school since I had not reached my sixth birthday by September 1. That meant they would have to pay tuition if they wished for me to continue to be enrolled. Note that she did not say "attend school." That was not in my plan, and she knew it.

Faced with the possibility of having to pay tuition, my parents relented. Faced with a stern lecture, not in my presence, from that principal, they suddenly realized what my problem was. That kindly principal made me promise to stay in school the next year, and to behave myself. I was so grateful to her that I did.

Hallelujah! I had not only won the battle of wits over having to go to school, but also I had regained a tad of my former baby-of-the-family status.

The plan had worked: "Push, push, push. Get ever more radical." I would employ those tactics to my advantage time and again whilst growing up.

My new status as non-schoolboy and small person in the family worthy of some notice paid off immediately. Within a few days, my father said one evening, "If you can get up early in the morning and get dressed, I will take you to see the president."

"I'll be ready," I said, not having a clue what he was talking about or who this president might be. All I knew was it meant a ride in the new Ford black-and-white with its squawking Motorola radio, its red fog lamps, and its ten-foot-tall bamboo whip antenna attached to the back bumper. That was treat enough for me, and I went to sleep that night very excited.

The president my father was talking about was Harry Truman—*the* president. He had been renominated by the Democrats and was running an uphill battle for re-election in November. As part of his campaign, he would be coming to the most unlikely place on the face of the earth the next day—Uvalde, Texas. You see, Uvalde was the home of the former Democratic vice president and currently ailing party *padrone*, John Nance

HAVIN' FUN, DOWN ON THE RANGE

One of life's great adventures for a five-year-old was riding in the new Texas Highway Patrol Ford cruiser, with its red fog lamps, siren behind the grille, squawking Motorola two-way radio, and really tall bamboo whip antenna on the back bumper.

George Arnold • 19

Garner. Truman was making an obligatory courtesy call on Cactus Jack, as he was known. And my father, as one of the two resident state policemen, was assigned to security escort duty.

Next morning, Truman arrived in another new black-and-white state police car which, as I remember, was followed by a black Buick with one Secret Service agent and two FBI agents. He drove in from San Antonio, about a ninety-minute drive. He had flown into Randolph Air Force Base the night before aboard an Air Force troop transport. There was no Air Force One in those days.

Nor was there any particular press hoopla. There were a couple of photographers, but I think one of them was from the Uvalde newspaper and the other from the Hondo newspaper. There were no Sam Donaldsons or Dan Rathers or Barbara Walters following him around. Just one Secret Service man, a couple of FBI agents, and three state Highway Patrolmen, two of them with less than a year of experience.

I got up and dressed at the crack of dawn, ate my bowl of cereal, drank a big glass of milk and climbed into the front seat of that new Ford beside my dad. We drove straight to Mr. Garner's house, a distance of less than a mile. I hopped out, sat down on the front bumper between those two red fog lamps, and I commenced to await the arrival of this president, whoever he was.

My father told me to sit there while he handled "crowd control." Now I can tell you that if everybody in Uvalde descended on Cactus Jack's front lawn, it could not, with a straight face, have been called a "crowd," especially since Mr. Garner's front yard was immense compared to anything else in town, including the dreaded school yard.

Very soon, the Highway Patrol car, followed by the black Buick, arrived and parked right next to where I had been stationed. A small man with round glasses and wearing a gray suit hopped out of the cruiser and walked briskly up to the house, followed by one Secret Service agent and one FBI agent, both of them—of course—in blue suits with white shirts.

Since the crowd numbered less than 150 and, hence, controlled themselves pretty well, my father came back over to introduce me to his sergeant from San Antonio and the remaining FBI agent.

"Did you see the president?" he asked me.

"I guess so. Which one was he?" I responded, proving myself a five-year-old dolt in national political affairs. In all fairness, there was no television in Texas, and I had never seen a likeness of Mr. Truman before. I imagined anyone who would be president would be very tall and walk like John Wayne, whom I had seen in the movies.

"He had on the gray suit," my father responded.

"Would you like to meet him?" the FBI agent from San Antonio asked me.

"Sure. Why not?" I responded, not nearly as overwhelmed as the blue-suit thought I should be.

About that time the crowd of 150 broke ranks and, led by the sergeant from San Antonio, formed two lines from Mr. Garner's front door, a kind of local, informal, how-do-you-do-Mr. President honor guard through which Harry Truman would pass as he left.

"Should I go up there?" I asked the blue suit.

"No. You wait right here with me," he said. "He won't be long. Mr. Garner is very ill, so the president won't stay long," he assured me, as if I cared one way or the other. As a non-schoolboy, I had another ten hours of sunlight to burn. I was in no hurry.

Sure enough, in about fifteen minutes, here he came. Right down that corridor of Uvalde bodies, slapping hands, smiling and talking a blue streak as he walked along toward where we were waiting by the black-and-whites.

Something was wrong. I sensed it as I saw him passing through the lined-up bodies. Something didn't look right. What was it? I was pondering that question as *The President of the United States of America* walked right up to me.

The blue-suit FBI agent said, "Mr. President, this is George. His dad is that Highway Patrolman over there, and George stayed out of school today to come to meet you."

The ignorant fool. I stayed out of school *every day* because I was one clever little son-of-a-gun.

The president looked at me and smiled. I was a tall kid for five. He said, "Hello, George. Thanks for coming over here to see me." He stuck out his hand. I stuck out my hand, And we shook hands. Hmmm. I knew what was wrong. He was about the size of my eleven-year-old brother.

MY NEW BUDDY, MR. HARRY

Not too many people thought Mr. Harry, as he had asked me to call him, could win the presidency in 1948. But he and the little prankster from Uvalde never doubted.

(Photo by Abbie Rowe, National Park Service Photography.
Courtesy Harry S. Truman Library, Independence, Missouri)

"Are you really the president?" I asked point-blank, clearly indicating serious doubt on my part.

"What makes you think I'm not?" he winked at the blue-suit.

"You're too little to be *The President*," I replied, straightforward.

Well, you would have thought I was Jack Benny, George Burns, and Henny Youngman all rolled up into one comedian. While the weenie FBI blue-suit winced, afraid he had made a mistake in introducing me in the first place, Harry Truman went into gales of laughter. I had struck his funny bone, for sure.

He stopped laughing and said, "You don't have to be big to be president. You just have to be a bit ornery and have a big heart." Then he laughed some more, put his arm around my shoulder and asked, "You know where a fellow could buy a new friend a pop?"

"They have Cokes and Grapettes at Hall & Schawe's," I replied. "I like Grapette best."

The president turned to the blue-suit. "Tell his father we're going to Hall & Schawe's for a pop," he said. Turning to me he added, "Come on, ride with me," as he got into the other new Ford cruiser.

And so we went to Hall & Schawe's Gulf station for a pop, the president and me. And we had us a good conversation about Missouri and about Texas along the way and while he drank a Coke and I sipped on my Grapette, both of which I noticed the blue-suit paid for.

About the time we finished our drinks, my dad, having dispersed the crowd, I suppose, pulled up to collect me. I introduced him to my new friend, Mr. Harry, which he insisted I call him. Mr. Harry said to my father, "I want you to bring George to the White House as soon as you can. We're going to sing some songs about Missouri. But, be quick. I may not be there come February."

He laughed his infectious laugh, and then he turned to me. "Whatever you do, be sure to vote for Democrats," he said with a stern look.

That advice given, he said his good-byes, climbed into the Highway Patrol cruiser, and headed back to Randolph Air Force Base and his Air Force troop plane, ready to hit the campaign trail once again, I supposed.

I never did get to the White House until Lyndon Johnson was president. I didn't know him personally, so I had to just take the public tour. And I didn't get to sing any Missouri songs, although I hummed "The Missouri Waltz" to myself out of respect for the funny little man who had been so kind to me, the undeserving child-chief of my own reign of madness.

Life's Lessons Learned:

- *It is always good to have a plan, even if it is somewhat misguided.*
- *Sometimes kindly old school principals can reveal a blinding flash of the obvious when it is most needed.*
- *Tough-minded, hard-nosed, decision-making leaders don't have to look like John Wayne.*
- *Bald-faced honesty is charming only in children.*
- *Presidents don't pay for Cokes and Grapettes. Secret Service agents do the paying.*

IKE AND PATTON WITH THE BOSS

Mr. Harry didn't have problems with all the generals. Just the ones who occasionally forgot who was really commander-in-chief.

(Photo by U.S. Navy. Courtesy Harry S. Truman Library, Independence, Missouri)

CHAPTER 3

Pyromania and Kidnapping

AUSTIN, 1949

It was time for me to enter the first grade for the second time. I was ready. Apparently my mother was not.

With her usual sense of direction, she couldn't find Becker Elementary School. Instead, she tried to enroll me at the State of Texas School for the Deaf on South Congress Avenue. Perhaps she thought my chronic failure to obey was somehow linked to a hearing disorder. More likely, she just didn't know where she was.

Once again.

So I was late for my first day of first grade, second time around. That distressed me.

We had moved back to Austin from Uvalde. This time we moved into a brand new house on Juliet Street, just southwest of Barton Springs Road and South Lamar Boulevard. I had never lived in a new house before, or even one that was less than fifty years old. It smelled of pine and paint, adhesives, shellac, and new carpets. I spent a lot of time just wandering around inside, sniffing. I decided I liked new things, at least the pent-up smell of shellac.

Our neighbor on one side of the new house was a reclusive old woman who had cats. Lots of cats. Dozens of cats. In fact, by my inventory, she had sixty-five cats, a goodly number for any one domicile except maybe the SPCA.

My brother and I had built our little sister a sandbox in our back yard. We envisioned her digging with her little shovel and pail, making sand castles and getting the seat of her ever-wet training pants encrusted with sand.

Alas, with all those cats next door, her sand frolicking was not to be. The abundance of cat poop kept *us* shoveling, instead of her. Within two weeks, we had completely cleaned all the sand out of the wooden frame, along with a dump truck full of cat droppings. The score was: neighbor's cats-1, little Mary Arnold-0. Surely the old lady wasn't supposed to have so many cats, but we—not being snitches—left her to her feline fetish and abandoned the used-to-be sand pile.

The neighbors on the other side of us were even more interesting... a family by the name of Donohoo. The Donohoos had seven children, the oldest of whom was nine. They were a wide-ranging band of hooligans such as I had never before seen. They roamed the neighborhood, cursing like drunken sailors, and leaving a scorched-earth path of destruction in their wake. Some of the other neighbors called them the Shermans. I finally understood why, years later, when history classes got to the Civil War.

My mother had told me to stay away from those Donohoo kids. Yeah, right. I was sure going to do that. They were right there. I was right there. We were all kids. Fat chance!

One day the oldest, whose name, I think, was Darrell, pinned me against the wall of our house and said, "Tell us the weirdest thing you've ever done."

"What if I don't?" I asked, somewhat belligerently.

"Then you'll be blowing your nose through your butt," he replied.

"Oh," was all I could think of to say. I understood his form of friendly persuasion right off the bat.

"Mr. Harry bought me a Grapette last fall," I said, not thinking that too weird, but suspecting strongly that none of the Donohoo hellions had ever sipped a soft drink with a president.

"What's weird about that? And who the hell is this Mr. Harry guy?" Darrell pushed me harder against the wall.

I thought he was kidding. Didn't everybody know Mr. Harry was president of the whole United States? Then it occurred to

NO SANDPILE FOR LITTLE MARY

Thanks to the eccentric neighbor's sixty-five cats, the sand pile George and Jim built for Little Mary immediately became useless. Except to the cats, of course, who promptly filled it to capacity.

me that the Donohoos might not be as right up to date on political affairs as I was, so I answered him. "Mr. Harry Truman; he's the president."

"Nuh-uh," he shot back, "Harry Truman never bought you a Grapette."

"Yes, he did so." I replied. "He drank a Coke, and we talked about a lot of things. He told me always to vote for Democrats."

"You're lying. Liar, liar, pants on fire!" Darrell wasn't buying my story.

"You can ask my dad," I said. "He'll tell you."

"Your dad's a bigger liar than you are," he retorted.

That was too much. This guy, even though he was nine and I was just six, wasn't that much bigger than me. I wriggled free and gave him my most menacing glare. It worked. He backed off.

"You ever smoke anything?" he asked me, still on the offensive.

Nobody in my family smoked. Well, my Uncle George occasionally puffed on a cigar, but mostly he just chewed on them. I liked the smell of cigar smoke.

"Nope," I responded. "Never did."

"Today you're going to be initiated," he said with a smile.

"What's 'initiated' mean?" I asked, not sure if I was particularly interested in it or not.

"It means we're going to teach you to smoke," he said, and a whole chorus of little barefoot, snot-nosed Donohoos chimed in, "Yeah!"

Darrell opened a small wooden door in their foundation and started to crawl in under the house. Five little Donohoos grabbed me and pushed me in right after him. Then they followed. We crawled over scraps of lumber, through spider webs and around beams to their secret "hideout." It was darker than a nun's habit under there. Suddenly, Darrell struck a match and lit three candles so we could all see a bit better.

We were right under the middle of their house. A small pit had been dug in the dirt, and in it was a variety of paraphernalia—an old coffee can, a bunch of pieces of grapevine, a big box of matches, a sack full of bubble gum, some papers, and a stack of comic books. All they needed was canned food and water to survive an atomic blast, it seemed to me.

"Okay, here's what we're going to do," Darrell said. He was

obviously leader of the pack. "Since all of us have smoked a lot, we're going straight for the grapevines. We'll start you out on coffee grounds."

He proceeded to pour some used coffee from the can into a paper, like a Prince Albert roll-your-own cigarette wrapper. He even packed it tight, licked it, and made it look somewhat like a cigarette; at least, in the semi-darkness, it looked somewhat like a cigarette. He then passed out short pieces of grapevine to all his siblings, choosing a nice, fat one for himself.

One by one, they lit up the grapevines and commenced to puff like a bunch of little steam locomotives. They didn't cough or even squint their eyes. Then he told me to put one end of the rolled-up, coffee-grounds cigarette in my mouth and "suck in" when he held the match to the other end. So I did.

Shazam! Double Shazam! The first puff nearly knocked me over. I started coughing, spitting, blowing snot wildly out my nose, all at once. I thought I would go blind. In my total confusion, I knocked two burning candles down into the pit.

Well, the paper bag with the bubble gum was the first to catch fire, followed immediately by the stack of comics. They flared up into a raging inferno. I remember wondering if the Donohoos had soaked them in gasoline for some reason.

A little Donohoo screamed, "Fire!" Another one shouted, "Let's get the hell out of here!" I didn't mind if I did. All seven of us made for the door in the foundation. In spite of the intense light from the now roaring fire, we all bumped into joists and beams and each other. The billowing smoke made us have to shut our eyes and crawl by dead reckoning like a bunch of half-crazed crabs on the seashore.

"Last one out's a ... *cough, cough, cough-cough*," someone tried to yell. We never did find out what Darrell, who was last, might have been.

Smoke was billowing from under their house. Their mother was now in the front yard with the baby, yelling incomprehensible obscenities at her kids at the top of her voice.

I ran across the driveway to our house and yelled to my mother, "The Donohoos' house is on fire, and I didn't do it." Oops. That last little clause would have been better left unsaid.

Mom looked out the window, gasped, and grabbed the

"STAY AWAY FROM THOSE DONOHOO KIDS!"

Not an easy thing to do for a six-year-old in 1949, or any other year. Especially with the lure of a litter of puppies tucked safely away under their house.

George Arnold • 31

phone. She called the ever-ready Austin Fire Department, whose Barton Springs firehouse was less than a half-mile away. It wasn't two minutes before we heard the siren's wail, and a big, red fire engine pulled up. Firemen jumped off it like drowning rats off a sinking ship. Some of them ran into the house with big fire extinguishers. A couple of others grabbed a hose and made for the fire hydrant on the corner. The driver ran over to where my mother and I were standing in our driveway and shouted, "Is there anybody left in that house?"

"No," I shouted back to him. "They're all in the front yard."

As it turned out, primarily because the crack AFD was so quick, it wasn't much of a fire, at least compared to the smoke that continued to pour out from under the house for another fifteen minutes. A hole was burned in the kitchen floor. It was large enough for about half the little Donohoos to shinny through it, so the hole had to be covered with plywood, pending repairs. Somehow, I don't think the Donohoos even noticed it.

Once the fire was out, the time for reckoning had come. Two of the firemen came over to our house and asked to talk to Mom and me. They allowed as how they had not been able to get any kind of straight story from the Donohoos. "Every one of those kids told us a completely different story," they told me, "but—to a kid—they all said you tried to burn their house down."

Those little vermin! I now understood the old saying, "Blood is thicker than water." Or, in this case, thicker than coffee grounds. Or grapevine.

So I invited the firemen to sit down, offered them a Grapette, but they only wanted water, and began to tell them my story, sipping as I went. I left out nothing. I took names and kicked virtual butt. Never had I been so candid in my short life. I took complete responsibility for knocking over the candles and concluded by asking them, straight out, "Am I going to have to go to jail now?"

They looked at my mother for a clue. She was shaking her head side-to-side.

"No. You won't have to go to jail. But you will have to come down to the firehouse one day and wash our truck. Do you know where it is?" the fireman who did most of the talking asked.

"Yes, sir, it's down the bluff on Barton Springs Road," I answered.

The fireman suggested Saturday would be a good day to drop by to pay my penance. About 10:00 A.M.

"Should I bring some of the Donohoos with me? Or all of them?" I inquired.

"Please don't," he said.

The visit of the little arsonist to the firehouse was an entertaining love fest. I got to hold the hose and squirt it on the fire engine to rinse off the suds after the firemen really did the washing. And I got to climb all over it. They even gave me some ice cream. Shucks, I thought I might just go out and set fire to something else.

A few pages back I mentioned starting the first grade at Becker Elementary School. That was true, of course, as is a lot of other stuff in this book.

Within a couple of months, however, a brand new, modern and fancy elementary school was completed, and some of us Becker kids were transferred to Zilker Elementary, just east of Zilker Park. I liked it a lot better. Not only was it unlike any other school of its day, it was also close enough that I could walk to school. I hated for my mother to take me. She would get lost at least once a week, and I would be late. My teacher said my excuses for being late were getting a little "worn out." I didn't know what to say about that. "My mother often gets lost" wouldn't be too good, I thought.

In this new school in the first grade we had graham crackers and juice every morning about 10:00 A.M., and after lunch every day, we had to lie down on little mats on the floor. I liked the crackers and juice, but I hated lying down on those stupid little mats. School was no place for naps, in my opinion.

In our class, there was a another novelty—identical twins. They actually dressed alike, and they had cutesy little twin-type names, Freddie and Teddy, or some such. The minute I saw them, I resolved to throw up on their shoes.

Freddie and Teddy were pests. They imagined themselves the cutest things since a bug's ear, and they were practically joined at the hip. Because they wore the same clothes and looked exactly alike, I couldn't tell them apart. I just called them Tweedle-Dee and Tweedle-Dum—Dee and Dum, at random, for short.

My best friend at the new school was a kid named Whitey. That wasn't his real name. I just called him Whitey because he had snow-white hair. He called me Brownie, for the same reason, I suppose. In a way, we were as alike, spiritually, as Dee and Dum. Or Dum and Dee.

Whitey lived a few doors up the street, past the Donohoos. We often walked to school together and always walked home together. One day in the spring, about March, I think, Whitey and I were walking home after school. We had our official Whip Wilson lariats with us, among other stuff, like bubble gum, baseball cards, and a bee in a jar.

What should happen but Dee and Dum walked up behind us. They probably had to run, now that I think about it, because they were much smaller than most of the rest of the kids in the class and had short, stubby legs.

Anyway, they caught up with Whitey and me just as we came to our street. Even though we considered them a couple of little weenies, and they knew it, they were mad at the two of us because we had "fixed" their midmorning graham cracker sandwiches with white library paste, which they thought was powdered-sugar icing.

Insanity had undoubtedly overcome them somewhere along the trail from the school to Juliet Street, because they started to taunt us. Whitey and I were a lot bigger than they were. And they knew we despised the sight of them.

Their ill-chosen dialogue began with one of them shouting out, "Look. It's Whitey and Brownie."

The other chirped up, "Those sound like dog names to me."

"Or pigs, maybe," said the little shrimp who started it all.

This sterling little confrontation degenerated into the totally weird.

First Dee, and then Dum, kept up their name-calling. Finally, one of the little twerps piped up, "What do you have those ropes for? Gonna hang somebody?" Now, that was a classically stupid statement, given the fact that Whitey and I had the ropes and we were almost twice their size.

I knew a lot about hanging. My brother had already tried to hang me. Twice.

I looked at Whitey. Whitey looked at me. We both smiled.

There was a giant live oak tree a block from the end of Juliet Street, right on the edge of the bluff overlooking Barton Springs Road.

Whitey and I continued walking, past our street, heading toward the big oak.

"Forget where you live?" It was one of the little pests.

"Or are you going to rope yourself a pig?" croaked the other.

Now we were close to that giant oak. It was time for action. Simultaneously, Whitey and I whipped the genuine Whip Wilson lariats off our left shoulders. He grabbed one of the infernal little twins, and I grabbed the other.

At first, Dum and Dee thought we were actually going to hang them from that oak. But Whitey and I weren't sadistic. Just tired of the little pests following us around.

I held them both by the scruff of their cutesy-pie little collars while Whitey went round and round that tree. In half a minute, they were tied, top and bottom, backs to a live oak on the edge of a bluff in South Austin.

"Shall we puke on their shoes?" Whitey asked. I had let him in on my loosely conceived little plan.

"Nah, Whitey, we'll do that next week," I responded. The twerps-times-two screamed in unison, even though they were on opposite sides of the tree and couldn't even see one another.

So we went on home, Whitey and me, and we never looked back. Just left the little warts tied, snug-up, to a tree.

About 7:00 P.M. that same evening, Whitey's mother and one of Austin's finest descended, Whitey in tow, on our front porch. My father, who was still in his Highway Patrol uniform with the new sergeant's stripes on the sleeves, saw them coming. He looked at me. "Lord, God, what have you done now?" he asked me. "Kidnap somebody?"

How extraordinarily perceptive! I supposed that was exactly what Whitey and I had done. My father wasn't usually that clever, I thought.

We all sat down in the living room, and the whole saga came

CO-CONSPIRATORS
Whitey and I didn't much care for cutesy little people. And we didn't much care who knew it.

pouring forth. First, Whitey talked. Then, I talked. Our story was right in unison. There was no need to question us separately.

After the policeman heard what we had to say and responded with a stern lecture, Whitey and his mom went home.

My mother looked at me, and she said, "What in the world were you two thinking about—tying those kids to a tree? And then leaving them there?" she added as an afterthought.

She had asked me a question. That, best I could tell, gave me an opening. It was my one chance to say my piece. I had to be creative.

"Well," I said, "I look at it this way. Gene Autry wouldn't have put up with listening to those little pricks, and neither would Whitey and me."

It was a good answer, except for the word "pricks," which meant nothing to me, one way or the other.

Once more, I had displayed a certain confident flamboyance. I wasn't a smart-aleck. Just a clever little kid with an advanced vocabulary and a way overactive imagination.

My father didn't appreciate my casual approach. He grabbed me by the shoulders, spun me around, and demanded, "Where did you learn that word?"

I had to make him say it. "Which word?" I asked, giving him my Michael, the Archangel, look.

"Pricks." He actually said it. I tried not to laugh.

Truth was, I had learned the word from my brother. It meant nothing to me, but seemed appropriate in the context in which I had used it. Rather than get Jim into this, I punted. "From the Donohoos. They go around yelling "prick" (I had to say it again) all over the neighborhood. What's a prick?" I had him on the run. In full retreat.

Hosanna.

A couple of days later, the mother of Dum and Dee called my mother. She wanted to know two things: Did we want the two genuine Whip Wilson lariats back? And did Whitey and I still intend to vomit on her precious little twits' shoes?

My mother said, "No, your boys can keep George's lariat. He's not allowed to play with it anymore. And I'm sure there won't be any such thing as vomiting on their shoes. We're going to be moving in a couple of weeks to San Antonio."

What?!! Another move?

"Don't you realize I have already been to three schools—four if you count the Deaf School—and I still haven't finished the first grade?" I pleaded with her.

She just looked at me.

I rushed down to Whitey's house. I had to tell him about the move, and we had to get those lariats back. After all, we were sure Dee and Dum never played with anything but dolls. They wouldn't know what to do with a genuine Whip Wilson lariat.

We hatched us a plan. It might just work. Mrs. Dum-Dee-Dum-Dum hadn't yet called Whitey's mother. Whitey was to get his mom, when their mother asked about the lariats, to say, "Yes, Whitey will come get them," and I would take over from there.

Sure enough, the twins' mother called Whitey's house. And, sure enough, Whitey was able to get his mom to say he would come get them. The evil twins' mother opted for dropping them off, a scarcely transparent attempt to keep Whitey off her property.

Now Whitey had both of them. I needed to borrow them, just for a few minutes.

"I'll call you in a little while and tell you to come get yours," I said. "Just don't mention mine to my mother."

I stole home and hid one of the lariats in my secret treasure-trove. The other I plopped prominently on the kitchen table, where Mom would be sure to see it. She spied it almost immediately. "I thought I said you couldn't have that rope anymore," she looked at me, frowning.

"Oh, that's not mine. It's Whitey's. His mom (emphasis on *His*) let him have his back. I'll call him and tell him to come and get it."

So I did. And, once again, Little Lamont Cranston had clouded his mother's mind so she could not see the wool being pulled over her eyes.

Hallelujah.

Life's Lessons Learned:

- *Never smoke. Anything. Especially under somebody's house.*

- *If, on the other hand, you get caught smoking because you set something on fire, like, oh, say, your neighbor's house, tell the firemen the absolute and total truth. It might get you a trip to the fire house and some ice cream.*

- *Do not tolerate "cutesy" little people. One at a time. Two at a time. Or in a mob. It's okay to throw up on their shoes. In fact, it's a great thing to do.*
- *Never tie someone to a tree and go off and leave them. Oh, tie them up, to be sure. But, then, hide in the bushes until they are rescued. That way, you can always say you were watching over them all along so they wouldn't get hurt.*

CHAPTER 4

Nifty New Flying Machines and Grumpy Old Soldiers

SAN ANTONIO, 1950/1951

Escaping Austin, again, this time just ahead of the juvenile detention authorities, we moved to the old city of San Antonio, into the northwest part of town to an area called Los Angeles Heights. I don't know why it was Los Angeles Heights, except that all the streets were named for towns in California.

We first lived on El Monte Street, where I finished the first grade at Woodrow Wilson Elementary School, the fourth school I had attended to get through my first year, not counting the Deaf School, where I was enrolled for less than two hours.

I was headed for a record of some kind, for sure.

Then, over the summer, we moved to Fresno Street, just off West Avenue, where I entered the second grade at Benjamin Franklin Elementary School.

Seemed to me that, since San Antonio was as old, or older, than those towns in California that our neighborhood streets were named for, the schools ought to be named Cabeza de Vaca or LaSalle or Cristobal Colon. Maybe even Attila, The Hun. "Attila, The Hun, Elementary School" had a nice ring to it, I thought.

Wasn't just the street and school names that were confusing

to a seven-year-old, either. Lots of things conspired to create a growing disorder in my heretofore mostly orderly little existence.

Because San Antonio was so old and had just sort of grown up around the Mision San Antonio de Valero, otherwise known as "The Alamo," as well as a string of 17th century missions scattered about, mostly south of downtown, former cattle trails had become thoroughfares that run helter-skelter, like spokes, from the center of the city.

There was no grid system, and the winding streets served to disorient even those of us with good senses of direction. You might not think that important for a seven-year-old in a fairly large city, but I was an incorrigibly independent little cuss. I would hop on my old bicycle and head out with a quarter in my pocket. Sometimes I stopped at the Woodlawn Theater, halfway downtown from our house. Sometimes I would cut across Hildebrand Street to Brackenridge Park, where I would ride a little train or sit by Monkey Island in the zoo, watching to see how my ancestors may have behaved. Other times I just kept going all the way to the Alamo to see a more interesting movie at the Majestic or the Aztec theaters.

I especially liked the Aztec because its domed ceiling was flooded in soft blue light, and there seemed to me to be a billion or so little white pin-lights shimmering like stars. I would sit and stare at that ceiling, pretending I was riding in X-2, the Bell rocket plane, on the fringes of outer space. I would commence to daydream about Martians and such, forgetting entirely to watch the movie I had pedaled so far to see.

Of course, that meant I had to sit through the feature one more time.

Sitting there another two hours was okay by me. I still had a nickel left to buy a second Holloway sucker. You remember them, the hard caramel on a stick that lasted at least two hours. Some kids called them "Slo-Pokes."

But those additional two hours were not necessarily okay with my mother, who usually had no idea when I might decide to come home, but always, somehow, just knew I was in dire straits, bloodied and dying in a gutter somewhere near St. Mary's Street.

Often, as I pedaled home, I would meet her heading downtown in our family's 1947 green Ford, which my dad had gone back to Missouri to pick up from the local dealer in Smithville, just before we moved to Uvalde. We had waited for that car for two years after the war.

Now, if anyone on the face of the earth had no sense of direction whatsoever, it was my mother. She couldn't find true north with a $2,000 compass.

The first few times she came to find me, I would hide out when I saw her coming, then just pedal on home. Invariably, however, she would get confused by the one-way streets and end up somewhere on South Presa. She would have to call, and it would irritate my father no end to have to get in his black-and-white Ford and go find her and lead her home.

Of course, I became the object of the irritation. And rightly so, I suppose. I remember hearing my father tell my brother, "Your little brother doesn't have sense enough to know when to come home, and your mother doesn't have sense enough to find him without getting lost herself." It didn't sound very kind to me, but I guess it was absolutely true.

Each time, I would be banned from straying past the Woodlawn Theater, which was only a couple of miles from home. Each time, I would just do as I pleased, go wherever I wanted to go, and generally ignore instructions.

That kind of behavior has, I believe, served me well for, lo, these past fifty-eight years.

I reasoned that pedaling to downtown San Antonio from Los Angeles Heights was a lot easier, and safer, than pedaling across the Brooklyn Bridge from Mulberry Street to take in the sights of the U.S. Navy yard ... or to find my way to the Bronx to see an afternoon Yankees game. I knew about those places, even though I had never been to New York, from listening to Yankees and Dodgers games on the radio. Red Barber was the best, I thought.

In an effort to dissuade me from disobeying, my father had begun to tell me all the terrible things Mexicans, who made up the majority of San Antonio's population, were known to do to little kids. He was a typical "Big Depression," white, Anglo-Saxon racist, or "bigot," as they were called in those days.

As long as he stuck with the nomenclature "kids," technically, he wasn't lying, I suppose. I have had many friends of Mexican heritage who were downright gleeful to take a small kid goat, gut it, skin it, and then slow-roast it over a fire pit. They call it *cabrito*, and it's pretty darned tasty.

The consequences of my wanderlust came to a head one Saturday in 1950. I had left with my usual quarter, telling my mother I was going to see a Hopalong Cassidy morning matinee at the Woodlawn. That should have gotten me back home by about 2:00 in the afternoon.

Somewhere between my house and that particular movie, I remembered there was an air show that weekend at Kelly Air Force Base. Being a normal seven-year-old boy, I was smitten with flying machines of all types.

San Antonio offered a cornucopia of flying machine opportunities for a kid with wanderlust. The XC-99, a giant, pencil-like, six-piston-engine forerunner of the B-36, would regularly rumble across the sky, shaking windowpanes to their breaking point. There were military transports of all kinds in-and-out of the several air bases that surrounded San Antonio. Helicopters were new army gadgets that buzzed around Fort Sam Houston like some kind of monstrous flying mantis. And then, there were the fast, jet-powered fighters that seemed to scream through the air at impossible speeds, like baking-soda-and-vinegar-powered hummingbirds. Let us not forget, too, the flying saucers that I regularly spotted racing among the stars on dark nights. There were lots of them. Hundreds, in fact.

Well, sir, the lure of a genuine air show, where kids like me could actually enter the gates of Kelly Field and get up close and personal with a jet fighter—it was all too much for me to pass up.

So I altered course. I headed southwest with a revised VPR (Visual Pedal Rules) plan. I was going to find Kelly Field by dead reckoning. Never mind that it was at least twelve miles from our house. Never mind that I couldn't possibly ever get there and back, even if I stayed only an hour, by dark. Never mind that I had been forbidden to venture past the ol' Woodlawn Theater.

I was going to see those airplanes close up. I was going to touch them, climb in them, smell them. And if I saw that nobody was looking, fire one of them up for a test flight.

You can guess, I suppose, what happened. I found Kelly Field. I went to the air show. I sat in an XC-99 and climbed in the cockpit of an F-86. I was an ace for an afternoon.

All at once, however, I noticed the crowd had dwindled, and the air show was beginning to close. It was getting dark. Time to pedal like an F-86 for home!

By the time I got back to the vicinity of West Avenue, it was approaching 9:00 P.M. Sure enough, here came my mother in her green '47 Ford, headed for town. Then came my father in his '50 Ford black-and-white. I hid behind the trees at an elementary school until they both passed, then whizzed on home and jumped into a big bed my brother graciously shared with me. I say graciously, with all due respect, because I was known, on occasion, to wet the bed. "Occasion" might have been as often as five or six times a week, best I can remember.

I feigned sleep. Deep, deep slumbers that nobody could wake me up from. Eventually, my parents came back home, found me "asleep," and did not attempt to wake me. The next morning, however, on returning from Sunday school, having once again successfully avoided being patted on the head by some dratted Church Lady, I found my bicycle firmly affixed to the rafters of the garage. My father said, "Until you can learn not to wander halfway across Bexar County, that bike is staying on the rafters."

On the spot, I kissed that bicycle goodbye. It was not in my plan not to wander. I would just have to find other means of transport.

You are among the first to learn where I really went that Saturday in 1950. At the time, I steadfastly refused to tell.

The next time I was able to get onto a flying-machine-type military establishment was about eight or nine months later. I was in the second grade at the aforementioned Benjamin Franklin Elementary School at the corner of West Avenue and Fresno Street. At supper (as we called it) one night, my father said, "I have to go out to Randolph Air Force Base tomorrow afternoon, and then on down to the Alamo. Want to go with me?"

Out of the blue, this invitation almost startled me. It would mean missing at least a half-day of school. For that reason, alone, I immediately said, "Yes, sir!" Didn't matter to me what

MATINEE ACE

For a Saturday afternoon at the air show at Kelly Field, I was an ace, sitting in the cockpit of a new F-86 jet fighter, blasting North Korean MiG's out of the South Texas sky.

(Photo courtesy Lieutenant Maxwell and the Retired Aviators' Organization)

was going on at either Randolph or the Alamo; a half-day off from school was enough reason to be excited.

Turns out it was another security detail, one that had ironic consequences for me.

General Douglas MacArthur, recently fired by my old friend, Mr. Harry, was making his famous "Old Soldiers Never Die" speech to the combined houses of the Texas legislature in Austin that morning. Then he was coming on down to San Antonio to repeat it in front of the Alamo.

Since I had the highest regard for my buddy, Mr. Harry, and Mr. Harry had just sent this general packing, I had to wonder if he were really as fit as John Wayne to address a crowd on the Alamo's plaza.

"You'll probably just get to see him from a distance," my father warned me. He seemed to know that the arrival of the good general would create a bit more whoop-dee-doo than had

JUST FADE AWAY
Mr. Harry personally brings the bad news to General Grump, on Guam, in 1951.

(Photo by U. S. State Department. Courtesy Harry S. Truman Library, Independence, Missouri)

Mr. Harry's arrival in Uvalde a couple of years before.

Boy, was he right about that. First came the somewhat luxurious army troop plane, converted to a personal office/living quarters for MacArthur. I remember thinking that maybe generals were more important than presidents since Mr. Harry's plane had been so plain by comparison. But the jazzed-up army plane carrying the general was not the end of the entourage. No, sir. Right behind it, in came an army transport plane. When it rolled to a stop, big bay doors under the tail opened, and out drove an army officer in General MacArthur's big ol' Packard. Wow! Not even Mr. Harry, who was president of the whole U.S.A., got to bring along his own car.

I guessed that Mr. Harry's car was probably a 1933 Plymouth, and not worth taking around with him everywhere.

MacArthur had not yet emerged from his plane. Reporters and dignitaries were everywhere. There were no TV stations in San Antonio yet, best I can remember, but flashbulbs were popping from a hundred press cameras.

A major in a fancy army dress uniform was scrambling around. "We need a kid," he said. "Six or seven years old would be just right." I was eight. I didn't know what he wanted a kid for, but I was disappointed that I was apparently too old.

My dad stepped forward. "My son's eight. Would he do?" The major was overjoyed. He escorted me to the foot of the stairway of the general's plane, where it met the red carpet that had been rolled out. He told me to stand still there and just do what the general told me. Then he rushed up the stairway and into the plane.

Holy smokes! The general was going to speak to me. Hosanna.

Actually, he was going to do more than that. Seems his advance team had decided to portray the general as a bit more human, you might say, than perhaps he really was. I was to be the shill in a game of "see-how-the-nice-general-likes-kids." All for the benefit of the press. Just a little showmanship, either at my expense or to my advantage. I never have answered that question, finally.

A roar went up as the general popped out, put on his military cap, and—straight as a ramrod—saluted the flag. He had a corncob pipe clenched between his teeth. When he finished his salute, he removed his cap and waved it in the air. The crowd roared.

Now I was sure generals were more important than presidents. No crowd had roared that much for Mr. Harry back in Uvalde.

Flanked by two aides, the general bounded down the stairs, all the while waving his cap and smiling for the cameras. When the descending trio got to me, the aide on my side leaned over and said, "Shake hands with the general. Keep shaking hands and look at the cameras until he lets go of your hand. Then follow him to his car."

That was easy enough. And I was tall enough that I could shake his hand without the general having to bend over. He looked to me like he might break in half if he bent over, anyway.

We shook hands. Forever, it seemed. My father had taught me always to use a firm grip. I did. The general whispered something to one of his aides, who bent over and asked me not to squeeze so tight. I wondered why he hadn't just told me himself. Maybe he didn't speak English, I thought, and considered saying something to him in my broken Tex-Mex.

When the flashbulbs stopped popping, the band began playing some march or other, and the general stepped off down that red carpet to his car with me right behind him. As we reached the big Packard, one of his aides asked me if someone should tell my parents that we were going to the Alamo.

"That's okay," I said. "I wander all over town most of the time, anyway. My dad's coming to the Alamo, too. We can find him there."

General MacArthur got in the back seat. A driver got in behind the wheel. Somebody shoved me into the back seat with the general, slammed the door, and then got in the front seat himself.

The general opened the back door, as if to get out again, and the aide shot out of the front seat like the man in the cannon at the circus.

There followed a heated discussion that I couldn't hear very well, since I was still in the back seat. Pretty soon, however, after the general had barked like a seal, I thought, at three or four people who were trying to tell him something, it dawned on me that the general wanted me out of his car.

Well, I could take a hint. Especially when it was yelled at 100 dB just a few feet away. So I slid out the opposite side of the car and started looking for my father.

The aide who had been in the front seat was now completely flustered. He asked me if I would mind riding with my dad to the Alamo and meeting the general there.

"Sure," I answered. "I can do that." I ran to my dad's black-and-white and jumped in.

MacArthur, seeing he had an entire, big back seat all to himself, again, got back in his Packard.

Motorcycles roared by, and we were off.

In those days, a drive from Randolph AFB to the Alamo might take fifteen to twenty minutes in traffic. There was no traffic. We had red lights and sirens in front, behind and on both sides of us. We owned Broadway Blvd. All the way to downtown.

As we headed out, my dad looked over at me and asked, "Why did you get out of the general's car?" As if I had a choice.

"He didn't want me in there. When I got in, he got out. Then he started yelling at one person after another. So I left. I'm supposed to meet him as soon as he gets out of his car at the Alamo. At least, they asked me to," I explained.

My dad noted that we would be right behind the general's car all the way downtown, so meeting him would be pretty easy.

"Why did Mr. Harry fire him?" I asked.

"Well, they had a difference of opinion about the future in Asia," my dad answered. "The general wanted to do things that Mr. Harry didn't want him to do."

"Are generals more important than presidents?" I wanted to know.

"Nope," my dad responded. "The president is boss."

"So Mr. Harry is General MacArthur's boss?" I wanted to be sure.

"Yep. Mr. Harry's the boss."

"Turn off here!" I shouted over the siren in our car and about a dozen more within a half block of us.

"What? Why do you want me to turn off?" My father asked the obvious question.

"Because I don't want to meet him at the Alamo. I think Mr. Harry fired him because he's such a grump. In fact, I'm going to call him General Grump if you make me meet him when we get there."

My father thought about this. My threats were not to be taken lightly. He had learned that lesson the hard way, more than once.

"They just want to take some more pictures," he tried to reassure me.

"No more pictures with me! Mr. Harry wouldn't like me fooling around with the enemy." I had reasoned the whole scenario out.

"He's not the enemy," my dad tried once again.

"If he's not a friend of Mr. Harry's, he's no friend of mine!" I was adamant.

And so it was, when we arrived in front of the Alamo, I refused to get out of the car. The aide tried to cajole me. "It's just for a few pictures," he pleaded.

"I don't want to. Mr. Harry wouldn't want me to," I said, matter-of-factly.

"Mr. Harry?" He looked puzzled.

"You know," I responded, wondering how you get to be a captain or major or whatever he was without knowing who the president of the United States is. "Mr. Harry Truman. He's my friend."

The guy looked at me as if I had just hit him between the eyes. Then he looked to my dad who, without a second thought, said, "He and Mr. Truman are friends. That's a fact."

This guy couldn't think of anything further to say, I suppose, because he left, and went over and spoke a few words to the gen-

eral, who got out of his car and walked directly to climb up on a platform that had been built for him to speak to the crowd.

He talked for a long time, it seemed to me, longer than it had taken to drive from Randolph Air Force Base to downtown. And he finished with that now famous line, "Old soldiers never die. They just fade away."

OLD SOLDIERS NEVER DIE

But they do speak for a long, long time in front of the Alamo in San Antonio, June 1951.

(Photo courtesy MacArthur Memorial, Norfolk, Virginia)

"He's a worn-out old soldier." My father started to make excuses for him as we left to escort the general back to his airplanes.

"He's a grump," I said. "I'm still going to call him General Grump."

And so it was, in the most ridiculous of coincidences and the darkest of ironies, that I had come to meet both the feisty president who fired him and the beloved general himself. General Grump.

Amazing.

Life's Lessons Learned:

- *Riding your bicycle all over East Jesus will cost you that bicycle, ultimately. Same goes for West Overshoe.*
- *A Holloway sucker really will last two hours. Even more.*
- *Some little presidents are funny. Some big generals aren't.*
- *Nobody can hide behind a uniform. If you're a grump, you're a grump. QED.*
- *Never tell General MacArthur's aide that you're a friend of Harry Truman. Bad karma.*

CHAPTER 5

Folks See What They
Want to See

WACO, 1953

I was on a quest early in June when Ronnie Simmons moved onto our street. You see, our Little League team, the Waco Chevrolet Powergliders, on which I was the starting catcher and up-and-coming slugger, needed a second baseman. Oh, we had Ralphie, and Ralphie could run, throw and hit, my three prerequisites for being a good ballplayer. But Ralphie was left-handed. Everybody, including our coaches and Ralphie himself, knew that a southpaw couldn't play second. It was as unnatural, and embarrassing, as if one of our moms were to be the umpire, or so we thought.

So I'm looking for a second baseman, hoping we could finally turn a decent double play, and Ralphie could go back to his natural position in left field, when the moving van pulled up in front of what was to become the Simmons' residence in the 3500 block of Windsor Avenue.

Immediately, I hoped the new neighbors might include a potential ballplayer, preferably right-handed, of course. My hopes were heightened when a kid who looked to be about my age hopped out of the back seat of the family station wagon with a fielder's glove on his left hand. Maybe, just maybe, the infield dilemma of the Powergliders would be solved.

I jumped aboard my red Western Flyer, whose saddlebags always held a baseball and my Rawlings fielder's glove, and headed up the street to check the new guy out.

"Hi, I'm George, and I'll be eleven in September," I blurted out, extending my hand as I had been taught to do.

"I'm Ronnie," he replied, "and I'll be 11 in December."

Nobody with any sense ever gave his real age. You always just stated how old you would be on your next birthday, even if your last birthday was yesterday.

We shook hands and began to play catch without speaking another word. A baseball was, and is, a universal language unto itself, a form of communication that needs no tongue.

At once I could see that Ronnie, although fairly small for a ten-year-old, was a ballplayer. At least he could throw and run, and he seemed to have quick hands. I tested him by throwing erratically, but he tracked down every errant toss and had the good manners not to point out that I couldn't throw worth a hoot.

Turns out, I learned when we sat down to rest and get acquainted, Ronnie's father was an air force captain just transferred to James Connally Air Force Base, the local military establishment. "He flies jets," Ronnie said with some pride, "fighter jets." I was impressed.

Believing I had solved the Powergliders' infield problem, and feeling more than a little proud for doing it, I invited Ronnie to practice that afternoon, where he did, in fact, take over second base (although he claimed to be the world's most natural shortstop), sending Ralphie back to left field and shoring up an infield that turned a record number of double plays that summer—twenty-seven of them in fourteen games.

He, in return, invited me to go swimming with his family at the officers' club the next day.

It was there at the OC that we met Quinton. This chance meeting launched very lucrative summer careers for all three of us. In fact, I would bet that the three of us each earned almost as much as our fathers that summer, although we couldn't gloat about it and had to hide the money. If our parents had any idea

LOOKIN' FOR A SECOND BASEMAN

My red Western Flyer with black saddlebags, complete with new baseball and trusty, well-oiled Rawlings fielder's glove at all times, got me down the street to recruit Ronnie Simmons, sorely needed, right-handed second baseman for the Powergliders.

DOUBLE PLAY CHAMPS

The only time all season we were still, as a group, the infamous Waco Chevrolet Powergliders, who turned twenty-seven double plays in fourteen games, pose for the obligatory annual team picture. Ronnie Simmons is third from left, kneeling, and I'm the tall kid in the back row.

how we were earning those big bucks, we would have faced instant unemployment, to be sure.

Seems Quinton, who would be twelve (an older guy) in October, had come across the opportunity of a kid's lifetime, a job paying $10 a day, $20 on Saturday and Sunday, seven days a week, for only one hour of work each weekday and two hours on weekend days.

Shazam!

We were an unlikely trio, to be sure. Ronnie was a New Yorker, street savvy and creative . . . and perpetually puzzled by the ways of Texas and Texans, which I did my best to explain to him week after week, although I eventually had to admit they didn't make any sense to me, either. I knew Ronnie was a philosopher when he said one day, quite offhandedly, "You must have been from New York in an earlier life. You don't get what's going on here any more than I do." In two sentences, he had nailed, dead-on, the confusion that had plagued me ever since I could remember.

Quinton was from California. His dad flew jets, too. And Quinton was a Negro (the designation of preference at the time), a fact that assured we would not all be in the same school come September, since all the Waco schools were still segregated—a perfect example of one of the things I "didn't get," according to Ronnie. Of course, he and Quinton didn't "get it," either. But I was more of a native and was supposed to be able to explain why something like this was. Five decades later, I still can't explain it.

Quinton seemed to me to be excessively proud of his father. Almost boastful, in fact. When I looked a bit puzzled by his exhortations and started to ask a question about it, Ronnie grabbed me by the arm and took me aside. "You don't understand, do you?" he asked, incredulous. I shook my head "no," assuming immediately we should be very quiet in our conversation. "Look," he questioned in his New Yorker style, "Quinton's father's an officer, right?" I nodded "yes," still quiet as if we were in a library, or a mortuary. "And he's a jet fighter pilot, right?" Again, I nodded agreement. "AND," he emphasized to be sure I understood that the point was coming, "he's a Negro, right?" Another affirmative nod from me. "That's it!" he said, clapping his hands together and closing his case for himself, but leaving me obviously trying to figure out what "it" was.

"What's *it?*" I was forced to break my silence.

Shaking his head in disbelief of my naiveté, he laid it out in black and white, so to speak. "Don't be so stupid," he said. "There aren't many Negroes who get to be officers, let alone jet fighter pilots."

"Oh," I said. "Thanks. I didn't know that."

That was the end of the conversation. He made his point. I understood it, finally. And there was no need to prattle on. I liked that about Ronnie. He was a direct, matter-of-fact guy, never tippy-toeing around subjects like all us Texas kids had been taught to do.

Back to the high-paying jobs.

As agreed, we met Quinton at 1:30 the following afternoon down by the Brazos River, not too far from Cameron Park, the local natural habitat in those days.

Back then, and still today, Waco was one of the places that attracted wacko religious fringes, even cults. Sure enough, within a stone's throw of the spot we had agreed to meet, there was a big tent. A sign proclaimed it the location of the Reverend Mallory's "End of the World Revival and Spiritual Renewal Meetings."

"Come on," Quinton said, "I'll take you two to Reverend Mallory. We have to work from 2:00 to 3:00 and be back here at 7:00 and work 'til 8:00."

The Reverend Mallory was a short, corpulent black man dressed in Waco's oppressive summer heat in a perfectly tailored, black silk suit with a vest, brilliant white shirt, a mustard-yellow tie, and a long black coat that fell to almost touching the ground. He had rings on every finger and a giant diamond stickpin for a tie tack. He looked just like a very well-outfitted Humpty-Dumpty to me.

Quinton, who obviously had made his acquaintance with the Reverend earlier, introduced us as Wilfred and Sean, which I took to be a bit peculiar.

Then the Reverend Mallory began to speak to us: "I doan care what you boys real names is," he said. "It's best that I doan know. If you do as you are tol' by my assistant, Miss Mozelle, and you keeps what you does here completely to yo'selves, you will be rewarded han'somely, very han'somely, nine times a week. You must not tell anyone what yous're doing here, or even that yous're here, not even yo' parents. Especially yo' parents. Now," he said, turning to Quinton, "Billy, take Sean and Wilfred to Miss Mozelle, please."

With that, he turned, passed out of the back of the tent and went directly into a small house trailer that he apparently lived in while on the road.

We turned on Quinton. "What's this all about, Quinton? Or is it Billy?" Ronnie asked, still puzzled by our little encounter with the Reverend.

"Wait," Quinton answered, holding his finger in front of his lips to signal us to be quiet. "Miss Mozelle will explain everything."

I must admit I have little recollection of what it was that Miss Mozelle said. She was young and gorgeous. Thin in all the right places to make the budding hormones of any almost-eleven-year-old boy lose his concentration, and his sense of direction, his appetite, and his natural desire to play baseball and virtually every other normally functioning faculty he ever possessed.

I do remember her "office" was a little walled-off room full of crutches, casts, wheelchairs, canes, various kinds of tapes and plasters, and a couple of ambulance-type gurneys. I also remember thinking that maybe she was a nurse and, simultaneously, hoping I would suffer some kind of seizure requiring her to administer mouth-to-mouth resuscitation. And this was the fantasy of a guy who had yet to even try to get close enough to know what a girl smells like.

She had been talking for some time. Ronnie and I had been drooling for the same amount of time. She was concluding, "So, boys, do you understand what it is you are to do?"

"Yes, yes!" Ronnie and I answered in unison, neither of us having any clue whatsoever.

We both stared like complete fools as she turned and walked away. I must say, watching her leave did nothing to sharpen our concentration or bring us back into reality.

"You guys can stop your drooling," Quinton said. "She's at least twenty-two, and, besides, she's a Negro."

"No, she's not!" It was Ronnie, vehemently denying her black heritage.

I agreed with him. "She was white, Quinton," I said. "And she is gorgeous."

"Gorgeous, yes. White, no," Quinton laughed.

As we learned later, after our shirtfronts had dried from over-salivation, Miss Mozelle was, indeed, black. She remained gorgeous in our eyes. I reminded Ronnie that New Yorkers were just as much Rubes as we Texans, and asked him if he could tell a dog from a cat. "Not if she's that good-looking," was his only response.

Now that she had left us, and Ronnie and I had not a clue what she had said or what it was we were to do for the $10 per revival meeting, Quinton, being older and obviously not so taken with her, proceeded to explain our new jobs and their duties.

Over the next three weeks, at twenty-seven revival meetings, it seems we were going to be "healed" by the Reverend Mallory—healed of a wide variety of debilitating conditions and disgusting ailments. Healed and made whole again. Again and again, apparently. And, if we did a good job (and kept our mouths shut), the Reverend Mallory might be persuaded to pass us along to the Reverend Jackson, who would pull into the present site for three weeks of more of the same as soon as the Reverend Mallory pulled out.

Dollar signs danced before our eyes. This was no piddlin' little summer job. We could be Vanderbilts or Rockefellers by September! Ninety dollars a week was rich man's pay in those days. You could buy three brand new Schwinns and a couple dozen banana splits for $90, although one of each would likely be enough. We saw ourselves rolling in dough.

A crowd was fast filling up the folding chairs inside the tent. A hugely fat lady, perspiring profusely, sat down with her back to us and began playing a rollicking version of "Bringing in the Sheaves" on a portable electric organ. I remember we all guessed how many pigs it would take to fill up the back of her empty dress to match her natural curvaceousness. I think my guess was eight.

Then Miss Mozelle glided back into the room, and Ronnie and I began, once again, to slobber as she said, "It's time to choose, boys."

"Choose what?" I blurted out, and then I turned red as a beet.

"Choose what's got you down today," she crooned softly. "What you will be healed of this afternoon."

"Broken leg," said Quinton, grabbing and strapping on a fake cast.

"I'll take polio," I said, latching onto a pair of crutches.

"I want to be raised from the dead." It was Ronnie, and he had just shown Quinton and me up for the Rubes we were. He had impressed Miss Mozelle. I could see it in her smile. God, what a smile it was, too!

"That is a very generous offer, Sean," she said to him, "but before we can do that, you will have to talk with the Reverend Mallory first. How about multiple sclerosis this first time?" she offered, rolling him a wheelchair.

"Yes. Sure. Multiple sclerosis it is. That's even better!" he blabbered on until he had brought himself all the way back down to Quinton's and my level of juvenile insipidity. Secretly, I rejoiced.

The Reverend Mallory was a brilliant orator. I found myself tempted to join in the "Amen, brothers" and the "Praise the Lords" shouted at random, and often, from the folding chairs as the good Reverend worked the crowd into a fever pitch that eventually led to some folks howling and crawling around, barking like dogs. Oh, it was a sight to behold.

If I do say so myself, when it came time for us to be healed, the three of us did a much better than workmanlike job, especially for this first-ever healing experience.

The Reverend Mallory grabbed Quinton by the head, jerked him upright, and intoned, "God of Gods (only he said it "God-ah"), heal this young man of his broken, mangled leg so that he may once again walk the straight and narrow path that leads to Thy kingdom." Then he ripped off the cast from Quinton's leg and shouted, "Get up. Get up-ah! And run thyself down that aisle and out-ah this tabernacle!" Quinton did just that. He jumped right up and raced down the aisle like a gazelle.

I remember, as the crowd went wild with "Hosannas," wondering if Negroes could play Little League in Waco. I didn't know if he could hit or throw, but, man, that Quinton could run.

Next, it was Ronnie's turn. He was shaking so in that wheelchair I couldn't be sure whether he was scared or just trying to mimic the symptoms of multiple sclerosis. The latter I thought would be a dreadful thing to do, as if this whole get-healed-for-cash scheme wasn't so bad, itself. Ronnie was healed and, like Quinton, raced out the aisle, pausing to do a 360-degree cartwheel midrun. By now, the tent was rocking, and the ushers were getting the plates ready to pass.

It was my turn. The Reverend Mallory called me forth, and I hobbled up on my borrowed crutches. "What is yo' name, and what is yo' infirmity?" the Reverend asked.

"My name is either George or Wilfred, I don't remember which, sir, and I have polio."

He looked at me funny and, recovering quickly, said to the congregation, "This poor lad has suffered, yea, has he suffered far too much. Not only is his body wracked with the wicked polio, but also that terrible disease has clouded his mind so he no longer be sure of his own name. Oh, Jesus, I beseech Thee. In Thine infinite mercy, free this boy" (here he seizes and tosses away the crutches and, I, not sure if I am healed yet, reel and stagger about until he grabs me by the shoulders and commences to shake the bejeesus out of me) "and make him whole again, body and mind. I pronounce you healed. Go forth and sin no more!"

So I ran down the aisle, jumped up and clicked my heels, shouted "Hallelujah!" and got out of that tent as quickly as I could. All the while I'm wondering why he selected me to "sin no more." He didn't admonish Quinton or Ronnie to sin no more. What did that mean? Was I going to get $15, maybe? Or was he mad at me for using two names?

And so, that first day, in a tent down by the Brazos River near Cameron Park, we were healed. Two white boys and a black boy. All friends. One of a broken leg, one of multiple sclerosis, and the biggest Rube of all, of polio.

And all throughout that summer, we were healed. Nine times every week were we healed. Healed of everything from asthma to zoological rot. Made whole, again and again, by the grace of God and the fancy footwork of Reverends Mallory, Jackson, Green, and Oliver. For twelve weeks we were healed, and each of us stashed away more than $1,000. What a summer job we had.

Oh, yes, the Reverends Mallory, Jackson, and Green all refused to raise Ronnie from the dead, in spite of our persistence, including a devilishly clever flip-chart presentation we cooked up to try to sell the idea. Reverend Oliver was an easier sell. At our first meeting, Ronnie asked point-blank, New Yorker style, "You got anything against raising me from the dead?"

The response was instant: "You very *clever*, young man. We'll do it the las' night!"

And lo, it came to pass, that Ronnie Simmons was resurrected by the Reverend Oliver on the 27th day of August, 1953 AD, in a tent on the Brazos River bank in Waco, Texas.

Hosanna!

Life's Lessons Learned:

- *It was possible for an almost eleven-year-old white boy to fall madly in love with a twenty-two-year-old black woman—because she was pretty, she was nice to us, and she smelled good.*

- *Judge not, lest ye be judged. Although we surmised Miss Mozelle was really the Reverend Mallory's mistress, who were we to question the morals of a man who had the power to heal and, in fact, had healed each of us more than two dozen times?*

- *With apologies to Abraham Lincoln, it is possible to fool all of the people all of the time. Once I got to the point where I could be in the same room with Miss Mozelle and not totally lose my senses, I asked her one day, "Don't these people see that the same three of us are healed at every service?" Her answer was not only prophetic, but it also formed the foundation for my lifelong career in advertising. Smiling at me, she said, "Folks see what they want to see." At that moment I thought her not only a beautiful person, but also a true prophet. For every single ad, for every campaign I was ever associated with, I always remembered Miss Mozelle and her prophecy that "Folks see what they want to see." Try it. It works.*

CHAPTER 6

Too Much of a Good Thing

WACO, 1953

By now you have probably figured out that only I, amongst the members of my family, was given to excesses. The rest of the family . . . well, I hesitate to use the term *reactionary,* so let's just say they were *conservative.* Moderation in everything, that was the family mantra. A simple house. A chromeless car with manual transmission, a heater, and an AM radio. Inexpensive, if not downright cheap, clothing. Simple food. And not a drop of the evil spirits anywhere on the premises.

When it came to religion, however, there was a total disconnect in the otherwise staid and low-key family outlook. My father had been reared in the Christian Church. You know, the Disciples of Christ. My mother, on the other hand, came up through the ranks of what my great-grandmother called *Dyed-in-the-Wool* Baptists. The good folks who brought you total immersion for baptism. Not a "sprinkler" in a trainload. Danceless proms. And dry precincts. Heck, entire dry states. Liquor, in any form, was just downright evil, reserved for the Whiskeypalians and those demon Catholics, all of whom hid guns in their basements (even though nobody in Central Texas had a basement, or likely had ever even seen one).

Yes, sir. We were abstainers. And our parents just knew, and reminded us regularly, that every Catholic family made wine in their nonexistent basements, right behind their stash of guns, and had a still in their garage to produce even more evil hard liquor. They knew it was true. Their grandparents had seen it, reported it, and passed it down in legendary stories dating back to the Civil War.

Since both our parents could read and had some significant reasoning capacity, taking the family to the Baptist church was out. Wouldn't want to lord it over the rest of the congregation, don't you know. And because almost nobody knew what the unique dogma of the Christian Church might be, or even if they drank wine, God forbid, that path, also, was eliminated. Too obscure. And too hard to find a church the next time we moved.

True to form, a compromise was struck.

We would be Methodists.

You know them. The folks who will speak to you in a liquor store. If you catch them there. As opposed to Baptists, who will pretend they are invisible. And holy-rollers, whatever they are, who are likely only there on some nefarious, spy-like mission to undermine the enterprise. And maybe even steal a pint or two.

So we duded ourselves up in our limited finery every Sunday morning and traipsed on down to the local Methodist gathering place. It was a small church, the kind today that would be labeled "evangelical," or even "charismatic." An insignificant place in Methodistdom, so that the bishop rarely made an appearance. Or even seemed to notice what went on there.

The pastor was a comical, at least to me, stereotype. A forerunner of television evangelists to come. He had long (for the day) hair, combed in a swooping pompadour that fell just below his collar in the back. That was a little suspicious, although you couldn't really discern "ducktails," the true sartorial symbol of evil. But he was a man of God, right? Given to working himself and the gathered flock into a frenzy of arm-waving, cuff-shooting, Rolex-exposing, prancing perspiration, his emphatic pronouncements getting ever louder and more outrageous with each passing, interminable minute. His sermons regularly ran on for seventy or eighty minutes. We guessed he had to get louder and louder to keep most of us awake after the first fifteen minutes or so.

He was a hellfire and damnation orator, raining down brimstone on his assembled flock. Unmercifully.

The only saving grace for a ten-year-old, held captive weekly for two hours or so, and forced to "sit up straight," was keeping count of the number of "hells" and "damns" so as to be able to report to Ronnie Simmons each Sunday afternoon a total of four-letter words that were belted forth at that morning's worship services.

Ronnie's family was Episcopalian. They participated in some mysterious, black-magic ritual called "mass." Very low-key. Sedate, even. So I always won the cussword count. Every Sunday. By huge margins.

My winnings got so lopsided that he actually entreated his parents to let him, on occasion, go to church with my family. Just to see for himself the bizarre act that I had described to him, in horrid detail, every Sunday afternoon.

As it turned out, that idea of going to church with the Arnolds backfired on him. He later would regularly express sorrow at ever having had the thought, much less having articulated it. Using his own four-letter descriptors, don't you know.

Here's where he ran afoul of reality. Leastwise, ten-year-old Episcopalian reality.

About the time he just had to "see for himself" the frenzied sideshow I had been describing to him every Sunday afternoon, complete with authentic verbal and physical demonstration, my own everything-in-moderation parents had decided that two hours in church on Sunday morning was not nearly enough for me, their semi-smart-aleck, heathen child. Clearly, I needed more time with the Lord to reflect on my attitude. And my actions.

A lot more.

And what could be better, for me, the aforementioned wise guy, than to have my closest associate join me in my penance? Or better for him, for that matter?

My mother and Ronnie's conspired to straighten out their errant offspring. You need to appreciate the dilemma and ultimate sacrifice this conspiracy represented to my mother. After all, the Simmons family were Whiskeypalians. Just having a conversation with them could threaten one's standing in the line of souls headed for either heaven or hell. To actually go into their home in the presence of single-malt Scotch, well, that was a dangerous mission. The only way to avoid eternal damnation as a result of consorting with these devil-worshipers was to be on firm ground that your mission was of a higher calling. Namely, to save your son's best friend from the clutches of the liquor-drinkers. If not Satan himself.

Who knew the difference?

So my mother actually spoke up in support of Ronnie's idea of attending the "right" church, although she didn't put it quite that way. No, she had a better idea.

You see, it was the beginning of summer. And that marked the commencement of a horrible annual event known as *Vacation Bible School.*

Never mind that it was no vacation to have to go to this pious little extravaganza. Or that we had just finished nine grueling months of real school. All of that was made totally irrelevant by that magic word, *Bible,* sitting right there in the middle of the name of the thing.

Never mind, too, that all Ronnie really wanted to do was to go see the Reverend Layne pontificate and postulate and utter four-letter words aloud on an occasional Sunday.

And then, there was the secret fact that Ronnie and I were already enlisted to spend an eventful nine hours a week in the clutches of the Reverend Mallory in a rocking tent down by the Brazos River. Getting healed. And rich.

We couldn't protest that we already were spending more time in church than a herd of monks in an upstate New York monastery. Oh, no! That would cost us money. And money was more important to us than grace. By a long shot.

But Ronnie had asked. And my mother had picked up the gauntlet, so to speak, and slapped us both right across our unsuspecting faces with it. We would be enrolled for three weeks of Vacation Bible School. One hundred fifty minutes of additional exposure to grace every weekday morning. Until the end of June.

Hosanna?

The PPIC (Pious Person In Charge) of Vacation Bible School was none other than the aforementioned Reverend Layne's wife. She was a huge woman. A Mrs. Martin look-alike, only dressed to the nines (or, in her case, the twenty-twos). And she was a Church Lady. Oh, my, yes, was she! All three hundred fifty sanctimonious pounds of her. Given to top-of-head patting, cheek pinching, and belching forth supercilious epithets designed, and guaranteed, to make ten-year-old boys hurl. On the spot.

Mrs. Reverend Layne was also the choir director. We guessed she was sort of double dipping. Or even triple dipping. Being the head of the choir and also the Vacation Bible School were both lowly, but paid, positions. We thought of her as a retired military officer who was drawing a government pension while working full time for the FBI. And, on the side, delivering a rural mail route, on contract, for the U.S. Post Office.

She had a beautiful singing voice. Kate Smith with perfect pitch. A voice that she totally wasted on church music. Or so we thought. There's no doubt she could have been the first Diana Ross (if Berry Gordy had invented Motown already). We wanted to hear her throw her head back and put her considerable weight behind an evangelical version of "Maybelline," with Chuck Berry for instrumental accompaniment.

Alas, however, she was devoted to getting a group of bored and uncooperative little heathens to sing out such favorites as "The Old Rugged Cross," "In the Garden," and "Bringing in the Sheaves."

Ronnie and I already had a lot of experience, down in the tent by the Brazos, with "Bringing in the Sheaves," although we still thought the last word of that little tune's first line was "sheep." Who knew what a "sheave" might be? Everybody knew about "sheep." Right?

So, every morning, beginning the second week of June, I, on my trusty red Western Flyer, complete with black saddle bags containing my well-oiled Rawlings fielder's glove and a semi-new baseball, and Ronnie on his old Huffy — soon to be re-placed with a new Schwinn from our stash of cash — would pedal on down to the Methodist church.

Vacation Bible School started at nine o'clock sharp. We dallied about on our route so as to miss the first fifteen minutes. After being on time the first day, we learned that the first quarter hour would be devoted to a group-sing, led by Mrs. Reverend Layne, of some of the aforementioned old Charles Wesley-penned favorites.

Dirges were not our favorite form of music.

If just having to be there weren't bad enough, you need to know that Mrs. Reverend Layne, although likely of childbearing age, had no children. We often thought she might be "with child." But who could tell for sure?

Being childless (and, we guessed, an only child), she was clueless about how to generate and hold the interest of a mass of hooligans in enforced attendance. Didn't have a clue.

The little kids, from toddlers on up to about age six, clearly were being bribed to be there. And to pay attention. Everybody got a Snicker's or a Baby Ruth at 11:30. Even a three-year-old could hold out for a couple of hours for that kind of reward.

But, as to the ten- and eleven-year-olds, segregated into a "big kids" class, gaining and holding our attention was another matter. Not to mention actually teaching us anything. Or indoctrinating us in some trivial, insignificant dogma that separated Methodists from Lutherans (which we guessed was the real reason for Vacation Bible School). It was a lost cause. Totally.

Only, Mrs. Reverend Layne didn't comprehend that Ronnie and I, at least, had put up an impermeable, invisible shield, designed to repel dogmatic hoo-hah. Totally. And effectively.

She did catch on to one thing. "You two are quite a challenge," she said to us on about the sixth or seventh day.

Hallelujah!

Our resistance was at least acknowledged.

On the other hand, we had the obligatory daily report to deliver once we escaped the confines of the little church in the vale and got back home. "What did you learn today?" Invariably, one or another of our parents would ask that question. We wondered why. Nine months of real school had just concluded, and not once was that question put to either of us. Had we suddenly fallen in with a group of religious zealots? Or maybe Hungarian gypsies? We didn't know. But we did know we had to have some kind of answer.

So, stealing a half hour from what could have been a rousing game of Monopoly, we took the little Bibles we had been issued on the first day of Vacation Bible School and proceeded to whip up a list of one-liners with which to respond, properly and enthusiastically, to the daily quizzes.

"Isaac digged a well."

"Joseph had this neat coat, but some crazy Egyptians stole it."

"Delilah was a barber."

"Asses often lost their jawbones back in the olden days."

We couldn't resist an occasional contemporary twist. But we were credible. And it worked. Best part was we could both issue any concocted answer, at random. Who would know better?

If we hadn't yet fooled the humongous Mrs. Reverend

Layne, we were pulling some big- time wool over unsuspecting eyes on the home front.

I mentioned that Mrs. Reverend Layne didn't know much about kids and how to deal with them. Actually, she knew nothing. Or even less. After a couple of hours, that fact was painfully apparent. After a couple of days, Ronnie and I decided we had to make a choice. We could roll with the insane activities the size twenty-two headmistress so dutifully had prepared in advance. Or we could embellish them. Put our own relevant spin on them, so to speak.

I'm sure you can guess that going with the flow was not our style. Boring. Boring. Boring.

So we set about to embellish, and otherwise perk up, the dreck we were expected to participate in daily.

These embellishments, enacted to the delight of the other bored ten- and eleven-year-olds, somehow seemed to be invisible to Mrs. Reverend Layne. She was so unaccustomed to being around kids that she either didn't see how we were helping her get through the daily grind, or she saw but was incapable of comprehending what was happening. We guessed the latter. Because we weren't trying to be subtle. Or hide anything.

To make it through the now-expanded half hour devoted each day to *Worshipful Glad Tidings Through Music,* we simply found it more palatable to modify, so to speak, the lyrics. "Bringing In the Sheep" was a no-brainer, although the Big Lady, as we called her amongst ourselves, never seemed to notice.

One, which she obviously did notice, was a slight modification of her trademark solo favorite, "In the Garden." We simply substituted the words "sheep's butt" for "roses." You know, "I come to the garden alone, while the dew is still on the sheep's butt." Sure, she noticed that one. But, unaccustomed as she was to ten- and eleven-year-olds, she had no idea what to do about it and, so, tried to ignore it. We wanted to ingrain it so deeply in her psyche that she would actually sing "sheep's butt" one day. Instead of "roses." We even had a pool, with two dollars at stake, for whoever guessed the right day she would slip.

Nobody ever won the money. She just quit including that song in our daily repertoire.

Part of our daily regimen was to color in biblical coloring

books. Can you imagine? Might have been appropriate for four-year-olds. But what did Big Lady know?

Ronnie, although an alien Episcopalian, quickly became the leader of the coloring scam. When it was time to take Crayolas in hand, he would quickly embellish Moses with horns. Or Mary Magdalene with a mustache and goatee. That embellishment was instantly flashed to all the other heathens who absolutely could not believe they had to color a stupid picture just so she could tape them on the walls in the hallway as a demonstration of the brainwashing effectiveness of Vacation Bible School. And Ronnie's daily visual devotion would immediately be included on most of all the others' coloring efforts, as well.

I say most of all the others' efforts because, as you well know, in any group of thirty ten- and eleven-year-olds, it is a statistical fact that there will be somewhere between 2.5 and 3.0 weenies. The kind of pious little perfect performers who will grow up to be Church Ladies. Or Christian-Right ministers.

We devised other such diversions as stealing one or two of the Baby Ruth little-kid-bribe candy bars and dropping them in the punch bowl. Nobody drank much punch, but everybody got to point, hold their nose with thumb and forefinger, and utter such memorable phrases as "Oooh . . . Look what somebody did!"

Undaunted, Big Lady kept coming at us with more and more determination. She was kind of like a giant garbage truck in grandma low gear with her throttle set wide open. Until she ran out of gas, figuratively speaking, of course, wasn't anything going to impede her forward motion.

What fun can it possibly be to subvert such an impregnable force? After the first few days, not much.

Tiring of always winning, but never being acknowledged as winners, Ronnie and I began to get restless after about six days of repetitive daily Big Lady indifference to our efforts to help. We had our comprehensive list of one-liner responses to use at home, which had taken us a whole half-hour to concoct. So what would happen if we spent a little less time each day in Big Lady's Vacation Bible School class?

Not much, we reasoned. Nobody ever took roll. Nobody seemed to care who was there and who was not. It was, after all, summertime, and lots of families had begun taking a week or two of vacation. Real vacations.

Perhaps there would be some other more meaningful and rewarding endeavor to occupy one hundred fifty minutes of our time each weekday morning—after we had put in an initial appearance for the start-up sing-song (so as not to miss a chance to continue our creative endeavor to improve the lyrics of old hymns). And we could show back up in time for a Snicker's or Baby Ruth. That was only sensible, don't you see?

The diversion Ronnie and I chose to otherwise occupy a part of our mornings, instead of attending all of each day's Vacation Bible School, was not only more fun, it was hellishly symbolic.

Willie's Pool Hall was right behind the Piggly Wiggly and next door to ABC Lawn Mower and Small Engine Repair. Willie's opened each morning at 10:00. Just in time to receive us following a rousing lyric-modification session at the Vacation Bible School. Normally, pool halls in those days did their best to keep out kids under eighteen. Ronnie and I told Willie, with totally straight faces, that we were nineteen and twenty, respectively. Willie bought our tale. We weren't sure if he really believed us or not. But we were sure that Willie wasn't the shiniest apple on the intelligence tree. So we went right on in every morning, making comments about cutting ourselves shaving and racing our cars the night before. Just to shore up a bit of credibility.

On day eight of VBS, we began to show up at Willie's front door promptly at 9:55 A.M. That early arrival assured us of a chance at getting our hands on table number four, the one with brand-new felt. And perfectly level surface. As opposed to tables two and five, both of which had a list toward downtown Waco.

We didn't think of our attendance at Willie's as any act of rebellion. Not at all. We reasoned that learning the nuances of nine-ball and just how to bust a rack so as to sink at least six balls with the first stroke ... well, those were equally as important to our futures in this world as how many people Jesus could really feed with two fishes and five loaves. Or was it five fishes and two loaves?

Didn't much matter. Even if we were quizzed, our inquisitors wouldn't know, either.

We spent an inspiring last eight days of VBS honing our skills with tapered sticks atop a green-felt-covered table with six little holes around the edges. And we got good at the sport. Very good. Pool shooting was, after all, a skill we could use for a lifetime. And, in a pinch, hustle up some ready cash with.

Hosanna.

Just for diversion, we would wander from Willie's on occasion to the ABC Lawn Mower and Small Engine Repair Service next door, where would watch Silas, resident mechanic and proprietor, overhaul somebody's Lawn Boy or Briggs & Stratton.

Silas was a talker. And, compared to the VBS' Big Lady, a darn good teacher. He would tell us everything he was doing. And why. Before the end of Vacation Bible School at the Methodist church, circa 1953, we could tear down and rebuild any small gasoline engine. Two-cycle, or four. Didn't matter.

We just had to be careful when we were quizzed about what we had learned that day to remember not to slip and respond with something like, "How to overhaul a dirty carburetor." Or, "Willie Mosconi's got nothing on us." Moses never had those experiences. Did he?

Someone once said, "All good things must come to an end." By the last week of June, we could also tell you, for sure, that "All boring things must also come to an end."

We decided that Vacation Bible School might have just been one of our best experiences in life to date. Where else could a couple of ten-year-olds learn to three-bank an eight ball in the side pocket, how to grind a Briggs & Stratton's valves, and—in the case of Mary Magdalene—what a "harlot" really is?

Hallelujah!

Life's Lessons Learned:

- *Sometimes some of your best experiences in life start out to be something entirely different.*
- *Church Ladies don't get it. They never will. Just forget it.*
- *A half hour of serious, studious preparation will often last for three weeks. Or longer.*
- *A Baby Ruth in a punch bowl is always funny. Always will be.*
- *Proper handling of a pool cue is a skill that lasts a lifetime.*

CHAPTER 7

What Goes Around, Comes Around

WACO, 1954

Winter was about to give way to summer. There are seldom springs or falls in Central Texas—just three months of winter and nine months of summer.

Ronnie Simmons and I had just been released from Purgatory, otherwise known as "detention" at Dean Highland Elementary School on North 33rd Street, where we were intent on finishing the fifth grade and waiting, impatiently, for the first of the new season's baseball practices of the infamous Waco Chevrolet Powergliders. We had delusionary visions of an undefeated season.

I guess I should explain how we got involved with long-term detention in the first place.

Back in early February on a Friday afternoon, one of those famous Texas cold fronts, lovingly called "blue northers," invaded like a runaway freight train from the Arctic Circle. There were flurries of snow, which was not all that common in Waco, and sheets of freezing rain coating our little world with ice, which was as common as sand.

Of course, when we had left home for school that morning, the sun had been shining brightly, and the temperature had promised to climb into the mid 70s. It did, about noon, but by 3:30, when the last bell rang, the temperature was 27 degrees and sinking in the face of gale-force winds blowing sleet and freezing rain.

Nobody had heard of "wind-chill factors" in the mid 1950s, leastwise not in Waco. I'll bet the wind chill was somewhere south of zero, though. None of us kids, except the geeks, had brought even a sweater, let alone a coat. Hooligans seldom paid attention to weather forecasts.

So about 3:15, our ever-cautious principal, Mr. Parker, came blasting over the loudspeaker system and held forth, even for him, an incredibly long time. He said if we had not brought warm clothing with us that morning, we could go to the office and call parents to come pick us up. If they were to be delayed, he rambled on in his own circuitous lingo, he would graciously open up the cafeteria so anyone who wanted to do so could wait for their ride in a warm place.

Moreover, he reminded us (for the gazillionth time that winter), we were to listen to the radio early Monday morning to find out if school might be canceled because of the inclement weather descending on us with such a fury. So as not to allow us kids to become too hopeful that the whole shebang would be called off on Monday, he concluded by saying that, if there were to be classes early next week, the custodial staff would come in at some ungodly hour, like 3:30 A.M., to fire up the boilers so there would be warmth coming from the steam radiators that heated each classroom in winter.

As it turned out, that last promise was probably not a wise thing for him to have said, and it clearly turned out not to have been a good thing for some of us more creative hellions to have heard.

He concluded, "Have a good weekend, and do not hope too hard for cancellations on Monday." This was his idea of a hilariously funny statement, and we could hear him chortling and snuffling at his own creativity before he managed to click off the microphone. Reaction to his hyena-like laughter and snortling among the student body was predictable. As I looked around Mrs. Tallant's classroom, all eyes were rolled upward in complete disgust.

All eyes except those of Ronnie Simmons, that is. He waved his hand at me and held up one finger, our secret signal for a parley as soon as possible.

The final bell rang, and everyone but the usual geeks raced outside in shirtsleeves to try to make snowballs from solid ice. Ronnie grabbed me by the arm on the way down the stairs from our third-floor classroom. He cupped his other hand in front of his mouth like a small megaphone and shouted above the regular afternoon din, "How much money you got?"

Not knowing what he had in mind, I thought a minute and shouted back, "More than nine hundred dollars." We were still living high off our earnings from being healed all last summer.

"No, I mean on you," he looked at me, as he often did, as if I were an idiot.

"About three dollars," I said, trying to remember if I had spent any of my own money at noon in the Ptomaine Palace, our name for the school's cafeteria.

"That's enough. Let's go," he headed for the bike rack, his new Schwinn and my trusty Western Flyer with the black saddlebags.

"Where're we going?" I wanted to know.

"To the Piggly Wiggly," he shouted. Then realizing the whole afternoon's plan, to be carried out in shirtsleeves in a blizzard, remained locked in his head, he stopped, waited for me to catch up, and began to explain the diabolical scheme he had created instantly when Mr. Parker blabbed on about starting up the radiators so early Monday morning.

"Here's the deal," he said, as I waited to be let in on this latest bit of mischief. "Parker will be here until the last geek gets picked up. So I figure we have at least an hour." He smiled wickedly.

"To do what?" I asked, still totally lost.

This time, his smile was a dark, almost cruel, smirk, and I knew the contortions that had seized his face were driven by his brain and had nothing to do with the fact that icicles were starting to form on his eyebrows.

The entire scam came pouring forth from Ronnie's mouth like water over Niagara Falls. "Okay, we blister on down to the Piggly Wiggly," he said (and here I pause to note that most

DRESSED FOR AN ICE STORM

*Since hooligans seldom paid attention to weather forecasts, Ronnie on his Schwinn
and I on my Western Flyer were always ready, no matter the elements. Of course,
my dog, Elmer, would have to stay home where it was warm. Or ride in the saddlebags, which would go back on when her special platform was removed.*

76 • Growing Up Simple

Northerners, like Ronnie, put an article before the name of places and things, as "the" Piggly Wiggly). "We buy us," he continued, "a big block of cheese, you know, the really stinky kind. Lindbergh, I think it's called."

"Limburger," I corrected.

"Yeah, sure, whatever," he responded, catching his breath.

"I don't like stinky cheese," I offered a gourmet's opinion.

"We're not going to eat it!" Again he looked at me, incredulous that I could ever possibly imagine we might buy some cheese and then eat it. "We're going to bring it back here before Parker locks up." He smiled, satisfied that I now understood everything.

My puzzled look, even with icicles hanging off my earlobes and a ring of ice forming around my hairline, shouted to him that he had left something out. I still wasn't aboard.

"The third floor!" he said, as if that would make it all crystal clear. "We're going to put little chunks of it on the radiators on the third floor." This time his grin was completely satanic.

Being relatively quick-witted myself, and having learned how his twisted New Yorker mind sometimes worked, I suddenly formed the whole scheme, and more, in my head. It was good. Really good. It was so good, in fact, that it came pouring out my ears and commenced to slapping me in the back of the neck!

"Brilliant!" I congratulated him. "Even if school is not canceled Monday morning, by the time we get here the third floor will stink so bad that Parker will have to let us all go home."

Occasionally I could catch even Ronnie flat-footed. He glanced up with a blank stare on his now beet-red, wet face.

George Arnold • 77

Then my safety-net-extension-theory-for-assuring-a-minimum-three-day-weekend hit him, and he pretended he had planned it all along.

"Right," he said, clapping me on the back. "Monday, we're off, for sure. And if school is actually canceled Monday, then we can count on the big stink-out for Tuesday. This is too good," he concluded the explanatory part of the caper. "Let's go!"

And so, full of piss and vinegar, off we pedaled as fast as we dared on the slippery, glazed streets, practically naked in the face of Arctic blasts, to "the" Piggly Wiggly, five blocks away.

Big chunk of Limburger cheese in hand, or rather, in saddlebag (because it stunk so badly, even half frozen, that neither of us wanted to hold it), we pedaled back to the school and arrived well before Mr. Parker started to lock the building. Six radiators were "cheesed-up," as we decided to call it.

Then, like all criminals, we let our egos talk us into a potentially fatal error in judgment.

"Before we go home," Ronnie suggested with a wry grin, "don't you think we ought to look in on Parker and the geeks? Just to be sure they're all okay, ya know what I mean?"

Never once considering we might be planting any kind of a clue, we tripped ourselves on down to Ptomaine Palace, where we found Mr. Parker and, predictably, a handful of snot-nosed third graders, noses running even though they hadn't even been outside yet.

And, of course, there was the inevitable Prunella, never missing a chance to brown-nose higher authority.

Prunella wasn't really her name. Seems to me now it was Jan, or Jane, maybe. We called her Prunella because she was the school snitch, a fat little girl with thick glasses who spoke with an affected British accent and told the nearest teacher every time one of us broke wind.

"Hi, Mr. Parker, everything okay?" I asked, cheerily, now that the ice had melted off my hands and arms. "We just thought we ought to, you know, be sure everything was in hand before we left for home." It was my best Tom Sawyer impression, and I was laying it on a little thick, which made Prunella mad. Sucking up was her exclusive prerogative, or so she thought.

"Awfully thoughtful of you boys to be so concerned," Mr.

Parker responded. "But we're all okay here. Are you sure you're going to make it home without freezing or getting sick?" he asked, seeming to be genuinely concerned.

This time Ronnie went one step too far. "Even if we get sick, we'll have until at least Tuesday to get well," he said, stifling a chortle of his own. "I'm sure there won't be any school here come Monday."

At the time, that last statement could have passed for wishful thinking, although, in retrospect, it turned out to be damning evidence, especially since Prunella would be able to spit it back, verbatim, from her own maggot-filled, fat, little mouth.

But I leap ahead too far.

By Monday morning, all signs of Friday's blue norther had disappeared, except the cold. It was still in the mid-20s, but without an icy wind or any rain or sleet. Ronnie and I wanted to get to school early, not because we were eager to learn more about Bernoulli's Principle, but because the sooner we got there, the quicker we would be back home to a rousing game of Monopoly.

Sure enough, we could smell the place from two blocks away. Phew! What a stench. As we parked our bikes and headed for the door, pinching our noses tightly against the odor, we found a hastily lettered sign that said, "Come to the Cafeteria." We stopped long enough to scratch out the word "Cafeteria" and replace it with "Ptomaine Palace."

The cafeteria was not in the old main building with the cheesed-up radiators. It was in a new wing that also contained the first- through third-grade classrooms. So those of us gathering in Ptomaine Palace that morning were the upper-classmen, the fourth through sixth graders.

Promptly at 8:15 A.M., Mr. Parker walked in and took his place on the stage at the east end of the room. The cafeteria also doubled as an auditorium. In fact, some fool on the school board had dubbed it the "cafetorium," a classically stupid moniker that was ignored by one and all.

Mr. Parker clicked on the microphone on the portable podium and said but a few words, an incredibly few words for him. I think I can remember them exactly. "Clearly," he said, speaking slowly and deliberately, "some joker or jokers has or have created a smell that, until it is aired out, makes today's use of the main building impossible." I thought he probably had been an English major.

He paused as if trying to compose his thoughts, and Ronnie slapped me on the leg as if to say, silently, "It worked!"

Parker continued, "Your teachers are spaced around the room. Each of you is to gather with your teacher and make arrangements to get safely home as quickly as possible. School will reconvene tomorrow morning."

Yahoo! We had done it. The ingenious duo of George and Ronnie had given a full 270 students an extra day off, and well deserved it was, too!

Then the bomb dropped.

"Ronnie Simmons and George Arnold will report to my office, immediately. That is all."

Why were we being summoned? Nobody, but nobody, had seen us that late Friday afternoon. As far as Parker knew, we had not even been in the building up until we checked out with him and Prunella at 4:45.

"Prunella!" Ronnie fairly shouted at me as the other 268 kids began making their way to nine clusters around the room.

Sure enough, when we walked into Mr. Parker's office, there she was in all her smug, thick-lensed, tattletale glory. She had her arms folded across her chest, her lower lip poked out, and she had "Gotcha!" written all over her face. She was witness for the prosecution numero uno. And we were road kill.

Mr. Parker came in, looking grim. He was brief: "You guys can make it hard on yourselves, or you can make it easy. It's all up to you," he said. "If you are responsible for that terrible smell that caused me to have to send almost 300 students home for the day, each of you raise your right hand."

"They did it! I saw them do it! They put stinky cheese on the radiators!" It was Prunella, who did everything to drive home her point, body language wise, except stick out her tongue at us.

"That will be all," Parker said to her. "We'll let them tell us if they did it."

We were caught, dead to rights, and there was no point denying it. I looked at Ronnie. Ronnie looked at me. We both stared daggers at Prunella. Then, in unison, we raised our right hands.

PRANKSTERS AND PRUNELLA

Mrs. Tallant's fifth grade class at Dean Highland Elementary School poses for their annual portrait with her and Jack Parker, principal. Is Prunella in this picture?

We were, after all, sworn to the Whip Wilson honor code of the West. No point in denying. That would be far worse than the cheesy act itself.

Ronnie spoke softly and respectfully, "Prunella made us do it, sir. It was blackmail. She even paid for the cheese."

Trying not to look startled, I turned to Mr. Parker. "That's exactly right, sir. She knows something about us that we didn't want her to blab, as you know she always does, so we had to do the cheese thing to keep her quiet."

We could not have been more credible if we had practiced those lines all weekend. And our quick confession apparently impressed Parker.

"All right," he began, "I'll tell you what we're going to do. All three of you are going to go on home today. You have accomplished your mission, as terrible as it was. Congratulations on a bad job, well done. Starting tomorrow afternoon, though, all of you will report to detention for one hour after school every day for four weeks and four days. In the library at 3:30, out the door at 4:30."

"You don't mean me, sir?" Prunella had lost a bit of her chutzpah.

"Yes, ma'am, I mean you, too." Parker even winked at Ronnie and me.

She was crumbling fast now. "But I didn't do anything. They're lying. They always lie about everything!" I thought she would cry. Secretly, I hoped she would, the little pest.

"You are correct about one thing, Jan," Mr. Parker responded. "You said you saw them do it, and you didn't, in fact, do *anything*. That was wrong, Jan. If you had told me Friday afternoon, all this stink could have been avoided." He smiled his own little "Gotcha" smile at her. Ronnie and I both burst out laughing, then quickly covered our mouths with both hands.

"Now, I don't know who is lying about what," Parker offered, "and I don't care. These boys did something stupid, and they got 300 kids a three-day weekend. Ronnie predicted it Friday. Remember? Now they are going to pay the price. Twenty-four hours of detention. And you, little missy, either guessed it was them or, if you really knew it, didn't do anything to prevent the smell. So you get to join them. Congratulations."

At this point, Prunella started bawling. Ronnie and I were smiling in spite of facing an eternity in Purgatory. Smiling because the dreaded and infamous Prunella had finally done herself in, with just a tad-bit of help from us. Har-dee-har-har . . .

Mr. Parker turned to us. "You boys go on home, now," he said softly and semi-confidentially. "One more thing: I'm not going to voluntarily contact your parents. You can do whatever you think is right about that." (Note: Total silence was absolutely, positively, undoubtedly right.)

And, so, we went on home to our last rousing game of Monopoly before entering the Big House. Somehow that was the best Monopoly game ever, and we enjoyed that holiday from school more than any other I could remember. Maybe it was because we created it. We literally created it.

Hallelujah!

Later, we heard that Mr. Parker finally had to call Prunella's mother to come from work to get her. She was incoherent, we heard, the whole time we were celebrating our Monopoly game and our last day of freedom for four weeks and four days.

Life's Lessons Learned:

- *What goes around, comes around. I wonder if Prunella ever learned that?*
- *Punishment for stupid pet tricks is not too bad if you fess-up quickly.*
- *Parents and teachers are not always as out-to-lunch as kids assume.*
- *Limburger cheese really, really stinks. It can make an entire building temporarily uninhabitable.*
- *Great creativity, spontaneous and on-the-spot, is most often appreciated, even if it is a bald-faced lie.*

DRATTED GREEN GRASS

Kamikaze had the chore of keeping the overfertilized, overwatered, lush green lawn on Windsor Avenue mowed and trimmed at all times.

CHAPTER 8

Money Laundering

WACO, 1955

My father was a ridiculous perfectionist in many things, but when it came to our lawn, he was a maniac—or whatever's worse than a maniac. It would be no stretch to say we had the finest, thickest stand of the dark-greenest St. Augustine grass on Windsor Avenue, and flowerbeds filled with the most prolific Paul Scarlet roses west of the Mississippi. I might even go so far as to say that our landscape, although a bit monotonous, with just the one kind of roses and green-green grass, ten inches deep, was the most handsome, well-cared-for landscape in all of Waco by 1955.

Only problem with that was that I, at age twelve and just finishing up the sixth grade, needed to change my name to Kamikaze or Mitsubishi. You see, I was the full-time gardener. It was my job to keep that landscape pristine at all times from March through October when, thankfully, the stupid grass began to go dormant for the three or four short months of winter.

Since my father was a firm believer of applying a top coating of cotton burrs in the fall and 49-0-0 pure urea fertilizer three times over the summer, that grass grew like bamboo in a Thai rain forest. Every three or four days it had to be mowed and edged and trimmed. More than four days and the lawnmower and its pusher, namely me, could barely make our way through it. And the clippings would be so deep they had to be raked up.

In a word, maintaining that lawn was a "chore."

Before 1955, my brother would occasionally pitch in. But he had graduated from Waco High School by then, had his own car, a job, and was attending Baylor University. My only consolation at having lost his help was that I knew, at Baylor, he would be required to attend compulsory "Chapel." And I also knew there had to be Church Ladies, galore, at Chapel, to make at least part of his day miserable.

I would cringe each spring when my dad would take down the old, hand-push mower from its winter perch in the garage, sharpen the blades, oil the wheels and adjust the mechanism. My long-term servitude was about to begin.

Besides, Ronnie Simmons and I had the fate of the Waco Chevrolet Powergliders to be concerned with. Pushing a reel-type hand mower around for a couple of hours, followed by crawling along the curb and sidewalk to trim with hand clippers, had a tendency to make even a big and healthy twelve-year-old tired. And being tired before a big baseball game was no way to be.

We had just gotten our first television set, a behemoth black-and-white Motorola about the size of an LST with a screen no larger than a library book. I was spending too much time in front of it watching test patterns. Nothing at all came on the air until 3:00 P.M., when it was Howdy Doody time, followed by a rousing session of Uncle Elihu and Ralph, the bat, local Buffalo Bob wannabes.

I began to be perplexed as to how I could catch Howdy, Buffalo Bob and the crazy mayor of Doodyville, then still have time to see Ralph, the bat, get the yard mowed and trimmed, and make a 6:00 P.M. game against the dreaded Pontiac Pistons.

My days were too crowded.

Ronnie suggested I spend some of the $900 or so I had left from being healed to buy a gasoline-powered mower and an electric edger to make my never-ending mowing quicker and less of an adventure. Now, that was a great idea, and I had thought of it the year before. But I couldn't just whip over to the local hardware store and plunk down $100 or so for some shiny, new, laborsaving tools without having to divulge the source of my bankroll. There was no way I could ever divulge the source, or even the existence, of that bankroll.

So we sat ourselves down on his screened-in back porch with a couple of Grapettes, and we started thinking. Wasn't long before an idea hit us both at about the same time.

Credit! That was it! I could buy the lawn equipment on credit, pay it back from my hidden bankroll, and spend whatever I could make mowing a couple of other lawns in the neighborhood.

Shazam! Another inscrutable problem solved by creative thinking. And Grapettes.

Bright and early Saturday morning, Ronnie, on his Schwinn, and I, on my trusty red Western Flyer with the black-and-white saddlebags, complete with a new baseball and my well-worn and well-oiled Rawlings fielder's glove, departed Windsor Avenue for the big Sears, Roebuck store on 18th Street. We parked our bikes out front, waited ten minutes for the store to open, and marched ourselves up to the credit office on the second floor.

A lady back at a desk in the corner stood up and came to her side of the counter.

"What can I do for you?" she asked.

"I want to open a charge account!" I said with all the confidence of a 500-pound gorilla.

"Oh, really?" she said. "And what would you be purchasing with this charge account?" she inquired, still politely.

"Not sure exactly, but at least a gasoline-powered lawnmower, an electric edger, an extension cord, and a gas can," I beamed.

"Going into the lawnmowing business?" she asked.

"Yes, ma'am. A small business, at least," Ronnie responded.

"How old are you?" she asked.

Uh-oh. Was there an age limit on credit?

"We are both going to be thirteen in a few months," Ronnie responded.

"And how long have you lived in Waco?" The interrogation continued.

"I've been here almost four years," I answered with a smile, thinking being friendly might help in getting that charge account, and being more than a little pleased at not having had to move in so long. "And Ronnie's been here almost three."

I fudged Ronnie's tenure a bit.

The woman behind the desk was trying not to laugh, which made us both a bit uncomfortable. But she looked nothing like a dratted Church Lady, so we held our ground.

"I'll tell you what," she said, "if there is someone over the age of twenty-one who will sign your credit application, we might be able to get you that account."

Rats!

"Thank you," I said, and we both turned and went back to our bikes with heads down, beaten, if only temporarily, in the game of higher economics.

"I'll bet we've each got more money than she makes in six months," Ronnie opined sarcastically.

"It's not about her, Ronnie," I responded. "But we have us some more thinking to do."

"Grapettes?" he asked.

"Grapettes," I answered.

Syrupy, sweet soft drinks in hand, this time in my garage, we sat down by the Lionel steam train layout and started, once again, to ponder. From that sipping and thinking session came another plan. A brazen plan, to be sure, but one that ought to work.

I slipped in the back door and asked my mother, quietly, "What kind of a mood is Daddy in?"

She smiled. We often compared notes before major conversations. Or confrontations.

"Pretty good, I think," she said to me.

I yelled out the back door for Ronnie, and we went looking for my father. It took about three seconds to determine he wasn't in the house. It was a small house. His car was in the driveway, so we knew he had to be around somewhere.

We found him pruning those dratted climbing Paul Scarlet rose bushes out front.

BARBECUE, ANYONE?
There was plenty of time for cookouts and to trim the dratted rose bushes since Kamikaze was committed to all the hard lawn chores.

"We're going into the lawnmowing business," I blurted out, directly. With my father, beating around the bush would only lead to trouble. "But we need to buy us some equipment."

He didn't flinch, so I plowed directly on. "The lady at the Sears credit department says we can have an account and pay for the equipment over the summer out of what we earn, but we need someone over twenty-one to sign for us." There, I had blurted out the whole scam. Almost.

"Would that someone be me?" my father asked, seeming to be genuinely amused. "And if it is, what do I get out of the deal?"

There was always a *quid pro quo* with my father. He did nothing without either recompense or repercussions.

We had anticipated the question. "You will get this yard done for free all summer, and with an electric edger, it will look even better than it does now when we do the clipping by hand," I responded. I had thrown in the irresistible lagniappe of a better looking lawn to head off his obvious reply that he already got the yard done for free, usually by Kamikaze only. Sometimes Mitsubishi helped.

It was a clever ploy, and it worked. He even started to say, "But I already ..." when he stopped in midsentence and said, "Oh, even better looking, huh?"

"More professional." I heaped on the adjectives.

He could not resist the temptation of an "even better, more professional-looking lawn." We knew he wouldn't be able to. Clever planning paid off once again. We had played him like a banjo, and he even stopped pruning his beloved roses to load us into the car and take us down to the Sears store.

We were determined to shop carefully. So as soon as he had signed the golden promissory note and we had sworn not to spend more than $125 and to pay it back at the rate of at least $10 a week, he went home, leaving us with instructions to call him to pick us up once we had decided what we wanted.

What we wanted was a red Craftsman mower with a 21-inch blade and a 2.5 horsepower, 2-cycle engine. No oil-changing chores for us. And what else we wanted was a little green electric edger that sounded like a bee when you turned it on. And a gas can and a couple of small bottles of ash-free, two-cycle oil.

Now, that may not sound like a very elaborate set of equipment, but in 1955, it was Sears, Roebuck's "Best." You know, "Good, Better, Best." Both the mower and the edger were the Cadillacs (there's that word again) of their lines.

The tab came to just over $100. Both of us, with secret stashes of more than $900, thought, "Big deal!"

Before we even had a chance to fire up the mower or plug in the edger, Ronnie came down to my house with an announcement.

"*Buon giorno,*" he said. "*¿Come sta?*" He tried to smile, but I could see he was straining. He repeated the polysyllabic polyglot for me.

Now, I knew it wasn't English, and I had picked up enough Tex-Mex to know it was not Spanish, either.

"I give up," I said, beginning to wonder why he had a funny look on his face. Seriousness was usually not his thing.

"We're moving to Italy," he said. "My dad is going in two weeks, and the rest of us are going at the end of May, when school is over. Someplace called Aviano, I think. My dad's going to be a major." Even that piece of good news didn't evoke a genuine smile.

I thought we had at least six weeks to spend creating more mischief, but Ronnie had a funny streak. He immediately began to withdraw, cutting off our friendship quickly rather than trying to hang on until the final day. He was a frequent mover, too.

I missed his wit and creativity mightily. And the Waco Chevrolet Powergliders needed a second baseman, again.

My first *bona fide* lawn-mowing client was Miss Pruitt, a spinster who lived with her aged mother directly across the street from us. She was the bookkeeper for the local Coca-Cola bottler. That seemed like it must be a fine job. She had a brand new 1955 Ford Crown Victoria, a pretty good house, and she took care of an elderly parent. She must have been stretched thinner than appearances would indicate, though, because she wanted her yard mowed and edged every week, but she was willing to pay only $2. That wasn't terrible. I could finish up her yard, thanks to my new red Craftsman mower, in about ninety minutes. Without rushing.

But $2 wasn't going to be able to be passed off as enough to make my weekly $10 payment. Oh, I didn't worry about coming up with the $10. I had almost 100 $10 bills in my secret cigar box in the back of my closet. No, $10 was far from the problem.

The real problem was that I intended to use this "lawnmowing" scam to launder as much of the $900 I had left from my "getting healed" earnings as possible into a bank account, disguised as lawnmowing money. My plan was to do several yards, appear to be making loads of money, and give my father about $30-$40 a week. He would put $20-$30 in my bank account and retain his $10 for the Sears, Roebuck charge account.

I had to make the enterprise at least appear to be real. Real enough, for sure, to provide me some pretty good spending money while I laundered the $900, plus some of the lawnmowing proceeds, into a bank account ... and paid off Mr. Sears.

So I went out looking for lawns to mow after school and on Saturdays. As luck would have it, I found two more the first afternoon. Mrs. Frankenberger, who lived next door to Miss Pruitt, would pay me $6 for the same size yard I was getting $2 for doing for Miss Pruitt. I must say, in all fairness, that Miss Pruitt would occasionally throw in a case of Coca-Cola. I didn't like it as much as Grapette, but it was free, and Grapette cost a nickel.

The second yard belonged to a member of the Hank Thompson country music band. It might have been Hank himself, for all I know. I never asked. But whoever he was, his yard was at the far end of Windsor Avenue at about 41st Street, right across the road from the Little League fields where the Powergliders managed only twenty double plays that year, sans Ronnie.

The music man's yard was big, at least three normal-sized lots for that neighborhood. There was a bunch of edging to do, as well. We struck a deal for $15 a week. It took me about three hours to cut and edge, so I had moved back up to half-scale of the healing game.

That provided a base of $23 a week, so I was set to open up the laundry. Any other jobs that came along would just be icing on the "get the money out of the cigar box and into the bank" cake.

That summer, missing my sidekick of nearly three years mightily, I actually made about $450 mowing yards. I managed to get $850 laundered and still spend $100 or so, in addition to paying Sears for the mower and edger.

HO, HO, HO!

Why was everybody else looking so glum? I'm the poor kid who got two saws, a hammer, a square, and a brace-and-bits set for Christmas.

The remaining $400 or thereabouts was laundered over the next fall as proceeds from a three-afternoon-a-week job selling Spudnuts, a local confection made from potato, rather than wheat, flour. Truthfully, I might have made all of $40 carting those grease-filled, sugar-coated doughnut lookalikes door-to-door three afternoons a week.

I started to feel, again, like Lamont Cranston, *The Shadow.* I truly had the power to cloud my parents' minds so that they could not see the wool I was pulling over their eyes.

My plan worked, though. By Christmas, 1955, the entire $900 from my cigar box, plus another $400 from mowing and the door-to-door selling of sugar-coated, greased-filled potato Spudnuts, had been safely placed in the Texas Department of

Public Safety Employees Credit Union, to be replaced in the cigar box with an infinitely explainable $75 or so that was left over.

Speaking of Christmas, my father chose that Holiday to pull two boners, as far as I was concerned. First he announced we would be moving back to Austin in the spring. Oh, joy. Another move. Another school. Another group of strangers for class-mates.

At least Quinton and Ronnie had moved first.

Second, since I was so handy and such an entrepreneur, I needed something special for Christmas. Not ball gloves. Not candy or fruit. Not even jeans or underwear.

Tools. A hammer, a square, a hand drill, two saws. It was awful. The worst. I still have those damnable tools, and every time I see one of them, I feel like crying a twelve-year-old's tears.

So, I took me $25 out of my cigar box, and I went, the day after Christmas, and bought me what I would have preferred in the first place—a new-fangled, battery-powered radio encased in genuine, simulated leather, with an antenna and an earplug so I could listen to the Chicago White Sox or the St. Louis Cardinals games at night, or maybe some good jazz from New Orleans.

And some candy.

Life's Lessons Learned:

- *Enjoy a real friendship while you can. You never know when some-thing as unimportant as world peace may separate you forever. (Hey, Ronnie, if you're out there somewhere, give me a call. I live in Fredericksburg, Texas.)*

- *You must be ever vigilant to never lose sight of the "rabbit" when dealing with parents. You may get to trade slave labor for a guaran-teed note at the local Sears, Roebuck; and you might also get tools for Christmas. Yuck!*

- *Remember that laundering money is a criminal act—a federal of-fense. Do it only if you have to in order to retain the money itself.*

CHAPTER 9

Dangling Participles

AUSTIN, 1956

By the time I was fourteen and in the eighth grade, I had been to ten different schools, hardly conducive to forming lifelong friendships. Ronnie Simmons, my one good friend (aside from John Joe and Lady Archibald) and fellow Waco Chevrolet Powerglider, was long gone. His father, the fighter pilot, had been promoted to major and transferred to Italy to help keep the peace along the "Iron Curtain."

Quinton had even left a year before Ronnie. I'm sure he was glad to get out of the South and out of Texas.

In fact, we had moved so often that I had become hesitant to even try to make friends anywhere, lest we move away from yet another good buddy. This time, however, my father promised it was our last move. He had been assigned to manage the training academy for the Texas Department of Public Safety. That meant headquarters—in Austin.

My uncle, the former state trooper, was now a Texas Ranger whose primary duties involved supervising the DPS fixed-wing and helicopter fleets and being the pilot for a string of Texas governors. So he and my aunt and cousins were in Austin, too.

It looked like we might just be settled for a long time, and I began to think, again, about finding a replacement friend for Ronnie Simmons.

A willing candidate was Don Hickling. We were both in the eighth grade at University Junior High School in the shadow of The University of Texas. We got acquainted on the football team, the UJH Eagles, where I was starting right tackle on offense and starting left tackle on defense. Don started at tight end, right beside me on offense, and at linebacker, right behind me, on defense.

We had a mediocre team, mostly because we had no speed, no size and, crucially important, no skills. I was the biggest guy out there at 170 pounds, and we regularly played teams whose lines averaged 210 pounds. So we got beat a lot, and we got beat up every last game. Blood and bulging bruises became our bread and butter. Arm slings and Johnson & Johnson adhesive tape variously applied to our anatomies were our badges of courage in the game of blood-and-guts football. They made us heroes amongst the student body, especially the girls, a few of whom were starting to look interesting to us.

We had a lot of time on our hands those two years at UJH. Allen Junior High, in deep East Austin, had burned down near the beginning of our eighth year, and we were called upon to sacrifice with shorter classes. School would start earlier and be dismissed each day at 12:30 so the kids from Allen could start their classes at 1:00. You can imagine how sad that made us all. Heh-heh.

After dismissal, of course, the football team practiced hard to try to keep from getting killed at our next game, but even that activity let us go home, or somewhere, by about 2:30, fully three hours earlier than we had finished up before the fire.

Turns out Don, like me, was a refugee from the North—Ohio, to be exact. But he had been in Austin for some time, already—ever since the first grade at Palm School on East 1st Street. He had a best friend in the band, Andy Bailey, and the three of us became a creative trio those last two years of junior high school. Let me hasten to add that we were not inseparable by any means. Don and I fancied ourselves athletes, but sweating and pain were not in Andy's plans.

Too, both of them were in the band, and I was not. For all practical purposes, my musical talent involved turning on a radio. Oh, I tried, but after twelve weeks of piano lessons, my music teacher suggested to my parents that either I was pretty much disinterested in learning to play the instrument ... or I was a completely tone-deaf dolt whose presence before a keyboard she could no longer abide.

I didn't like her, either, even though she didn't look to me anything like a Church Lady. She smelled funny. Like Simoniz car wax.

When the two of them, Don and Andy, that is, were doing band things, I had another good friend, Kenny Squier, who had just moved to Austin from England, where his father had been stationed in the air force. Austin was their last move before his father retired, so I felt reasonably comfortable he might be around for a while. In fact, he still lives in the Austin area.

All four of us had paper routes. Folding, delivering, and collecting for the daily *Austin American-Statesman* was the sole livelihood for each of us, although we always suspected Andy's mother either gave him extra cash or he lifted it from her purse.

Don's and Andy's routes were for the morning paper, *The Austin American*. The two routes were adjacent to The University of Texas campus, so most mornings they just teamed up and threw them together. Sometimes I went with them because they delivered papers to every sorority house on the campus.

It's not what you're thinking.

We had little, if any, interest in seeing some nineteen-year-old coed with her hair in curlers and green stuff plastered on her face, even if she was wearing a shorty nighty that came up to her whatevers. No, it wasn't the lure of *femme fatales* that made those two morning routes so golden.

It was the doughnuts and chocolate milk. We were just fourteen, after all.

Seems every early-morning delivery person, including us, had been instructed by every housemother of every sorority house to leave deliveries on the back porch. So we would take us two or three newspapers around back and help ourselves to some of the doughnuts and chocolate milk that had arrived earlier.

It was a good way to start the day.

We were careful not to take too many doughnuts or too many cartons of chocolate milk from any one porch, lest someone miss them. In several years of our petty pilfering, nobody did, so far as I know.

My route, and Kenny's, were both in the afternoon, throwing *The Austin Statesman*. It was usually a smaller paper than *The American*, but the pay was the same—35 cents per customer per month, provided you collected from everyone and nobody moved off without paying.

Don and Andy had well over 100 customers each. Kenny had 110. And I had only 65 to start with. That meant they always had about 50% more money than I did and, hard as I worked at it, I couldn't get my smaller route over 90 papers.

Having earned $10 an hour getting healed on my first job, I was the first to get restless with the meager pay and upside risks of being a (very) downscale entrepreneur. So I went out looking for an after-school job. With a steady paycheck.

As luck would have it, the manager of the Varsity Theater at Guadalupe and 24th streets was one of my brother's best friends from Waco High School. Jim and Jerry Cooper, his friend, were both students at UT and had worked together at the old WACO Theatre. Jerry stayed with the Interstate chain when he went to college, taking over as manager of the Varsity.

So I called him, and I put on a suit and went to see him. Miraculously, he hired me. I say "miraculously" because he was one of the few people on earth who knew too much about me. One of the benefits of moving frequently was just plain walking away and leaving your stupid past behind you.

But Jerry knew about the money I had earned with the healing job, although I had refused to divulge its origins. And he knew about the Limburger cheese incident. Still, he hired me, anyway, for the princely sum of 70 cents an hour. I was to work from 6:00 P.M. until closing, three or four weeknights, Saturday morning for the kiddy matinee, and Sunday evening from 6:00 to midnight, or whenever the last feature ended and all the people left, whichever came first.

It still wasn't $10 an hour, but I could clear $25 a week, a full month's net on the infernal paper route. So I took the job, strapped on a paper dickey, a clip-on black tie, dark blue pants with a red stripe down each leg, and a powder-blue, double-breasted jacket with gold buttons and epaulets. Wow! I was an Interstate Theaters usher, looking like a Russian Air Force general.

Cat on a Hot Tin Roof started playing the same day I started

PUT ON A SUIT
*And go get a **real** after-school job as an usher at the Varsity Theater, Guadalupe and 24th streets, Austin. At fourteen, we had no idea these jobs would last almost five years and be a proving ground for so much creativity and so many hellishly clever pranks.*

ushering. It starred Elizabeth Taylor as the neglected wife, Maggie, The Cat; Paul Newman as her drunken husband, Brick; and Burl Ives as "Big Daddy," Brick's father. Today, more than four decades later, I can still recite the entire screenplay, and I can point out the three minor continuity lapses on the release print. I watched that movie forty-eight times before I learned that an Interstate Theaters usher wasn't required to watch the movie at all.

Soon as a week rolled around and I got my first paycheck, I flashed my bankroll amongst my three buddies. Don and Kenny both wanted to know what they would have to do to get a great job like mine—free passes to any movie in town and 70 cents an hour, to boot. Andy, with his mother's purse as his near-bottom-less reservoir, allowed as how it sounded too much like confining work to him. Besides, he figured, the chocolate milk and dough-nuts were worth at least another $4-5 a week in compensation, so he would, thank you very much, just stick with the ol' *Austin American-Statesman*.

So it came to pass that, within a month or two, both Don and Kenny joined me as ushers at the Varsity Theater.

Alas, the Varsity, once an 850-seat, wide-screen crown jewel in the Interstate Theaters chain, is no more. It has given way to two stories of little retail shops which, I suppose, earn more in rent than the beautiful old theater ever made in box office and concessions.

No movie house, anywhere, at any time, ever had a more cre-ative set of employees. Besides the three of us, there was Sam Hanks, the world's crudest practical joker; a guy named Bob, a Korean War veteran going to law school on the GI bill and also a right good boozer; Angie, our grandmotherly ticket seller; and Lillie Mae, a maid who kept the place looking decent from about noon to 8:00 P.M. every day.

So much creativity took place that I could tell you about. Like the day Don rigged up a fan to blow the aroma of popping corn into the auditorium. I had popcorn popping duty that Saturday, and the double-feature was *Sinbad, the Sailor* and *Dumbo*. We had us 900 screaming kids on our hands all day long. They wanted popcorn. I popped 500 pounds of corn between 9:00 A.M. and 6:00 P.M., even though I was supposed to be able to go home at noon, and still I could not keep up with the demand. It was just as I was about to go home, at around 6:00 in the evening, exhausted, that Don revealed his little trick.

I swore vengeance.

I could also tell you about the many fun times we had changing the marquee, especially on those Thursday nights preceding a big UT football game. Darrell Royal had recently been hired to coach the Longhorns, and football was king along Guadalupe Street, usually just called "the Drag."

Don and Kenny and I had about a dozen alphabets worth of plastic letters, and we could spell out almost anything we could think of to the delight of the impromptu-pep-rally student crowd on the street. I guess our best was the question, "What comes out of a Chinaman's butt?" on the Thursday night before a big Saturday game with Rice University. That question actually became an unofficial cheer for the Longhorns.

We also lost a lot of plastic letters. Somebody in the crowd would yell, "Give me a T!" So we would sail one, Frisbee-style, from our perch atop the marquee, into the crowd. And an E, an X, an A, and an S, too. We ran out of X's early on.

Eventually the administration of the university called on our management to request we cease and desist entertaining a relatively ruly (as opposed to unruly) crowd of students every Thursday night. Our manager knew nothing of these long-standing hijinks since he usually went home after the box office closed, leaving the entire enterprise in our often sadistic, but always creative, hands. Thereafter, we tried to tone it down, but that was no fun. We just changed the marquee and went on back inside to wait for the last feature to end.

We got clean away, slick as can be, with the greatest on-the-spot prank ever created and executed at the Varsity, or any other theater. In fact, I am about to reveal the truth of the matter for the very first time to anybody except the three of us involved in the caper, so far as I know.

You see, Clint Bradley, who operated the hole-in-the-wall Sunset Grill on 24th Street, kind of behind and across 24th Street from the Varsity Theater, served the best hamburgers and the greasiest fries in the universe. But the crew at the Varsity, while still smitten with his burgers, badgered Clint to import a tasty sausage produced by South Side Market in Elgin, Texas, a few miles to the east. It was called Elgin Hot Gut.

EHG was greasy, it was a little hot, it was delicious, and it was cheap. Don and I convinced Clint, finally, that students by the hundreds were driving all the way to Elgin to bring back EHG, and that he could make a small fortune by just adding it to his menu and selling it by the foot.

Quite coincidentally, Clint's acquiescence to our demands for more conveniently available EHG came at the same time as a special screening of a Billy Graham Crusade movie for a group of about 400 of those dratted Church Ladies.

Occasionally, especially if we were showing a dog of a movie that might attract less than a dozen people on an afternoon, we would close down the house and rent it out to a private group who had a special movie they wanted to see. This particular private showing happened to be for Church Ladies. I didn't like Church Ladies. For ten years, I had done everything possible to avoid Church Ladies. And now I was confronted with 400 of them.

Vengeance was mine! Hallelujah. Praise the Lord and pass the potatoes!

I would have half the Church Ladies in Austin captive. Or maybe all of them from the infamous Hyde Park Baptist Church. That would be an opportunity of a lifetime, as far as I was concerned.

My two accomplices in "Operation Church Ladies" would be my good friend, Don Hickling, and that semi-crazy prankster, Sam Hanks. As I outlined the caper to them, two things became apparent. First, neither of them liked Church Ladies even as much as I did, which was zero. Second, the whole operation would require split-second timing and teamwork.

We decided to practice after the house closed that very night. There were three roles in Operation Church Ladies. We wrote them down on identical pieces of paper and then mixed them up in the popcorn popper so as to be totally fair. And we each agreed to accept the role we drew.

Don reached in first. His part would be *The Big Moon*. Sam was next, and he drew the part of *The Procurer and The Destroyer*. That left me the job of *The Bombardier*. We were all pleased, especially me, since I would have worried if Sam had drawn either

The Big Moon or *The Bombardier.* Too many ways things could go wrong with Sam on the loose. But *The Procurer and The Destroyer's* duties were very structured and only required split-second timing.

While all of Austin was out having fun that night, the three of us practiced. We locked the doors after all the patrons and the projectionist had left, we turned out all the lights except the side sconces in the big auditorium, and we practiced. Twelve times we ran through the entire drill. We had it down to plus-or-minus a half second. We were ready.

Sure enough, the next afternoon, 400 Church Ladies arrived promptly on a dozen chartered city buses, bringing with them two large metal canisters that held five reels of Billy Graham Crusaders praising and shouting their hosannas.

We had decided to let the feature run to some climactic point before flashing the signal to start the caper. Sam's trusty flashlight would be our sign.

Sam, as *The Procurer,* did his procuring and brought the package to me, *The Bombardier.* Don and I did our best to seat the most pious-looking of these old hens in row 23, seats 7, 8 or 9— near the center of the aisle.

It didn't take long to find our victim. She had on the obligatory Church Lady hat with the veil hiding her hairline pimples, and the expected, ever-sparkling, white gloves; her collar, like a turtleneck, was buttoned to cover her scrawny, vein-impaired neck, and her skirt fell to her ankles, not that anyone would want to see them. She even wore pince-nez glasses. Church Lady perfection, she was.

We were very insistent that she and her holier-than-thou friend sit in row 23, seats 7 and 8. They were unsuspecting. Grateful, even, for the extra attention.

Now we were ready. Don and I were up in the first row of the balcony, which we had closed and kept empty, just above row 23, seats 7 and 8. Sam, with a large cloth bag and his flashlight in his hands, waited downstairs, watching for something on the screen that might lead someone to swoon. Or a Church Lady to get excited. That would be enough.

About the time ol' Billy got really wound up and launched from common, everyday, Southern-colloquial English into the evangelists' exclusive goat-speak (wherein the voice breaks, *staccato*, like a billygoat talking), Sam flashed the signal.

Don, *The Big Moon*, stood up, dropped his pants and underwear, and hung his rather large and completely bare behind way out over the balcony rail.

As *The Bombardier*, I began to grunt loudly and blow hard on my arm to make the sound of passing gas, magnified a hundred times.

The intrusive sound of someone breaking wind at 80 decibels caused more than a few of the Church Ladies to look up, among them the overly pious old crone in row 23, seat 7. She looked right up at Don's behind as if she were a long-distance, secret-agent proctologist, and—just as she recognized what she was seeing and gasped—*The Bombardier* commenced to drop foot-long sections of the Elgin Hot Gut that Sam had procured from Clint's Sunset Grill, as *The Procurer's* part of this little exercise, right down onto her prissy little Church Lady hat.

One, two, three. Plop, plop, plop. Direct hits.

She screamed this time. Sam, being downstairs, rushed to her aid and tried to comfort her, all the while surreptitiously scooping up the now battered EHG and tucking it into his cloth bag for immediate demolition by his alter-ego, *The Destroyer*.

Sam brought her and her prissy friend out to the lobby and offered them a drink of cool water. Don and I, pants now back in place and hands wiped clean of sausage grease, showed up and took over the questioning and consoling, while Sam went to finish his job as *The Destroyer*.

Meanwhile, the movie continued, uninterrupted, and 398 swooning Church Ladies thought secret thoughts about what they might do to Billy Graham if they ever got him alone in a motel room.

Perhaps this particular Church Lady, or "row 23, seat 7," as we called her, had never been so blessed from on high before. She was incoherent. Babbling. Drooling down her chin. We finally got her to drink a cup of water and calm down enough that we thought she might be able to tell us what had her so riled up.

But every time she tried to tell us, she could not think of words to use that had ever crossed her lips before. "There was a man up in the balcony, and he … *sputter-sputter, gulp*."

Don asked how she could be sure it was a man and not a woman.

"A woman would never do that!" she blurted out.

"Do what, ma'am?" I asked.

"I can't tell you!" she sputtered.

"Is it a secret?" Don wanted to know.

She shook her head.

Sam, having destroyed the physical evidence, sauntered up and asked, "She ever able to tell you anything?"

I shook my head "no" and added aloud, "Sam, did you see *anything* in there?"

"Nothing. One of those Church Ladies farted really loud. Then, I just heard this woman, here, scream, and I ran straight to her to see what was wrong. She was so shook up she couldn't say anything. I brought her into the lobby."

He cupped his hand beside his mouth and leaned over to speak to Don and me, faking confidentiality. But he was talking loudly enough for row 23, seat 7 to hear him, for sure. "I thought maybe it was her who farted and then, maybe, she pooped her panties."

"Ma'am, would you like to see the rest of the movie?" Don asked, ever so politely.

"No. No-no-no. I just want to go home. Would you call us a cab, please?"

You betcha we would call her a cab, and get her bony booty right out of that theater before she recovered her memory and her willingness to say "butt" or "poop" aloud in the presence of a man—or even three boys.

Sam looked at her as she waited for the cab. He was into his Huck Finn character; I could see it in his eyes. "Ma'am," he said, "we are so sorry you have had something mysterious and unfortunate happen to you here in our little movie house. Lord knows what it was, but I will pray for you that it becomes a sign for all Church Ladies everywhere to look to the heavens to see what's about to come to them. And if you want to talk about it, whatever it was, you just call ol' Sam, here. Personally, I think it was a sign from God, especially for you, only, since none of the rest of us saw a thing. How lucky you are to be so blessed."

"Hosanna," I added, just as the yellow cab pulled up in front of the box office.

As she and her prune-faced friend climbed into the cab, Don added to Sam and me, "Let this revelation be a sign unto Church Ladies everywhere. 'Look up to heaven at the wrong moment, and you may get pooped upon,' saith the Lord, Amen."

Oh, yes. We asked Sam what he did with the EHG evidence. "Ate it," he grinned. "Manna from heaven."

Hallelujah.

Life's Lessons Learned:

- *Practice makes perfect. Never underestimate the value of drill.*
- *If you want to totally destroy a Church Lady, involve her in some scam in which she will be woefully vocabulary-impaired. Very easy to do.*
- *Leading impromptu pep rallies from a movie marquee is great fun.*
- *Nine hundred little kids, given the money and the opportunity, will invariably eat too much popcorn.*
- *Don't automatically assume that all poop tastes bad. It might be manna from heaven.*

Title Taken By Sandies

George Arnold's grand slam homer and six RBIs paced the Sandies to a lopsided 20-4 victory over the Peppers Thursday in Pony League action at LeNoir Field.

The victory gave the Sandies the National Division championship with a season's record of 15-3.

In other action, the Diggers defeated the Liners, 8-1 and the Pavers collected 17 hits for a 11-7 victory over the Indians at State Hospital Field.

```
Sandies .................. 095  15—20 13  3
Peppers .................. 202  00— 4  3  7
   Robbins, Basey (4) and Arnold; Smith.
Washington (3), Smith (3), Overton (4)
and  Overton,  Pool  (4).  Home  runs:
George Arnold (Sandies), Kearney Eitler
(Sandies), Jimmy Young (Peppers).
Pavers ............... 013  123  1—11 17  2
Indians .............. 102  120  1— 7  8  6
   Kirk, Hillsbert (5) and Moore, Streeter
(7); Willeford, Jackson (6) and Walder,
Stautz  (4).  Home  runs:  Joe  Bowles
(Pavers), Glenn Randell (Indians).
Liners ............... 000  100  0—1  3  4
Diggers .............. 400  031  x—8  5  0
   Clark, Legg (6) and Powell, Clark
```

NATIONAL LEAGUE CHAMPS
Capitol Aggregate "Sandies" went 15-3 and turned thirty double plays on their way to Austin's Pony League championship.

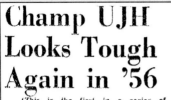

Champ UJH Looks Tough Again in '56

(This is the first in a series of stories analyzing the City Junior High Conference football teams.)

By ORLAND SIMS

Any team which has dominated its district, conference or league to the extent University Junior High School has dominated the City Junior High Conference during the past several years must be considered the team to beat in any given year.

That's about the size of things this year as far as UJH is concerned, although Coach Jimmie Munson's Eagles will be a slower and smaller team than the one which swept aside everybody in sight en route to a 5-0 record and a city title last fall.

Gone are two really outstanding backs, quarterback Raymond Culp and halfback George Lewis, plus many of the other stalwarts who brought the Blue and Gold back from its unaccustomed second-place finish in '54 (Allan won the title that year) to the top spot in '55.

Nevertheless, UJH has nine returnees including three "actual" lettermen — backs Charles Gurkin and Bill Ollison and tackle Sidney Douglas.

The Eagles also have adequate size, although the team certainly won't be as huge as it has been in years past.

Right now, the key men for the Eagles seem to be quarterback Ollison, fullback and defensive star Gurkin, offensive and defensive regular lineman Douglas, halfback Frank Rosales and halfback David Hilsberg.

Munson's team will run from the split-T, using the fullback as a flanker on occasion. The Eagle attack probably will be chiefly overland, although it's hoped the passing will succeed enough to keep opposing defenses "honest."

On its winning tradition alone, UJH would have to be listed as a prime contender. However, if the Eagles can get by a tough opener with Lamar, it could mean a good start on the road toward another championship.

UJH Squad Roster:

ENDS

13—Bill Huie; 22—Don Hardy; 23—Rayford Morgan; 25—Jim Fleming; 28—Fred Ritchie; 40—Claybourne Powell; 41—James McNeil.

TACKLES

31—Gilbert Velasquez; 39—Don Hickling; 49—Sidney Douglas; 51—George Arnold; 52—Jim Anderson; 53—John Cook.

GUARDS

12—Fritz Weigl; 26—Howard Thornton; 27—Kenneth Jourdan; 29—Bill Pool; 30—Terry Seiders; 45—Vernon Magness.

CENTERS

14—Ernie Kuehner; 35—Bronson Schultz; 38—Charles Ericson.

BACKS

10—Ray Oldham; 11—Wayne Walker; 15—Mike Carden; 24—Charles Powell; 32—Bob Scheaffer; 33—Glenn Harris; 34—Gary Pauer; 42—David LaBauve; 43—Frank Rosales; 44—Bill Ollison; 46—David Hilsbery; 50—Charles Gurkin.

SCHEDULE

Sept. 27—Lamar; Oct. 4—Baker; Oct. 11—Del Valle; Oct. 18—Open Date; Oct. 24—Allan; Oct. 31—Fulmore; Nov. 7—O. Henry.

CHAPTER 10

Life's Hard When You're Dumb

AUSTIN, 1957

Other than my one encounter with Miss Mozelle at age ten, I had never paid much attention to girls. At least, as *girls*, if you know what I mean. All my buddies had about the same level of experience when it came to the fairer sex.

We were all dumb. Maybe "ignorant" is a better description. Or "stupid." Or all of the above.

Looking back on 1957, I guess we would have to describe ourselves as a pack of ignoramuses, who were also naïve.

We didn't suffer from impaired IQs or deductive reasoning abilities. Not at all. Lack of firing neurons was not the problem. We were just completely unprepared for the clever onslaught of the still-amateur, but hellishly effective, feminine wiles that were about to completely consume us.

Nature is grossly unfair in that way. Fourteen-year-old boys are at least five years behind fourteen-year-old-girls in social development, raw awareness, basic instincts, conniving and plotting, personal hygiene, and practically any other thing that psychologists, sociologists, physiologists, and assorted *Bean Counters* decide they're going to measure.

That wouldn't be so bad if *anybody* ever bothered to warn all fourteen-year-old boys that, for the next two or three years, girls their same age were going to make their lives a living hell. What those girls could do to us boys was far more impressive than the Reverend Mallory causing grown people to crawl around like dogs and bark.

That was child's play, comparatively speaking.

So Don, Andy, Kenny, and I all entered the ninth grade, in the fall of 1957, at University Junior High School with high hopes, unsuspectingly unprepared for what was about to happen to us.

Our football team was a little better that year. We actually won five or six games. And we had grown a bit, so our size disadvantage was not quite so lopsided. Don, especially, had grown over the summer. Instead of a 150-pound linebacker and tight end, he was now a 180-pound linebacker and tight end. I grew a couple of inches to a hair over six feet, and I had soared to 190 pounds.

Fritz, our center, came to fall workouts looking like he had been pumping iron all summer. Actually, he had, in a way. He had worked for ninety days at the forge of his father's ornamental iron company.

Our biggest boost, though, came from a couple of guys who moved into town over the summer. One of them, Paul Parker, my counterpart at the other tackle, was actually bigger than I was.

The coach told us we had a chance to win, if we wanted to badly enough, and we believed him. In fact, we swore vengeance on all the teams that had battered us and left us bruised, beaten up, but unbowed, the year before.

A few of us cooked up some extra little strategies to aid the cause.

Don and I would go to the Kash 'n' Karry Food Store at I-35 and 38½ Street and buy us a few pods of garlic. These we broke down into their little kernels and we passed them out to the linemen and linebackers, three or four pieces each. We chewed them to nothingness on the way to each game, thereby entering each contest with pretty nasty garlic breath. Then we would breathe like heaving horses on the opposition. Every pileup smelled like an Italian restaurant. On fire. By halftime, the opposing line, running backs and ends would be reeling, half-sick.

That little strategy helped.

We also had a secret-weapon strategy. His name was Charles Davis. Charlie was our fullback, and he was also the hairiest biped being this side of Monkey Island at the zoo back in Brackenridge Park in San Antonio. His hairs were about the length of a horse's mane and as black as the ace of spades. He was built, short and squat, like a 55-gallon drum and, with no practice whatsoever, he could drag his knuckles while walking upright.

One of our more clever ideas was to roll Charlie onto the field just before the game. In a cage. He would shake the bars and scream like a tied up gorilla at mating time, while several of us poked at him with sticks and whips and a chair.

Mind you, this went on at the very end of garlic-chewing time, right in the middle of the field in plain view of the opposing team.

Then we would let Charlie out of his cage.

He would begin to run amok for five minutes or so, screaming and beating his chest and rolling around on the turf to get himself good and filthy. We would stand and watch until it was time to get ready for the kickoff. Then, armed with whips and blank pistols, the whole team would surround him and, whips cracking and pistols popping, pretend to subdue him and tie him up. All the while, our cheerleaders would be rolling his cage over to the pileup. Since he wasn't on either the kicking or receiving squad, we would toss him, trussed-up tightly, back into his cage for the cheerleaders to roll on back over to our bench.

We never let Charlie come into the game on our first offensive play, although we all assured him he was a starter.

It was much better theater to bring him into the huddle the first time we had third-and-long. We could hear the other teams' teeth chattering. If they ever were inclined to poop their pads, it was the first time we had third-and-long and Charlie came trotting and screaming onto the field, knuckles ripping up divots behind him.

Every time on that first third-and-long, we ran the same play. We called it "34-cross." That indicated the number three back (fullback) running through the number four hole in the line of scrimmage, with the linemen cross-blocking,

Wayne, our quarterback, would take the snap and pitch the ball back to Charlie as if he were afraid to get too close to him. Paul Parker, the left tackle, would pull right and run down the line of scrimmage to demolish the left defensive end. Don, tight end on my right, would take down the outside linebacker. Our right guard, Servando Varela, and I would cross block. He would pull right and smother the other team's left tackle, and I would go left and obliterate either the nose guard or left guard, depending on the formation of the defensive line. Fritz, the center, would take out the middle linebacker.

Everybody else could pretty much just stand around and scratch.

Charlie, who was fast for a 220-pound, hairy, screaming and untamed 55-gallon drum, would come roaring right through the number four hole, which is where my rear-end had been a split second before.

Thirty-four cross worked exactly right, every time. In two seconds, Charlie, our own uncaged madman, was loose in the opposition's secondary. This was no pass play, and the defensive halfbacks and safeties, at 145 to 160 pounds, dripping wet, usually just flailed at him as he passed them by, screaming (literally) down the field.

I don't believe that play ever failed to gain at least fifty yards. Most often it ended in a touchdown.

I should add here that Charlie was a really nice, gentle giant of a guy. He was, for sure, a team player. He was smart enough and loyal enough that, the first time we proposed this whole bizarre scheme to him, his eyes lit up and he said but two words: "Damn straight." He didn't talk much, so I'm sure all the screaming he did was actually good for his vocal development.

Besides the horrendous garlic breath and mad-man Charlie, we had a third strategy—attitude. We decided to be the meanest suckers on the block, and so we immediately became the meanest suckers on the block, at least in the theaters of our own minds.

This attitude ploy helped us often, but it didn't always work.

The baddest dude on the junior high gridiron that year was a kid named J.C. Hartmann. He had tattoos all up and down his arms, smoked unfiltered Camels, and was rumored to be twenty-two years old and to have fifteen or twenty children. He was a halfback for Baker Junior High School, our hated enemies, and he was accustomed to running through opposing lines at will, gaining in excess of 200 yards every game.

That year, our game with Baker was the last game of the season. On their very first play, they ran a 22-trap, a kind of right halfback dive play with a trap-block variation, with ol' J.C. coming right at me. I slipped the trap block and met him well behind the line of scrimmage. I hit him around the knees, helmet-to-groin, with everything I had, and Don—bless his heart—was right behind me. You could have heard the slap-clap of leather for a country mile as I wrapped him up low and Don hit him in the chest, polishing him off and sending him flat on his back for a loss of almost four yards.

That would have been a good play for the NFL defensive reel. But our attitude got the best of us. Don and I actually believed, for a second, that we were meaner than J.C. Hartmann, that our tattoos were more plentiful and colorful, that we smoked Cuban cigars, two at a time, and had fifty kids each.

Being on top of the pile, Don was the first up. He looked down at J.C. and said, "Try to come back this way again, and we'll give you another dose of the same!"

As I unpiled, I added to the attitude that was already electric in the air by saying, "Yeah, J.C., we'll break your scrawny legs next time and stuff you in Charlie's cage!"

I don't think J.C. had ever lost yardage on any play before, ever. He was stunned, and if we had just kept our attitude to ourselves and our mouths shut, we might have had him where we wanted him.

But, no. Not us. We had to announce our intentions.

There was, right away, an argument in the Baker huddle. J.C. and their quarterback were at serious odds over something. It got so bad that the referee stuck his head in to see what was wrong and, immediately, they had to use one of their time-outs. J.C. and the quarterback went over to the sidelines, together, to confer with their coach, who apparently made a decision that ended the debate.

Back they came.

First play after the time out was ... guess what? Twenty-two trap. This time I didn't slip the block so easily. I looked up from an awkward three-point position to see J.C. headed right for me, red-eyed and blowing smoke out his nose. As I reached up to try to grab him, he simply hurdled into the air, landing on my back, legs pumping up-and-down like the pistons in his Harley.

At full throttle.

The guy had actually stopped for a second to stomp on me with his cleats. He then jumped off me and resumed his forward motion, knocking Don aside with a vicious and tattoo-inspired stiff-arm. He gained about fifteen yards before somebody tripped him up. He would probably have scored if he had not decided to try to aerate my back. As he came back to the huddle, Don was helping me up.

J.C. clenched his teeth and said to the both of us, "Ain't nobody on this earth's tougher'n J.C. Hartmann."

My inclination was to say, "Yes, sir, boss. You are absolutely right." But I kept my mouth shut. This time. Don, defiant to the death, did say, "Horse hockey!" loud enough for him to hear it. For the rest of the game, they never ran him at us again.

Not once.

Poor old Paul Parker on our right side was pretty beat up by the end of the game. He, however, kept his mouth shut, unlike his attitudinally impaired counterparts on the left, and we held ol' J.C. to a career-low sixty-five rushing yards. And only one touchdown.

Don't think that these football war stories have nothing to do with fourteen-year-old girls completely overwhelming fourteen-year-old boys. They are, incredibly, intricately connected.

You see, those of us who had earned the leather-sleeved letter jackets with our two years of blood, bruises, broken bones, and physical humiliations as UJH Eagle football stars had not a prayer of ever wearing them.

I believe the girls spent the whole summer plotting how to get those jackets before we ever tried them on. Mind you, up to then, we boys had paid those girls little or no attention.

They were about to change all that.

It wasn't that they weren't cute, pleasant individuals who smelled good. It was just that we had our priorities, and those priorities didn't include preoccupation with, or mostly even taking notice of, the fact that girls were different and might have some interest in us other than as the guys playing baseball down the street.

Besides coveting the leather-sleeved letter jackets, girls also seemed to have a totally different outlook on the fact that, in those days, anyone could get a full-fledged driver's license in Texas upon reaching the age of fourteen. Show your birth certificate. Take a written test that would not have strained the intellect of most of the aforementioned monkeys on Monkey Island, if you know what I mean. Then go for a short drive and, if you don't have a wreck or beat up the examiner, *voila!* You are certified to drive a car on any street in the state of Texas.

Girls got drivers' licenses the same as we did. They, most of them, anyway, had a vehicle at their disposal to drive here and there. But would they? Good heavens, no. Somehow it became our duty to pick them up and ferry them around as if we were Roy's Taxi Company. Without a meter amongst us.

We could never figure this out. What were they up to?

Of course, they would slide over into the middle of the front seat, thigh-to-thigh with us. We supposed they thought that would be ample inducement for us to hurry back the next day to take them wherever it was they were going then. In fact, it was such a distraction to us ignoramuses that it's a miracle we didn't kill them and ourselves by running off the road into a watermelon patch.

Our lack of experience in *both* driving and thigh-touching created a dangerous situation. Comical, but dangerous, still.

Nope. When it came to the leather-sleeved letter jackets and to driving those girls somewhere, we didn't get it. We didn't even come close to getting it.

As far as the jackets were concerned, once a girl had her hands on yours, you could kiss it goodbye. Forever. Seems like the universal excuse was, "I'm sorry. I can't find it." Loosely translated, that meant, "Hey, Bubba, you ain't getting it back. Ever. So don't ask again. Ever."

And, apparently, having cars to drive and the license to go with them was supposed to mean that we were to call them up, invite them to a movie or to go get a burger. Or go just about anywhere. Didn't matter. Just call them, pick them up. Go somewhere.

For what? We didn't get it.

Most of all, we had no desire to have to go to their houses to pick them up. A trip to a girl's house meant we had to (gasp) meet her parents. What if her mother was a Church Lady? Would we just say, "I have to go now. I can't stand to be anywhere near a Church Lady"?

Probably not.

But meeting the father was worse. Far worse. The interrogations. The trick questions. The dirty, accusatory looks. It was not something we looked forward to. In fact, it ranked right up there with root canals and hemhorroidectomies on our lists of favorite things to be subjected to.

Besides, all those fathers could relax. We were too dumb to be any kind of a threat or menace. On the other hand, the fathers ought to have been worrying about their daughters' collective aggressiveness, not some poor, dumb guy who doesn't have a clue what he's doing. Or why he's doing it.

We also thought the girls got together in clandestine meetings, not unlike secret Communist cells, and divided us up. "Okay, Sally, you take Kenny. Dianne, you can have Andy. Tammy, Don is yours for the fall. And Nancy, you get George 'til further notice."

We didn't pick them out. The thought never crossed our idle minds. They rounded us up, cut us from the herd, and branded us before we even knew they could ride a cutting horse.

It was pathetic.

And it surely must have been illegal, as well. The whole scheme reminded us of competing companies in the same industry (in this case, making males do stupid pet tricks) getting together to carve up territories and customers and to fix prices.

NOT SO TENDER TRAP

Fourteen-year-old girls schemed and plotted, connived and planned until they got us into white sport coats with pink carnations. And made us do stupid pet tricks. Meanwhile, they wore our leather-sleeved letter jackets over their strapless formals to keep their shoulders warm.

George Arnold • 117

We had been studying the Sherman and Clayton Anti-trust Acts. We were the paying customers being hornswoggled. The girls were the corrupt cartels and giant trusts taking unfair advantage of us. Seemed like a decent enough analogy to us.

Oh, man, were we dumb. We didn't have a prayer. We couldn't decide if we should surrender and enjoy whatever the adventure might bring us, or try to join the Merchant Marines to avoid the whole magilla.

Before we could say, "What for?" Don, Andy and I were all paired up.

A pretty girl in the band, named Tammy, cut Don from the herd, hog-tied him, and caused him to do her will for months on end. Pathetic.

Dianne, a little girl who could have passed for nine or ten, except for her braces, grabbed on to Andy. To make matters worse, she lived a half-block from him, so she could spy on everything he did. Disgusting.

And one of those "Vote for me for Queen of the May" cheerleaders, Nancy, had my jacket and me as her personal chauffeur, valet and court jester. All I did was wake up and go to school that day. Outrageous.

So here we were. Naive babes in the woods, being led about by the nose. Having our time monopolized, our wallets emptied, our chains jerked, and our brains scrambled with eggs for breakfast. What in the world was happening?

We sure didn't get it.

But the girls did. Oh, my, yes, did they! They would get together to compare notes.

"Do you know what Andy said last night? It was so sweet."

"George brought me a bunch of flowers he'd picked himself. He is so thoughtful."

"Don told me my eyes are beautiful. Can you beat that?"

This stuff went on and on. At one point, to our collective horror and utter embarrassment, we actually found ourselves competing to see who could be the most "sensitive." Now, that was truly "horse-hockey," for sure.

These ninth-grade relationships were going nowhere. We knew it and admitted it freely. We just didn't know what to do about it.

The girls, on the other hand, apparently conjured up some fantasy world in which the dumb-butt *du jour* would father their children, build them a big, new house on a mountaintop in Switzerland, and buy them a Porsche—all because they had naturally curly hair. Yech. Patooie.

We knew these things; yet we continued to allow ourselves to be duped and manipulated, month after month. We couldn't seem to do anything about it.

Life became more and more difficult for the dumb.

While sipping on Grapettes one afternoon, pondering our own incredible stupidity, as we often had serious need to do, we all decided that somebody should say to every fourteen-year-old boy:

> *Listen up, kid. Girls your age are wicked. They will crank up your imagination and keep it revved, as long as you do what they want you to do. Take them to the dance. Buy them flowers. Tell them how pretty they are. Jump when they say, "Frog."*
>
> *They'll take your letter jacket and turn you into a sniveling marshmallow.*
>
> *It's a game with them, buddy. You can bet your soul that the duration of their infatuation with you won't amount to more than three or four months. Then they will get bored, and one day say to you, "We have to talk." Right then, you're road-kill. Dead meat. Hasta la vista, dumb-butt. There is no pony out there, kid. No pot of gold at the end of the rainbow.*
>
> *And, in spite of what you dreamed about and hoped for, you won't have gotten close to the secrets hidden under their seductive clothing.*
>
> *That is your goal. Isn't it?*

Was that it? The secret enticement of forbidden fruit?

We decided that Eve lives in every scheming female, and that her supply of apples is endless. And ever-changing.

To make a sad story disgusting, I must tell you that we were each sacrificed on the altar of female narcissism not once, but over and over and over again, between the ages of fourteen and sixteen.

We didn't have the sense God promised last year's bird nest. And we sure weren't as clever as Pavlov's dog, although we did a lot of fetching, jumped through countless hoops, and panted continuously.

Life's Lessons Learned:

- *If you are a boy, you will have absolutely no sense before you are at least sixteen. Do not try to match wits with girls your age. They will only break your heart.*
- *With all due respect to Norman Vincent Peale, a positive attitude will sometimes get you stomped on. Literally.*
- *If you can't beat 'em outright, try to psych them out with a madman in a cage. Or make 'em sick with really bad garlic breath.*
- *A touched letter jacket is a lost letter jacket.*

CHAPTER 11

Stepping Up to the
Big House

AUSTIN, 1958

It was during our second day at the big, and somewhat overwhelming, Stephen F. Austin High School that I met Jack
Clagett for the first time.

Our esteemed new principal, Lipscomb Andrews, had summoned forty or fifty of us neophyte sophomores to a little pep talk.

He was the head warden on a campus with 2,600 students,
150 or so teachers and assorted staff, and a large physical plant
that included the big, original, four-story main building, completed about 1905, a two-story annex, a gymnasium across the
street, a field house, and the venerable House Park football stadium and baseball diamond where we had competed from time
to time in the past.

From those past competitive experiences at House Park had
come the nickname "The Big House," for our new school. We
thought it was clever, although we were mostly still dumb.

Don had already made Jack's acquaintance the day before
since both of them played trombones in the band. They came
into the late-afternoon meeting in the school's auditorium, together. The three of us sat down with Jack in the middle, and
Don introduced him, simply, as "Jack Clagett, fellow trombonist."

THE BIG HOUSE
Stephen F. Austin High School, in 1958, was a big, inner city melting pot with more than 2,000 students from all parts of the city.

(Photo PICA 07558 courtesy Austin History Center, Austin Public Library)

I immediately asked which school he had attended last year. His answer, O. Henry Junior High, sent red flags waving.

Our experience with O. Henry, on the west side of town where all the rich people lived, told me that the girls looked great only because they had the money to buy the clothes and makeup that hid their natural plainness, and that the boys were mostly all Type-A, overbearing loudmouths, if not outright bullies, who wore lizard-skin boots, had their own expensive cars, and were committed to attending Texas A&M, where they would be issued swagger sticks to match their belligerent attitudes.

Somehow, though, Jack didn't look like most of them. I decided to suspend judgment, just in case one or two rational human beings might actually have escaped from O. Henry.

"Lippy," as we had already learned to call our new principal behind his back, apparently had summoned about ten to twelve new sophomores from each of the junior high schools that fed students to the tenth-grade class at AHS every year. There were four such schools—Allen, Baker, O. Henry, and University.

He began, "You have been singled out to me by the principals of your schools last year."

Oh, no. This would likely not be good news, and it perplexed me, especially since we had been there only two days, so far, and—to my knowledge—had not yet assaulted a teacher or set fire to a classroom. Where was this little meeting headed?

He continued, "Your former principals tell me that from this group will come the leaders of Austin High School in the future. I welcome you, and I look forward to meeting you, personally."

George Arnold • 123

Who had this guy been talking to, anyway? Was this some kind of reverse psychological ploy? Or was he just an idiot?

"So we all get started on the right foot, let me tell you that I already know you are referring to me as 'Lippy.' It happens every year. I don't mind, as long as you don't ever address me, personally, in that fashion. I am 'Principal Andrews' or 'Mr. Andrews' to you and to all students.

"Now that we are clear about that, I understand that some of you also have been referring to this hallowed institution of higher learning as 'The Big House.' I don't know the origin of that term, but I want to assure you this place is not a prison."

Jack rolled his eyes, as if to say, "We'll be the judge of that, Lippy." Was that a good sign?

On the other hand, Lippy's apparent intelligence-gathering abilities seemed to be formidable. Oh, the "Lippy" business was no big deal. As he said, it happens every year. But "The Big House" intelligence was impressive. Only a few of us knew about it, and it was barely twenty-four hours old.

How did he do it? Was it possible there was a whole squad of "Prunellas" feeding him information? Did he have microphones hidden in the students' restrooms?

Whatever—he was good. Really good. We would have to be cautious when it came to Lippy. It might not be so easy to cloud his mind. Or to pull the wool over his eyes.

Well, Lippy went on about ten more minutes, giving us a blow-by-blow and chronological account of the history and traditions of the Stephen F. Austin Maroons. They were legion. And he was beginning to put us to sleep, when he concluded with a bang.

"That's it!" he fairly shouted, to wake us up, I supposed. "Enjoy your three years here. High school will be the best years of your life!"

That said, he simply walked up the aisle and left all of us sitting there in the auditorium.

Everybody else, but the three of us, got up, immediately, and started to rush back to their respective classes. We had no intention of going back. Not a third of the way through the class. That would create a disturbance, coming in late, now wouldn't it?

Besides, it was the end of the day. Don and Jack had band

sixth period, and I had plane geometry, taught by a retired army colonel, now Mr. Sinclair (who, a few months before, had become my brother's father-in-law at a real, and mostly legal, I suppose, wedding). We didn't have textbooks yet, so Mr. Colonel Sinclair was allowing us another study hall. The books would be in tomorrow, he had told us, and he didn't want to begin the semester's work until we were all on the same page, so to speak.

Very military of him, we thought.

I wasn't due to the football field house for another forty-five minutes.

As everybody else got up to leave, Jack looked around at them and simply said, "I wonder what they are thinking? We all have a free pass from Lippy himself, and they don't seem to know what to do with it."

Well, now, could this West Austin, O. Henry escapee actually be of the same mind as the rabble from the East Side? All the signs, so far, were good. Very good.

Jack continued, "I hope there is a place in this world for lemmings. I just try my best not to get caught up with them."

Even though he spoke thoughtfully and with precision, I started to like this Jack guy, right away. I would look up "lemmings" later so I would have a clue what the devil he had just said.

We determined the best course for the next forty minutes or so would be to get some Cokes out of the vending machines, none of which contained any Grapettes. They seemed to be everywhere in this school. Then we'd go sit in the shade and get better acquainted.

Turns out, Jack had three younger brothers. They lived on a short street near the intersection of Enfield Road and the Missouri-Pacific Railroad tracks, which would later become Mo-Pac Boulevard, a major new north-south freeway. Their house was about half a block from Westenfield Park. It was a nice part of town, but the neighborhood certainly was not overly affluent.

Jack was tall and thin, wore glasses, and gave the appearance of being very intelligent, though clearly not a geek. I immediately thought I could enhance my vocabulary by just hanging around him. He said his father was a professional land speculator, a fact I later learned was absolutely true. So it seems the

Clagetts were either flush, or they were broke, depending on the senior Clagett's luck with the land-grab *du jour* or before the local Planning & Zoning Commission.

Pretty interesting to Don and me, who had never actually been either. Flush or broke, that is.

Within a half-hour, even though he might not have realized it yet, Jack had become the newest member of the little trouble-making mob consisting of Kenny, Andy, Don, and me—a mob that is still mostly intact after almost fifty years.

I think it was pre-ordained, although none of us is Presbyterian.

Promptly at 3:30, Don and Jack took off for the band hall, and I made my way the two blocks to the field house to suit up for football practice.

Don had made the decision to concentrate on band, rather than athletics, except maybe for one more year of basketball. He was already a very accomplished trombonist who would only get better, musically. He reasoned that he could even earn a living with his trombone, but would never have the physical attributes or the athletic ability to play in the NFL, the NBA, or major league baseball. Wasn't in his genes.

It was sound, adult thinking.

I, on the other hand, being a completely tone-deaf dolt with no musical talent whatsoever, decided to stay with athletics. I would play football that year on the junior varsity, and baseball and track on the varsity teams.

The decision for Don had been gut-wrenching, I know.

Coming to grips, at fifteen, with the realization that we could not continue, indefinitely, participating in, and excelling at, everything was not easy to face up to.

It was time to make some choices.

In addition to football, with the UJH Eagles, we had played baseball the last two summers, together, on the 7-Up Bottler's team in the Colt League, for fifteen- and sixteen-year-olds. I was the Bottler's catcher, and Don was our first baseman. We had a pretty good team, and both of us made the league's all-star squad at the end of the season, traveled to San Antonio for the state tournament, and managed to play four or five games in the double-elimination schedule before losing out in the semifinals.

RIDIN' THE BENCH AND STAYIN' CLEAN

According to the Austin American-Statesman, *"Coach Travis Raven's 1959 Austin Maroons have four good catchers." Life's Lessons Learned: Third-string catchers seldom get their uniforms dirty. But it's better'n being the fourth stringer.*

Hit by Arnold Provides Win

George Arnold's seventh-inning single drove in the winning run Thursday night as the Seven-Up Bottlers came from behind to beat the Crestview Braves, 8-7, in a Colt League game.

Crestview ....201 003 1—7 4 1
Seven-Up ....111 000 5—8 6 5
Sauer, King (4), White (7) and Nau; Lovelady, Russell (5) and Arnold.

Don was a better-than-average baseball player, a very good basketball player, and had given up on getting killed, again, on the gridiron.

I was very good at baseball, getting better at football, and had absolutely no basketball talent whatsoever.

When he went to the band hall, I went to the field house.

The S. F. Austin junior varsity that year was a fairly decent football team. We had some size, some burgeoning talent, and we won six or seven games, the highlight being a 34-0 trouncing of the hated Alamo Heights HS "B" team in Alamo Stadium at San Antonio. Their fans had pelted us with rocks when we got off our bus. That made us mad, and we returned the favor by making their football team, theretofore undefeated, pay. Big time.

The ride home to Austin was actually fun.

The Austin Maroons baseball team won the state championship that year. And Texas is a big state. The team was so good that I was relegated to being the third-string catcher—what, today, might be called the bullpen catcher. Accustomed, all these years, to being the starter, and playing every inning, I found sitting on the bench and watching a very difficult thing to do.

That baseball team had two not-so-secret weapons—a senior pitcher named Raymond Culp, who went on to play major league baseball for both the Phillies and the Red Sox; and a dwarf named Ralph Franklin.

Ray pitched several no-hitters his last year in high school with only one pitch, a 100+MPH fastball. His father wouldn't let him throw anything off-speed, like a changeup, a curve, or a slider. Didn't matter. He needed only the fastball, and he would psych-out our opponents by deliberately throwing a couple over the backstop during his warmups. Kept them on their toes.

As the third-string catcher, my job sometimes included, besides always catching batting practice, taking the between-innings warmup tosses from the pitcher. Early in the game, like before the second inning began, I would receive Ray's last warm-up pitch, throw my hand and arm straight up, and roll over, backward, as if the power of the pitch had knocked me off my feet. That would get our opponents' eyes bugging out. And it was one of my few chances to get my uniform dirty, since I rarely played in a game.

Ralph, on the other hand, was a utility player. He entered games as a pinch hitter any time we had the bases loaded and two outs. Ralph was outfitted with the biggest bat we had, a 36-inch, 36-ounce Adirondak. There was no way he could swing that bat.

Of course, nobody wanted him to swing it.

His job was simply to crouch there, in the batter's box, in his ridiculous, ill-fitting uniform and all his 39-inch height, and, with his four-inch tall strike zone, to draw a walk, thus forcing in a for-sure run. He would trot to first base, and then we would send in a pinch runner.

It usually made our opponents really mad, but there was nothing they could do about it. Ralph was a student at the school and every bit as entitled to play baseball as any other student who could make the team. I remember our coach explained it to an umpire once, *"That* guy is here because he can throw, *that* one because he can hit, *that* one because he can run, and *Ralph* because he can get on base—every time."

Immediately after we beat Lufkin for the state champi-onship, Ray Culp was handed a bonus signing check from the Philadelphia Phillies for $100,000. We all got to touch it. That was big-time bucks in 1959.

Bigger, even, than any "heal this boy" money.

We voted Ralph a leather-sleeved letter jacket for his steady contribution. I, who had played maybe two innings all year, didn't get one. Just as well. Some girl I had never laid an eyeball on before would probably just have made off with it, and then claimed she couldn't find it.

Back to Jack.

A trip to his house was usually more fun than going to a cir-cus. I say "usually" because the level of entertainment depended on how many of his three younger brothers were home at the time. If one were there, it was a good time. If two, a better time.

Austin Bees Triumph Over Jefferson, 34-0

THE YARDSTICK

	Austin B	Jeff B
First downs	7	2
Rushing yardage	230	50
Passing yardage	45	20
Passes	2-5	1-3
Passes intercepted by	1	1
Punts	1-30	3-21.6
Fumbles lost	1	0
Yards penalized	90	45

Special to the American

SAN ANTONIO—The Austin Maroon B team wiped out the Jefferson Mustang B team here Thursday night, 34-0, for its second shutout victory in a row.

The Maroon Bees beat New Braunfels last week, 32-0.

Five different players scored the Austin touchdowns. Fullback George Moreles led off with a 40-yard dash in the first quarter. Halfback Garland Earls then ran five yards and Tommy Fisher, another halfback, followed up with another five-yarder. Quarterback Knox Williams ran five yards in the fourth quarter and fullback Jesse Hellums followed with another five-yard touchdown burst.

The Maroons rolled up 275 yards of offense while holding Jefferson to 70 yards, only 20 of which came in the air. Austin did incur 90 yards worth of penalties.

Austin B	0	12	8	14—34
Jeff B	0	0	0	0— 0

Austin scoring—TD: Moreles, Earls, Fisher, Williams, Hellums.
PAT: Hellums, Morales (runs).

When all three were there, it was better than a Three Stooges and Marx Brothers double feature.

To begin with, the house was small. Too small for all the Clagetts, really. Jack's younger brothers all seemed completely unlike laid-back Jack; they were whirling-dervishes on steroids. It was not unusual for Don and me, at six-feet and 200 pounds-plus, to be knocked down, trampled upon and left for dead, just inside the front door. Like Inspector Clouseau's houseboy, Kato, the three younger Clagetts attacked at random and from every direction, it seemed. While it was usually fun to go in the house, it was always good to escape with no broken bones.

Instantly, Jack's positive influence on our little band of ruffians was apparent. He brought a certain level of heretofore missing sophistication to our antics, elevating us from a pack of crude pranksters, hell bent on instant gratification, to a higher plane—to the patience of intricate intrigues with plots that sometimes took days, or even weeks, to unfold.

He taught us all to play bridge, being steadfastly unwilling to participate in our favorite game, "Pooch-a-Rootie." We had invented Pooch-a-Rootie ourselves. It was a variation of the French game, *Mille Bournes,* except it had no rules. We were all indifferent, if not steadfastly opposed, to rules.

It was a game played with both cards and Don's mother's mah-jongg tiles, a kind of a cross between slapjack and dominoes. I would like to explain it to you further, but sans rules, it's difficult to describe. It involved the moving of tiles, like dominoes, and a sudden certain alignment that resulted in each player slapping the table and shouting, at the top of his voice, "Pooch-a-Rootie!"

Jack didn't get it. He was always shouting "Pooch-a-Rootie!" at the wrong time, causing Don, Andy, and me to turn to stare at him as if he were crazy, which he clearly was not.

Finally, with his own brand of logic, Jack convinced us that there was no future in Pooch-a-Rootie. If a new person to the game, like himself, and with his intellect, could not decipher what the devil the other three of us were doing, finding enough players to get up a good Pooch-a-Rootie game was only going to get harder and harder as we grew older.

He convinced us to take up bridge.

And he patiently taught us the basics. The bidding. The scoring. The eye movements with which to cheat. And—finally—the intricacies of the game.

We were good students, quick learners. And before we knew it, we had some outrageous bridge tournaments with rubbers that often went on for days, interrupted, of course, by the need to attend classes or, for Don and me, to put in a shift or two at the good ol' Varsity Theater.

Jack also got us into golf. He was a pretty decent golfer. The rest of us were not. Emphatically not. The oldest of his younger brothers went on to become a club pro.

After school, on occasions when the band was idle and there was no football, basketball, baseball or track practice, we would hack our way around Austin's municipal course, getting in eighteen holes before dark. We had awards for these little afternoon competitions: most flora destroyed; most fauna killed by flying golf balls; most creative string of expletives after a particularly bad shot; and first one to shoot par on any hole.

Jack always won the last award, for par-ing a hole or two. Andy, exquisitely creative with the turn of a crude phrase, usually won the expletive award; that left Don and me to fight it out for the flora or fauna awards. We seemed to have an uncanny knack for one of us, totally unintentionally, to barely miss hitting a bird, or rabbit, or squirrel with one of our errant shots.

Having cured us of Pooch-a-Rootie, and having enhanced our level of sophistication with bridge, golf, and ever-more intricate pranks, Jack also introduced us, years before its common popularity, to Austin's East 6th Street music scene.

His favorite place was Charlie's Playhouse, a soul/blues nightclub on East 6th, but several blocks east of I-35. Charlie's Playhouse was intended for, and patronized exclusively by, blacks from Austin's deep east side. We were likely the first white patrons, ever.

Of course, at sixteen, we had no business in Charlie's Playhouse. At least according to the conventional wisdom of the day, which we pretty much blew off, totally, as a matter of principle anyway. But the music was great, the kind of music you couldn't hear on the radio—period. We supposed there were some recordings of this kind of music, but we had no idea where to find them.

Besides, where would we play them if we had them? Our uptight and still-preoccupied-with-what-the-neighbors-might-think, Great Depression parents would never tolerate that kind of music in their houses, except maybe for Don's mother, Ginna, who was more like one of us than a parent. She, like us and everybody else we knew our age, didn't give a rat's-ass about the neighbors' thoughts.

Eight-tracks, cassettes, and CDs had not yet been invented.

So we would go to Charlie's on a weekend night to listen. They never asked us how old we were; of course, we never tried to order booze, either. I'm sure the music was more meaningful, or understandable, to Jack, Don, and Andy than to Kenny and me, them being musicians and all.

But, as with every amateur critic, I knew what I liked. And I liked what I heard at Charlie's Playhouse.

We all learned something else there, at Charlie's Playhouse, that Jack already knew, apparently. Black people didn't seem to mind having whites in their neighborhood. They were polite to us, and they treated us like any other patron. The reverse was surely not true.

Not in 1958 in Texas, anyway.

I said, a few pages back, that Jack's pranks were, if not downright intellectual, at least intricate and intrigue-filled.

He outdid himself in the latter part of the year.

In what was then far northeast Austin, another new school—to be called Pearce Junior High—was being built, and an enterprising developer was turning a few hundred acres, just past it to the northeast, into a big, new neighborhood. There would eventually be several hundred houses built. But right then, only the areas that would later become streets had been roughly bladed, knocking the native cedar and post oaks down and to the side.

From time to time, Jack had referred, vaguely, to some creature he called "The Will o' the Wisp." The rest of us had taken notice of these references, I think, but nobody had yet actually asked Jack what this Will o' the Wisp creature might be.

Finally, in one of our more animated bridge games one evening, Don said, "Jack, you keep mentioning this Will o'the Wisp thing. What is it you're talking about?"

Jack never faltered. "Well, rather than tell you about it, why don't I show one to you?"

The rest of us all agreed we would like to see this thing, and then went back to our bridge game.

A couple of days later Jack showed up with a hand-drawn map of the far northeast Austin housing development, and he reminded us of our interest in seeing this Will o' the Wisp creature. He said the last one he saw was out in the middle of the new, going-to-be neighborhood, and rather than spoil the surprise by telling us what we would see, he just assured us that we would all know when we saw it.

Now, I had been taken on a snipe hunt once, in Cameron Park in Waco. It was an ill-conceived and poorly executed debacle—part of the initiation to move up from Webelos to Boy Scouts. I got completely lost and ended up having to walk home, gunny sack empty, about 2:00 A.M., with half of Waco out looking for me. In fact, that's the very reason I never became a Boy Scout after four years as a Cub Scout.

That, and the fact that I thought sitting around tying knots was a stupid pastime.

So I challenged Jack. "You taking us on a snipe hunt, Jack?"

He chuckled. "I wouldn't do anything so crass as that, and you know it," he responded, straight-faced.

Yes, we all knew snipe hunts were way, way below Jack's level of curmudgeonry. Not nearly clever or upscale enough.

"Besides," he added quickly, "we're all going together, as a group. I sure don't intend to waste my time with some ridiculous joke." Sounded right to us. Just like Jack.

So Friday night we piled ourselves into Jack's old Buick, which had a great radio and no brakes, and we headed down the main bulldozed path, right to the center of the development. Jack shut off the car, turned out the lights, and suggested we walk twenty or so yards on down the road.

We did. And we waited.

While we were waiting, Jack described for us the conditions under which we should be able to see this creature, and he assured us there was nothing to be frightened of. He even pointed out precisely where he had seen his last Will o' the Wisp.

"First," he said, "we'll hear a rumbling sound, and then the sound of the Will o' the Wisp thrashing through the trees. When we hear those two sounds, we'll see it right away."

So we waited some more. Clouds were building, and it was starting to rain.

"Well, that's it for tonight," Jack said. "We'll never see one if it's raining. Besides, we need to get the car off this dirt trail before it gets too wet and we get stuck."

If our leader had been most anybody but Jack or Jonas Salk, who, with a grant from the March of Dimes, had just saved us all from the threat of polio, we might have been a little suspicious. But these two guys were above suspicion.

So we left, and Jack vowed to return with us. "Soon."

"Soon" turned out to be about ten days later. Jack took us all back to the same place after dark, and we recommenced our second Will o' the Wisp vigil. This night was pitch black when we first got to "the spot." We could hardly see one another, let alone anything where we thought the trees ought to be.

But there was to be a full moon that night, which rose and began to light up the trees. After we had been standing around, again, for thirty or forty minutes.

"No use hanging around here any longer," Jack said. "It's

just going to be too bright. Wills o' the Wisp don't like to come out in the light."

Once again, we left, empty-handed, so to speak.

By now our curiosities were getting the best of us. We all checked the lunar calendar in the sports section of the ol' *Austin American-Statesman*. You know, the sun and moon table-thing for fishermen. And we marked our calendars for the next round of moonlessness.

When the appointed night arrived, full of anticipation, we piled ourselves into Jack's Buick for the third time, and we headed back, once again, to what had become—by now—"our stakeout."

We had probably been there, standing around in the dirt, as usual, for forty-five minutes or so. The lunar calendar hadn't lied. It was darker than the inside of a coffin with the lid already screwed shut.

I saw Jack, a couple of times, sneak a glance at his watch, but I didn't think anything about it.

Suddenly, he spun to his right, turned on a flashlight and pointed it into the trees. "I hear it," he said, very excitedly.

We strained our ears while making entirely too much noise trying to get one another to be quiet.

Then we heard it, too. A low rumble, slowly getting louder, and the sound of something large and heavy threading its way through the stand of post oaks, coming toward us from the southwest.

It got louder. Then louder. And, suddenly, three extremely bright lights lit us up as if it were high noon, and whatever the Will o' the Wisp was came screaming out of the trees behind the lights. The sound of an air horn made us jump almost out of our skin. And the lights commenced to spin 360-degrees, as if on an axis. They bounced, spun, twisted, and turned incredibly fast. The air horn continued its intermittent blasts.

So far this thing had performed its admittedly pretty scary antics about 100 feet from us, and it had stayed in that one place. All at once, however, it stopped its crazy spinning. The lights hit us head-on, and the thing started directly toward us, gaining speed.

"Let's get out of here!" It was Jack. He sounded scared. Even panicked, maybe.

He didn't have to coax us. We took off for his car, and we nearly crushed one another trying to all get in at once, as Jack started up, spun around and took off, the rumbling, oncoming three lights right behind us, bounding up and down, that crazy air horn tooting over and over again.

We were gradually leaving ol' Will o' the Wisp behind when we reached the pavement by the construction site of the new junior high school.

Suddenly, Jack stopped—best he could, at least, without brakes. Stopping often took a while ... and a few hundred feet of pavement.

We urged him on.

He looked back at the three lights that were well behind us by now, but still coming, and then he said something we all took to be total insanity.

"This is ridiculous. I've got to talk to him," he said. And, with that, he got out of that Buick and started walking back toward the oncoming lights.

He had taken his keys with him, or so help us, we would have driven off and left him to deal with the creature by himself. Come to think of it, we were going to sit right there, doors locked, windows rolled up tight, and let him deal with it by himself, anyway.

Looking backward, we could see Jack's silhouette walking straight down the middle of the road toward the oncoming lights.

"The damn thing's going to run over him," I said. I usually only cursed when I was really stressed. Right then, I was. Big time.

"He's gone nuts!" Andy said.

Onward, relentlessly, came the lights.

Jack kept walking straight toward them.

Seemed to us that just an instant before that Will o' the Wisp ran him down, it stopped. He walked right up to it, appeared to be shouting something, then turned, quickly, and headed back for the car.

Likewise, the Will o' the Wisp, or whatever it was, spun around and headed back from whence it had come, down the rough dirt path that would eventually become the extension of the street we were sitting on.

Jack climbed back in the car, started it, and—as we pulled away—said, simply, "That won't happen again."

"What won't?" we shouted, completely out of unison, like the Three Stooges.

"That Will o' the Wisp won't be chasing me or my friends anymore," he said, as we pulled away.

Don shouted over everybody and the radio, "Jack, what're you talking about? Did you yell something at that thing?"

"I sure did. I told him if he ever decided to chase me again, I would never let him use my car." Jack turned to face the three of us, and he smiled. He looked like the Cheshire Cat in *Alice in Wonderland*.

"Billy!!?" Again a chorus, this time almost in synch. Billy was Jack's oldest younger brother.

"It was a Will o' the Wisp. That's my story, and I'm sticking to it!" Jack was, once again, somber and determined.

And so it was that Jack, with a little help from his brother, Billy, had scared the bejeesus out of us.

While he never admitted anything, we figured out that he began using the phrase "Will o' the Wisp" weeks before, patiently waiting for one of us to bite. Finally, after at least fifteen or twenty mentions, Don had asked the question, and the scam was on.

But he dragged it out with a weather forecast and his own lunar calendar into several dry runs that were always supposed to be dry runs.

Later that same moonless night, over cold Grapettes in the kitchen of Don's mother's brand new house, we surmised that the thing which had come out of the trees, lights blazing, air horn blasting, spinning, turning and twisting insanely had probably been Billy on a Bobcat he had "borrowed" from the new school's construction site.

Jack never admitted anything, sticking strictly to his story that we asked to see a Will o' the Wisp, and he delivered one. He only regretted that the thing had chased us, he said.

Our analysis may have not been exactly right. Most likely, we will never know for sure. To this day, Jack either feigns memory failure or, sometimes, adamantly claims total innocence. But he still smiles like the Cheshire Cat.

We didn't even bother swearing vengeance.

We had gotten what we asked for, as Jack pointed out in his own inimitable way. But we also knew we could sit, drink us a few barrels full of Grapette, and plot 'til polar bears water-skied, and we wouldn't be able to devise a prank more devious or clever.

Or, especially, more drawn-out.

We had met our match. And he was one of us.

Hallelujah.

Life's Lessons Learned:

- *Beware of high school principals who know your very thoughts, sometimes even before you think them. They've got a better network than you do.*
- *If you can't blow a horn or beat a drum, maybe you could be an athlete.*
- *A snipe hunt, by any other name, is still a snipe hunt. Even if it takes six weeks and three trips into the woods to find a snipe.*
- *When you're badly outwitted, don't try to retaliate. You don't have the patience. The wits. Or the IQ.*

CHAPTER 12

Grapefruit Heard 'Round the World

AUSTIN, 1957/1959

A brief, but thought-provoking, interruption in our otherwise happy-go-lucky, prank-filled existences occurred one frosty Friday evening in October.

Since the junior varsity's football games were usually on Thursday nights, I was free to go see the varsity play on Fridays. Kenny was with me and, of course, Don, Andy, and Jack were there, too, in the band.

The whole mob was at the scene.

Just after our big marching band and the Red Jackets, our girls' precision drill team, finished their halftime show, the public address announcer turned up the volume and made a startling announcement:

"It has just been reported that the Soviet Union has launched an artificial earth satellite which began circling the globe a few hours ago. It apparently goes around the earth several hundred miles up every ninety minutes or so. We'll pass on more information as we get it."

Either there was no more information forthcoming, or it was so terrible as to not be passed along immediately to a couple of thousand teenagers. That was the first, and last, word we heard that evening.

On hearing the stunning bulletin, everybody looked up, as if we thought we might see something streaking across the sky. The intense, new, mercury-vapor lamps at House Park assured we would see nothing, even if there had been anything to see.

Of course, the news was of Sputnik, the grapefruit-sized little ball that did nothing much except emit a beeping signal, sent by the Communists in Moscow to allow the running-dog capitalists in the West to assure themselves it was really there. And that the Soviets had beaten us in the space race.

"Take that, Yankee imperialists!"

That night, we didn't know what it was. Was it able to spy on us, individually?

That was an important question given the fact that our *modus operandi* had been to play our little tricks and pull our best pranks anonymously, leaving the powers-that-be the chore of trying to identify the culprits. As if that were much of a challenge, given our years-long track record.

Nevertheless, that very personal concern was the first thought both Kenny and I had. We had us some egos, I suppose, to immediately think the Politburo might be interested in some of America's premier pranksters and what we were up to.

> *"Boris, ve haf to ooncahver da zeekrits ov dat geng ov hellyuns in Tecksas. If ve dun't, dey vill be runnink da Kremlin in ah foo yearseh."*
>
> *"Da, yoo spick da troot, Mishka. Dose leetle bastirds vill be our rooinz if ve dun't shuht dem down zoon. Ve cannut fail, ohr it vill bee dee Sibeeryun vork geng fur uhs, dun't yoo zee?"*

Could that conversation be taking place, right then, in Moscow, as we sat, half a world away, watching a high school football game?

Very likely, we thought.

We discussed this possibility with our band-member cohorts during the third quarter as the band made its way back to their seats in the stands. We even grabbed (for discussion purposes and figuratively, only, you understand) a few of the more trusted members of the Red Jackets, knowing the girls still had a lot more sense than we did.

At least we had figured out that much in the past couple of years.

Apparently we were to be safe from invasion of personal privacy by this particular Russian orbiting spy-thing. The girls laughed at our outrageous notions as if we were a pack of kindergartners trying to save the world from nuclear destruction by forcibly taking over the United Nations.

Of course, they almost always treated us in this rudely condescending fashion. Unless they wanted another leather-sleeved letter jacket, or a ride, or a date and corsage for some dance or other. But their intense, mirth-filled exuberance in making fun of us this time was a sure measure that we were on the wrong track. Again.

Nuclear destruction came up as the next possibility. Whatever that orbiting thing was, might it be full of hydrogen bombs that could be launched, remotely, by pushing buttons in the Kremlin? Buttons marked *"Varshington, Deesee," "Noo Yerk,"* or even *"Ahstin, Tecksas"*? We did have a SAC base just outside of town which would, most assuredly, we reasoned, be a prime target of this nuclear-spewing devil circling overhead.

We decided that possibility was worth in-depth discussion, later, when we could concentrate, maybe even with cold Grapettes, in a venue other than a chilly football stadium. So we left it on the table and went on to our third, and final, instant theory.

That, of course, was the obligatory conspiracy theory. It would be six more years before JFK would be assassinated in Dallas, a heinous act that would spawn decades-long conspiracy theories, some of which rage into the 21st century.

Yes, once again, friends, our little creative play-group, with our own early-on conspiracy theories, was light-years ahead of the rest of the world.

Amazingly, only one common conspiracy plot surfaced amongst the five of us. Were we beginning to think too much alike?

I wondered.

Our conspiracy theory *du jour* was that the U.S. Air Force,

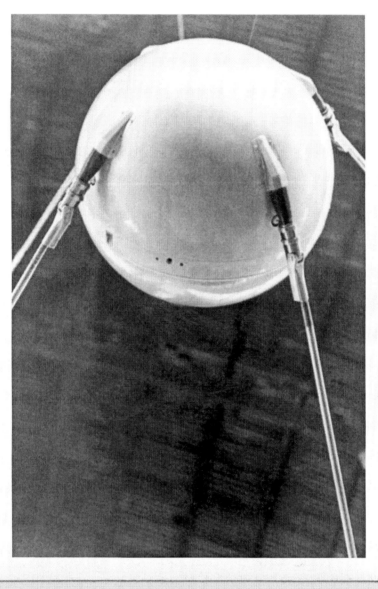

BEEPING GRAPEFRUIT

Even a bucketful of Grapettes wasn't enough to unscramble the little dilemma heaped upon us when the Ruskiys tossed Sputnik 1 into orbit one frosty, October evening in 1957. But it did get the little gang of pranksters some attention from the Red Jackets, scorn-filled, as usual, of course.

(Photo courtesy NASA)

the CIA, the Pentagon, and the White House, mostly military-industrial-complex players, had conjured up this whole story, with the cooperation of the Soviets. Hadn't they been our allies in WWII? Didn't Eisenhower know most of them? Personally?

The reason? Something was, in fact, circling, but it was alien in origin. Probably from Mars. Or some other galaxy, like Alpha Epsilon, or Pakistan, maybe.

"They" knew it was out there, and "they" couldn't do anything about it. But "they" could shake up a nation of lazy, living-for-pranks high school students to maybe cause us to switch to the calculus or physics instead of homemaking, tattin'-and-knittin', and Discovering Welding II. How could we beat the Martians, let alone the Russians, without regenerating interest amongst a nation of teenage degenerates?

Could not be done, we theorized.

Hadn't it been announced at a high school football game so we would all hear it? We resolved to poll everybody we knew who would have been at any other game that Friday night to see if the same announcement had been made at those games. We were convinced it had, verbatim, at no less than 25,000 Friday night games, simultaneously across the whole U.S. and all its foreign protectorates.

We knew it was a conspiracy. Had to be.

Russian toilets wouldn't even flush. Their cars, what few they had, would barely run (they weren't our fathers' Oldsmobiles; not even close!). Heck, Russians didn't even know how to play baseball.

The only two things we knew of that the U.S.S.R. produced successfully were vodka and tanks, both pretty low-technology. How could they get a satellite up successfully? Ha!

Don't laugh. Our entire generation had a serious (and, as subsequently demonstrated, confirmed, and well-founded) distrust of generals, CEOs of aircraft-bomb-missile makers, and even former generals who happened to be president of the U.S. at the moment.

We had no doubt Mr. Harry would tell us the truth, but nobody was briefing him on the really important issues. Know what I mean?

Earlier I mentioned an organization called the Red Jackets,

an all-girl, precision drill team that performed at halftime with the band. You need to know more about them.

This group consisted of about 125 of the choicest honeys on the campus. It was supposed to be an honor to be selected to be a Red Jacket, and membership was limited to junior and senior girls. The Red Jackets were "under the direction of Miss Connie Henderson," as the public address announcer always said.

Right away, we had figured out that they were only a fraction of what they could have been, showmanshipwise. Big Connie was no Gussie Nell Davis. That's for sure! Gussie Nell being the venerable and creative director of the world-famous Kilgore Junior College Rangerettes.

Take 125 or so shapely, young beauties. Instead of white boots with tassels, plunging necklines, and short, flared skirts to show off their various *accoutrements*, dress them up like Philip Morris' little bellhop, or whatever he was supposed to be, so that they become a seamless mass with no skin, whatsoever, showing.

Those poor little honeys wore white shoes, white stockings, straight white skirts that came to the tops of their ankles, and double-breasted (tailoring-wise, you understand) maroon coats with white piping, gold buttons, and epaulets. And they wore white gloves.

We wondered if their sponsor, Miss Henderson, perceived hands as too lewd to be exposed. Maybe she had a hand fetish.

Unfortunately, their uniforms made them look like 1942 versions of the WACs.

We knew most of them. We knew what they looked like in shorts and halter tops. Even swim suits. Alas, their dowdy Red Jacket uniforms did nothing for them. Or us.

Such a waste!

Later that night, over a bucket filled with ice and Grapettes on Andy's screened-in back porch, we began to ponder the significance of the night's startling announcement. We quickly discounted theory one—a personal invasion of our privacy (or piracy) based solely on the level of scorn and laughter it had generated amongst the Red Jackets.

Our sophomore social studies teacher, Mrs. Bristol, had been to Moscow. She reported to us, in great detail, the crudeness of Russian products, emphasizing over and over that the toilets wouldn't even flush. We wondered about that.

But based on the fact that we knew her two sons, who were slightly less "active," shall we say, than we were, and that she was a stickler for detail, we passed over the nuclear buttons labeled *"Noo Yerk"* and *"Varshington, Deesee."*

If your toilets won't flush, your bombs don't have a prayer, we reasoned.

That left the conspiracy theory.

After mulling it over for a couple of hours and two or three Grapettes each, we decided that either the Martians were scoping us out and the military-industrial complex was running scared. Or the Russians really had done the impossible and beaten us into space, and the military-industrial complex was running scared.

Either way, it didn't matter. The running scared part was the same.

Former General Eisenhower, the generals in the Pentagon, and dozens of General Bullmooses at the helms of dozens of military paraphernalia manufacturers were all running scared. And that was not good news for sixteen-year-old boys, any way you cut it.

I expected even General Grump might be concerned about now. 'Course, if he'd had his way, U.S. troops would have marched through China and just kept on going to Moscow, and this little problem might not exist. Shoot, he'd have even kept on going on through France to Geneva. Nobody believed in that "neutrality" business, anyway. Or that all the Frogs weren't still loyal to the Vichy. Did they?

I found myself wishing I could talk the whole thing over with Mr. Harry, the only former or present resident of Washington, D.C. I thought I could believe. He didn't take any crap off the generals, and now the damned generals were in charge of everything.

Not good. Not good at all.

Meanwhile, we learned a bit more the next day. The dratted orbiting whatever apparently was, indeed, a Ruskiy satellite. They called it "Sputnik," which we immediately assumed meant "Gotcha, Yankee" in Russian.

The calls for more emphasis on science and mathematics came pouring forth from the collective generals, both military and civilian.

Even though dubious, we didn't want the world passing us by. So we instantly descended on our guidance counselors and commenced to change our graduation plans to include trigonometry, physics, and even introduction to the calculus.

We dropped such mind-bending subjects as physiology (we would attempt to learn that by Braille, as if blind, using Red Jackets for study models, whenever possible), typing, health and hygiene, and Deploying Your Pots & Pans Efficiently II.

Most of those subjects were just common sense, we decided, but physics and the calculus had to be studied.

In the wake of Sputnik, every one of us resolved to become an engineer so we could design our country's way out of this space-race hole Moscow had, embarrassingly, lobbed us into, in spite of the fact that we had glommed onto better German scientists than the Ruskiys had a decade earlier.

As time wore on, and we saw that Sputnik was not much more of a feat than tossing the shot-put sixty feet or so, our enthusiasm for the harder, science-based courses began to wane. Slowly, and one by one, we began rearranging our class schedules, bringing back pots & pans and knittin' & tattin', and dropping the likes of trigonometry and number theory.

We would be, again, the lazy degenerates we all thought we were destined, and entitled, to be.

What a relief!

Back to the Red Jackets. Once again.

My fellow students had elected me president of the sophomore class. In that role, it was my duty, late in the spring, to welcome a convocation of incoming tenth graders who would be part of the class of 1962 at S.F. Austin High School.

Helping me welcome them, lined all along the side walls of the cavernous AHS auditorium, were representatives of the Red Jackets. Only, because they were inside a building with no air conditioning, the Red Jackets had been allowed to remove their coats.

Without their maroon coats, they were white from head to toe. White shoes, white stockings, white skirts, white shirts with little black ties. They looked like a line of milkmen to me. In my remarks, I complimented them on how nice they looked and asked the incoming class to give them a round of applause.

Nice things to do, no?

No.

Not according to Connie Henderson and half the Red Jackets who were in attendance. They badly mistook a comment I made, and they were after me to do serious bodily harm.

First to tell me I had transgressed was "Lippy," our beloved, well-networked, always informed and pretty cool principal.

"I didn't hear everything you said in there," he began, "but something came out of your mouth that has Miss Henderson and half the Red Jackets madder than a bunch of cats sprayed with a fire hose."

I thought his analogy rather clever and made a mental note of it for future use.

"Well, I had no intention of insulting them, for heaven's sake. I thought I paid them a very nice compliment," I responded.

"Some of them must not have taken it as a compliment," Lippy said. "Miss Henderson is about to wet her tennis shorts."

Miss Henderson was a girl's physical education teacher and coach of the girl's tennis team.

Lippy continued, "You know some of you guys walk right up to the edge of being smart-alecks. You and Don and Andy and Kenny teeter right on that edge more often than I would like." He looked at me. I wondered why he hadn't mentioned Jack.

"Supremely confident. Often humorous. But never smart-alecks," I answered. "We may be witty, but we're not half-wits, sir." I looked at him. "The second day we were here, you asked us to be leaders, Mr. Andrews. Students will follow us faster than they will the geeks or the nerds, if I may say so."

"You may, and you are right, George," he said to me.

That looked like an opening. He had pronounced me right. I dived right in, "You have never heard one of us call you 'Lippy,' have you, sir?" I said, smiling.

"As a matter of fact, I have. On several occasions," he shot back.

"But we have never addressed you directly as 'Lippy,' have we, Mr. Andrews?" I wanted to get as many legal "Lippies" into this conversation as I possibly could.

"No, you haven't, I admit. And since that was our deal, I have no complaints," he answered. "But this business with Miss Henderson and the Red Jackets is not going to go away. You and I have to solve it." He was advising me of the facts of life. Big Connie was going to make a federal case of it. Whatever "it" was.

"Tell you what . . ." Lippy was about to wax philosophical, I thought. Instead, he faced the problem he was apparently willing to share with me straight-on. "Come by my office at the end of the day—3:30 or so. I'll get Miss Henderson in, too, and the three of us will put an end to it. Today."

"I'll sure be there, because I don't know what I said that has her panties in a wad. Whatever it was, I intended to be complimentary," I smiled at him.

He looked up at me. "You'll be there because I told you to. And that comment's what I'm talking about," he said, looking perplexed.

"What comment, sir?" I asked, innocently.

"That panties comment. Right on the edge of smart-aleck. Please don't refer to Miss Henderson's panties this afternoon. We have enough to overcome here without adding to the charges, whatever they are."

He was actually pleading.

"I'll be there at 3:30, sir, and I promise to leave my comments behind," I said, knowing I had just committed to the impossible.

I rushed to find Don, *Capo di capo* of our own intelligence gathering, to see if he could shed any light on what I might have said that had 125 or so pairs of panties, cute as could be, I was sure, in wads.

I found him outside the band hall just before sixth period. I was going to be late for Mr. Colonel Sinclair's solid geometry, the one class I had sworn to myself I would behave in as a model student (lest the truth of my hooliganism get back via family). It was a risk I had to take.

"Do you know what has Henderson all in a twit?" I asked as I walked up to him.

"You don't know?" He was incredulous.

"I don't have a clue, and neither does Lippy, but I have to

OUTTA THE WAY!

A group of the choicest Red Jackets and band babes shoved me into a corner, as they always managed, somehow, to do, and ignored me, as usual.

(Photo courtesy Austin High School Archives)

George Arnold • 149

meet with him and her in an hour. What do you know?" I was begging now.

"You made a dumb-ass remark," he replied. "I heard it myself." The compound adjective "dumb-ass" was reserved for flagrant violations.

"What did I say?" Now I was really begging.

"C'mon, George, for pity's sake. You know very well what you said," he answered emphatically.

"If I did, I wouldn't be begging you to tell me," I pleaded.

"You really don't remember?" He was softening.

"No!" was all I could think of to say.

"Okay, here it is. You called the Red Jackets 'milkmaids.'" He looked at me, straining not to laugh his special "You-are-such-a-fool-once-again" laugh.

"Why would anybody get worked up over that?" I asked, unbelieving. "They were all dressed totally in white, and I complimented them on how nice they looked."

I was baffled.

"Nobody but Henderson took offense at first," he said. "But she went flying around and convinced the girls that you were referring to the size of their breasts," he smiled. "You know Henderson wants nobody to see a square centimeter of their bare skin. She's fixated," he concluded.

"Damn. Thanks."

I had fifty minutes, while Mr. Colonel Sinclair droned on about Pythagoras, or Anthony Quinn, or Melina Mercouri, or one of his other favorite Greeks, to come up with either an explanation or a counterattack.

I have to admit I didn't learn much solid geometry in that hour, but I was able to prepare a devilishly clever comeback. It would be based, as usual, on absolute truth.

Promptly at 3:35 (always keep 'em waiting at least five minutes) I walked into Lippy's office. Henderson was there, fat thighs bulging from her white tennis shorts. Just to make her uncomfortable (and thus gain an advantage in what was about to happen), I looked her up and down like a leering old pervert. What really went through my mind as I scoped her out was too totally disgusting to tell you about.

Then I took my seat at Lippy's invitation.

Lippy began, "We have a situation here that I intend to resolve in the next fifteen minutes. Put it to bed, forever. I believe there has been a gross misunderstanding of intent, and it need not fester."

Good for you, Lippy. That's a great start. And another opening. I leapt into the breech, apparently for the second time in the last couple of hours.

So to speak.

"Miss Henderson, I have, since the meeting in the auditorium and my conversation with Mr. Andrews, found out exactly what I said. And I believe you have misinterpreted it, deliberately or not." That was a challenge.

She turned red. "Why would I deliberately misinterpret a nasty reference on your part to my girls' breasts?" she exploded, half standing.

It was now or never.

"Because it is common knowledge that your concern about exposing even a square inch of Red Jackets' anatomies is greater than anybody else's, including the Red Jackets themselves. And their mothers and ministers, for that matter."

I fired the big gun. The Howitzer.

"What kind of accusation is that supposed to be?" She was clearly taken aback. Stunned, even.

Advantage, George. I served again.

"No accusation. Just a flash of the blindingly obvious. My comment this afternoon was a heartfelt compliment (truth, even if twisted), and you chose to turn it around to something it never was intended to be, making me out to be some kind of ill-mannered pervert."

Right between the eyes.

Lippy was silently enjoying this verbal *tête-à-tête*.

She turned to him. He immediately became stone-faced.

"I'm not going to debate this insinuating little smart-ass (oops, careful, there, Connie) any longer. What are you going to do about him?" she demanded.

"First, we are all going to stop calling names." He corrected her right in front of me. Another opening.

"I have a suggestion, sir!" I piped up loudly.

"Nobody's talking to you!" Dear Connie fairly screamed, spit flying out the corners of her mouth, causing Lippy to stand up, walk across the room, and shut the door.

"I want to hear what he has to say." Lippy looked at her. "I talked to him immediately after you talked to me, and I must say he convinced me he was completely in the dark. It is just possible, Miss Henderson, that this is all a big misunderstanding." He held his ground and motioned for me to go on and offer my suggestion.

"What I said was intended to be a compliment. I thought the girls looked beautiful all in white. I've never seen them, as a group, without their jackets on before. Perhaps my choice of phraseology lacked a certain *savoir faire*, but I intended no insult, I promise."

"That's enough excuses!" Henderson challenged. "What's your idea?"

"I was just getting to that before you interrupted," I shot back. She could not be allowed to minimize my advantage.

"My idea, *Miss* Henderson (big emphasis on *Miss*), is that I will be prepared to personally come and apologize to the entire assembly, *en masse*, of every last Red Jacket on the face of the earth." I was gritting my teeth and talking directly at her through them. "In fact, I demand the chance to set this thing right, once and for all. Two minutes to eat crow, or humble pie, whatever you want to call it. Then it's over. QED."

I tested her knowledge of both common French phrases and geometry proofs.

Clearly, this was not what she had expected to hear. I had instantly disarmed her, and Lippy jumped in before she could recover.

"Miss Henderson, that sounds entirely reasonable to me. In fact, I want to be there to introduce the subject myself. When and where?" he looked directly at her, as if to say, "Do not object, Miss Henderson. We are going to do this, come hell or high water."

At that moment, he became one of my heroes, and I never uttered that disrespectful name, "Lippy," again.

She glared at me. Then she looked at Mr. Andrews. "We drill at 3:30 tomorrow afternoon. Field house. Let's get it over with." She stood up and tromped out of the room, slamming the door behind her, and looking to me, from the back, like Yogi Berra after a long, hard, extra-inning game.

Except Yogi would be better looking in a pair of white tennis shorts. I was sure of it.

Mr. Andrews looked at me. "Keep it short. Keep it simple. No name calling. No accusations. Do not repeat the term 'milk-maids.' Can you do that?"

"Not only can I, sir, but I have insisted on the opportunity." Hallelujah.

The chance of a lifetime. And just twenty-four hours away.

I immediately called a meeting of *la cosa nostra piccola* for 10:05 that evening in the ushers' locker room at the Varsity Theater.

No need for Grapettes this time. This one was a no-brainer, and all five of us were unanimous: Follow Mr. Andrews' directives explicitly, and—when it came to Connie—take no prisoners. Be sure to charm all the girls in the process.

Not a big hill for a climber. And, if nothing else, we were climbers.

The following afternoon, as scheduled, Mr. Andrews and I walked down to the field house area, together, to face Big Connie and her harem of 125 lovelies.

Miss Henderson called the group to attention, literally. Had she been a Marine? Probably. A drill sergeant, by the looks of things.

She simply announced, almost resignedly, that Mr. Andrews had something to say.

The babes in their 125 pairs of matching white practice Bermuda shorts and white T-shirts, relatively modest outfits in which they would still, however, never be allowed to appear in public, were looking at me, puzzled. Had not Miss Henderson told them I had insulted them barely twenty-four hours before? What was he doing here? Strange.

Taking his cue from Connie's uncharacteristic understatement, Mr. Andrews simply said, "George Arnold has something to say to you."

Truly, this was going to be my show.

I began humbly.

"Yesterday at the assembly to welcome the new tenth graders

for next year, I attempted to pay those of you who were there a supreme compliment. I said I thought you were beautiful. I have reconsidered over the past twenty-four hours after an insightful discussion among Miss Henderson, Mr. Andrews and myself.

"I was wrong yesterday. You were not beautiful at all. (Pause here for effect). No, to a sixteen-year-old male, you were all far from beautiful (repetition for more effect).

"You were absolutely, unequivocally, undoubtedly, outrageously gorgeous."

Smiles broke out everywhere except on Henderson's face. She glowered and looked to Mr. Andrews to intercede. He stood, arms folded, intent on what he was observing.

I continued.

"Unfortunately, Miss Henderson apparently misinterpreted my intent. And I now admit, freely, that my particular choice of words might have lent themselves to being misunderstood (pause) . . . by anyone preoccupied with breasts!"

I twisted the knife.

"I guess that would include me and any other red-blooded male." I confessed the obvious.

Smiles broke out again, unanimously, except for Henderson, who was doing a slow burn. Even Mr. Andrews was smiling.

"In the final analysis," I began my conclusion, "I don't think you would have it any other way.

"So if, after hearing Miss Henderson's interpretation of my unfortunate, but well-intentioned remark, in case you might have taken offense, I came here to apologize to you. As a group. Or one at a time, out behind the field house. Only if you want to, that is."

Loud laughter.

"I also want you to know, in spite of those 1942, old-lady uniforms Miss Henderson makes you wear, I'm still madly in love with every one of you."

Cheers rang out.

I was finished with my statement. But I was just beginning a long relationship with the Red Jackets. I had hit their two hot buttons: Miss Henderson's perpetual overprotection of bare skin, even hands; and those gawdawful, matronly uniforms they were forced to wear.

Henderson was devastated. She would be months getting over the shellacking I had just given her, but with a velvet glove, to be sure. I didn't feel bad about it. She had it coming to her as far as I could tell.

As we walked back to the main building, I turned to Mr. Andrews and casually inquired, "How did I do? Was it okay?"

He took hold of my left arm to stop me, and turned me to look directly at him. "It was just right," he said. "You did exactly what I asked you to do, but you didn't back down a half-inch.

"Miss Henderson is going to give me grief. And you, too, I expect. But sometimes today's little ripples make tomorrow worthwhile. Right?"

See why I could never, again, call him "Lippy"?
Hallelujah.

Life's Lessons Learned:

- *The military-industrial complex must be watched, checked and challenged. Vigilantly. Every day.*

- *Russian toilets may not flush, but the Ruskiys did put up the first orbiting earth satellite. Even if it was no bigger than a grapefruit, and it did nothing but chirp.*

- *Use a script when you have to talk before a group. A casual, and completely innocent, ad lib can bring you grief.*

- *Apologize immediately when you have aggrieved someone. But do it with panache. Take no prisoners.*

- *Every woman loves a compliment. But be sure it's heartfelt and honest. Or you're just an insincere cad, who, ultimately, will pay for that insincerity.*

- *If you are right, stick to your principles. And with your principal.*

CHAPTER 13

Two for the Road

AUSTIN, 1959

From time to time, Don and I enhanced our meager Varsity Theater earnings with a unique and interesting side job—delivering new school buses to school districts around the state.

You see, South Austin was home to a company called Ward Body Works. Ward was one of a small handful of school bus assemblers in the country. Engines on truck frames would be delivered to Austin from the auto manufacturers, and Ward would then fabricate school bus bodies, from the hood back, for them.

Every bus was built-to-order for a school district, usually in Texas or a surrounding state.

Don and I had a deal with David Trippett, Ward's manager in charge of delivering those buses to their new owners. Whenever he had two going to the same place, he would call us a couple of weeks before they were painted and ready to roll. We would arrange for three consecutive days off from the theater, and, soon as they were finished, we would drive them to their new homes, turn them over to their new owners, and then make our way back home.

Depending on the size of the bus, we were paid anywhere from sixteen cents to twenty-two cents a mile, one way, to get the job done. We had to buy the gas and get ourselves home from East Jesus or West Overshoe out of that per-mile stipend.

Interestingly enough, in those days no special type of license was required to drive an empty school bus. Any fourteen-year-old with a valid operator's license could climb behind the wheel of a seventy-two-passenger school bus.

We were sixteen. And we thought we could do anything.

Now, besides being pretty lucrative, financially speaking, these little trips were fun for us. And educational, for sure. We not only got to see a lot of our small corner of the world up close, but we also met a number of interesting characters along the way. Everybody from dirt farmers scrabbling out a living from an unforgiving environment to school superintendents to hyper and overimaginative local police deputies.

But more about that later.

Anyway, over the summer of 1959, at age sixteen, Don and I made about three trips a month, taking these shiny, new behemoths from Austin to such out-of-the-way places as Muleshoe, Post, Center, Atlanta (Texas), and Waskom. Once, we even went to New Mexico, to a tiny place called Las Vegas.

These buses were built on truck frames, with engines and six-speed transmissions designed to achieve anywhere from four to seven miles per gallon on the highway, in overdrive and without kids aboard. On short runs, we would figure about how much gas would be required to get there, wherever "there" was, and try our best to deliver them bone dry.

The way to make the most money was to deliver the buses with four ounces of fuel left in the tank, and then hitchhike home, thus saving bus or train fare.

We hitched ourselves rides in everything from eighteen-wheelers to sheep trailers. Riding with the sheep, of course. We found they were pretty easy to get along with.

Back then, the hitchhiker was often more in jeopardy than the driver who picked him up.

One trip, we went out to Lamesa in West Texas. A guy in a brand new '59 Ford Fairlane picked us up. Unbelievably, he was headed to Austin, and he said he would take us all the way home.

What luck!

Except this yahoo had a theory about breaking in new engines. He was convinced the best approach was to run the engine wide-open for 400-500 miles. He called the procedure "stickin' yer foot in the carburetor," and then he proceeded to demonstrate. Mile after mile, we cruised along at 110-115 miles per hour. Now, admittedly, there was little traffic out there, but this guy was a totally distracted talker.

The more he talked, the more he gestured. The more he gestured and looked around to see if we were getting his points, the more the speeding, new car drifted from side to side on that two-lane road. After one quarter-mile stretch where he drifted off to the gravel on the right shoulder, overcorrected and hit the gravel on the left shoulder, and then straightened out right down the center line, all the while talking and gesturing and gawking around, we asked to stop to pee.

Thirty seconds before, neither of us had had the urge. Now we could barely hold it.

We sneaked away and hid from him the first time he stopped for gas. No ride at all was preferable to that one.

On another trip, we took two seventy-two-passenger Ford diesels to Snyder. A gray-haired, grandfatherly type in a new Cadillac picked us up. He was headed for Waco. We could get home from there easily.

He told us, proudly and only with minimal pomposity, that he was a retired Baptist minister, currently working part-time as a Bible salesman. That explained the Waco connection.

I thought we might slip down to the Brazos River near Cameron Park and see if we could get ourselves healed, maybe. An additional ten-spot wouldn't hurt. Would it?

Well, this Bible salesman, in a Cadillac, should have been the perfect ride. Right?

Wrong.

Don was soon asleep in the back seat. Retired Baptist Reverend Part-Time Bible Salesman kept glancing back at him in the rear-view mirror. Once he determined Don was snoring sufficiently, he started to become a little too friendly with me, if you know what I mean.

When the touching turned to grabbing, I hopped over into the back seat with Don, claiming I, too, was sleepy.

Instead of taking us to Waco, he put us out at the next town, Brady. As bad as we wanted to get to Waco, and on back home, both of us were relieved to get out of that Cadillac, to tell the truth.

Which we always did, don't you know?

The Reverends Mallory, Jackson, Green, and Oliver began to take on increasing legitimacy after our run-in with the Retired Baptist Reverend Part-Time Bible Salesman who, unlike the four aforementioned messengers from God, probably had a divinity degree and damn-straight ordination papers.

I thought any one of the Reverends Mallory-Jackson-Green-Oliver probably did more good in this world with their healing hijinks than this old molester, with all his *bona fide* legitimacies.

Yes, sir. When we delivered those buses, we were two sixteen-year-olds turned loose on the world, for sure.

One Thursday evening in July, we filled up the tanks of two big, new GMC seventy-two-passenger buses and headed north-west, about midnight, to Post, Texas, out near Sweetwater. For a change, both buses performed flawlessly (often these new vehicles were not completely assembled properly, so we always carried a small tool kit).

After stopping for donuts and chocolate milk (it was a habit, now) in Brownwood, we hauled into Post about noon, delivered our buses to the superintendent of schools himself, and trooped ourselves on down to what looked like a favorite local diner for a couple of burgers. While we were eating, the same superintendent pulled up in one of those new buses, and the entire place emptied out to inspect the first half of the town's new acquisitions. Just got up, left their burgers, BLTs, tuna-melts and fries on the tables, and went on outside.

We figured life must be pretty dull around Post if something as apparently mundane as a new school bus could empty a decent restaurant at noon, leaving half-eaten, pretty good food behind, to the delight of the local flies.

Before long, the superintendent opened the front door and motioned for us to come on out. At first we thought maybe they didn't trust us alone with the cash drawer in the café, because even the fry cook had left a few minutes before. We should have known that folks in small towns are trusting, though. The superintendent just wanted the townsfolk to meet the two guys who brought the new buses, and he offered us a ride to the main east-west highway, since Post is a bit north of any intersection, whatsoever. We took our unfinished burgers with us.

Half the people in the diner opted to ride along, leaving their burgers and fries to get cold and their Cokes and Grapettes to get warm.

Don said to me, "Lord, if I'd known we'd be minor celebrities just for bringing them a couple new buses, I'd have brought a cake, too. We could have really partied."

Out on the main highway, we began to hold out our thumbs. Don would always lift his right pants leg when a woman driver approached. Seemed fair to us, if women hitchhikers could hike up their skirts. Never did any good, but it was funny to a couple of Beavis and Butthead forerunners.

I first noticed the smell of ozone in the air and commented on it.

Don, often more observant and in tune with our surroundings than I was, pointed and told me to look to the northwest sky. Well, it was royal purple, darkening quickly to black. We were not in a good spot, out in the open like we were. All hell was fixing to break loose, and the closest shelter was at least a dozen miles away. Only we didn't know in which direction.

Turns out, wind, rain and hail might just be the least of our worries. A new concern cropped up suddenly with a strange whooshing sound coming from the north. All at once, over a small rise (read "West Texas hill"), here came what looked to be a gigantic, gray flying carpet, only it never got more than a few inches off the ground. This gray carpet was moving directly toward us, and it was big—at least half the size of a football field.

I said to Don, "What do you think that thing is?" I couldn't help but think of the flying saucers I was sure I had seen in the night skies over San Antonio—back in the second grade.

"I don't know, but I'm climbing up on a fence post," he said as he began to retreat through the ditch to a cedar-post, barbed-wire fence that was behind us.

I joined him. On the next post down.

The wriggling, writhing carpet thing kept coming at us, relentlessly. It was at least twenty-five yards wide and sixty to seventy yards long. And it looked to be perfectly rectangular.

Across the highway it charged and right on toward the fence posts we were perched on.

"Tarantulas!" Don yelled to me over the din of the swoosh-

ON THE LOOSE

Don and George are a couple of sixteen-year-olds turned loose on the world, delivering new school buses to far-flung, little-known and seldom-visited meccas like East Jesus and West Overshoe.

George Arnold • 161

ing sound and the increasing noise of the wind as the purple, turning black, curtain bore down on us. "There must be two million of those suckers," he shouted.

Sure enough, as the flying carpet reached the fence line and started underneath us, I could see thousands, millions, of hairy tarantula spiders, in a perfect marching formation that would have made General Grump proud. They were heading hell-bent-for-leather to higher ground so they wouldn't drown in the rain that had just started and soon would engulf us all—two sixteen-year-old city boys and a couple million dancing spiders.

"Jesus, Louise!" Don shouted. "Is there no end to these little monsters?"

Before I could answer, we heard the distinct sound of big air brakes grabbing, locking and sliding tires on slightly damp asphalt. It was an eighteen-wheeler loaded to the hilt with bales of High Plains cotton. He hit that column of tarantulas straight on. They began to pop and squish under his tires as he came to a stop, trailer almost jackknifed right in front of us.

The driver leaned over, rolled down the right-hand window of the big cab and yelled to us over the rumble of his diesel engine, the whistling of the wind, and the odd, swooshing sound of the monstrous spider brigade. First time, we couldn't hear him, so we cupped one hand behind an ear to indicate "louder," and, with the other, we held ourselves onto our respective cedar posts for dear life, so as not to fall amongst the tarantulas.

Second time, we heard him. He shouted, "Tarantulas!" Oh, really?

Then he added, "Wait a minute until they're gone."

What else did he think we were going to do? Jump down on all fours and join them?

They passed us in less than three minutes, just ahead of a hail-filled torrent that began as the truck driver, seeing we looked clean-cut and were in a devil of a pickle, waved us to the truck.

"Get in," he said as he swung the big door open for us. "You'll drown out there. Or get beat to death by that hail. Where're you going?" he inquired.

"Austin," we answered in chorus.

"I'm headed for Houston, to the docks with all this cotton," he said. "I can take you as far as Junction or even San Antonio.

Right now, though, let's just get the hell away from this storm." He put the big Peterbilt in gear, and we were off, leaving a squishy, greasy, hairy mess of hundreds of dead tarantulas on the road behind us.

It was dinnertime, according to our driver, about when we got to Ballinger. We stopped at what used to be a Dairy Queen, but was now converted to "Chicken Fried Steak Heaven," or maybe "Chicken Fried Steak Haven." I can't remember, exactly.

"They have pretty good chicken fried steaks here," the driver told us.

When we went in, we found that's all they had. There was one item on the menu—"House Salad with Miracle Whip Dressing, Chicken Fried Steak, French Fries and Texas Toast—$1.59. Take it or leave it."

Now, Don and I (and a few hundred thousand others who passed through Austin at one time or another) had been spoiled by Hill's Café on South Congress Avenue when it came to chicken fried steaks. Hill's, next to the Goodnight Motel, served up a platter-sized round steak, pounded, battered and deep-fried, with secret yellow gravy, a loaded baked potato, and either a vegetable or salad. We were chicken fried aficionados.

Since we had only one option, this had better be good.

It wasn't.

Oh, it wasn't terrible. Dairy Queen quality, at least. But it wasn't Hill's, best in the world, which caused us to start to think about shortcuts home.

Our driver, who had generously saved us from both an arachnophobia attack and a serious West Texas hailstorm, was willing to take us all the way to San Antonio. But he was loaded, making about a 35-40 MPH average. It would be a long, long ride with him to San Antonio. Besides, San Antonio, via Junction and U.S. 90, was way out of our way.

We thanked him, split the price of his mediocre chicken fried steak, and went out to the cross-highway to thumb our way more directly toward Austin.

As we were standing at the crossroads of two highways in downtown Ballinger, hoping for a quick exit from this little burg, up rolled what looked to be a local police car, and out stepped Deputy Barney Fife. No joke. This guy not only was a dead ringer for Don Knotts; he also had the mannerisms down perfectly.

I'm not even sure if *The Andy Griffith Show* was in production yet, but, at that moment, Ballinger could have been Mayberry.

"What're you two doing in Ballinger?" he asked, throwing his head back, sniffing and swaggering, Knottsian-style.

"Just passing through," I responded.

"Just passing through, huh? That's a likely story if I ever heard one," he said.

Why that inane answer would have seemed to him a "likely story," we couldn't imagine.

"We're leaving as fast as we can catch a ride," Don assured him. "We don't much like being here, either, as a matter of fact."

Deputy Fife turned on him, "Wise guy, huh?" he glared, eyes twitching, lips pursing. "We have rules around here, like, laws, you know? I could run you in on a 403K. Or a 713R."

That was it. No further explanation.

Don challenged him, "I think you're making those numbers up. We're just standing here. What's the charge for standing? 666T?"

"Okay, that's it!" he yelled in a squeaky-high voice. "Put your hands on top of the car. Move!" He pulled an old revolver, with one side of the handgrip missing, out of his creaky holster and pointed it at us. "C'mon. Move it, you two."

That little Napoleon was going to frisk us, which he did. And then he handcuffed us and told us to get in the back of his filthy, old squad car.

Now we could see straight into his old five-shot revolver. It had a big cylinder, and all the slots where bullets normally would be were empty.

"Do you see what I see?" I asked Don.

"Got it!" he responded.

Telepathically, we decided to chance that there was not one bullet in the chamber.

So, we refused to get in the car.

"We were just standing here, and that's what we're going to keep on doing," I looked him straight in the barrel of his gun, knowing he wouldn't pull the trigger, and—even if he did—he couldn't shoot us with a "click." We had no intention, whatsoever, of getting into that car with him.

"You'll just have to shoot us," Don smirked. "Murder-1. What's that? A 314P?"

Well, old Barney didn't know what to do. He tried, "I'll add 125B to the charges if you don't get in that car," he threatened. "Before you ask, that's resisting arrest."

"We're not resisting," Don shot back. "We're just refusing. There's a difference, you know, deputy."

"How'd you know I was the deputy?" He puckered up his mouth, sort of sideways, bugged out his eyes and looked, suspiciously, at Don.

I answered, "It says 'deputy' on your badge and on the side of your car. But we just made a lucky guess, though."

We were starting to get the upper hand, even if he had a gun and we were handcuffed.

"We're standing here. We aren't going anywhere with you," I told him flatly. "Maybe you better call the chief, or the sheriff, or whoever you report to," I suggested.

He waved the gun as if to try to scare us and got back in his car to use the radio.

"Buster'll be here in a minute," he yelled to us through the open car window. "He'll get your butts in this car!"

Was that a threat against a citizen from an officer of the law?

Before we could contemplate that question for very long, up pulled a green Ford F-100 pickup, and out stepped a big man we deduced must be "Buster."

He ignored Barney. Didn't even give him a second glance. Just walked right up to us, and—polite as you please—said to us, "What's the problem here?"

"The only problem we have is these handcuffs," Don said.

"Any idea why he put 'em on you?" Buster asked, still moving about to keep ol' Barn to his back.

"He said it was a 622T, or a 319K, or something like that," I said. "We don't know what he's talking about."

"He don't, neither." Buster rolled his eyes up and backward toward ol' Barney as if to imply that he might not be quite right in the head. "He don't have no bullets," Buster whispered. "I promised his daddy I would look after him, so I give him a little deputy job. Nobody 'round here pays him no mind."

Buster spun around. "Edward (so that was his name), come

take the handcuffs off these two boys, right now!" It was a bark from Buster, but a kindly one.

"Aw, Buster, cain't we at least run 'em in on a 764L?" It was Barney, pleading.

"And what's that, Edward?" Buster had to ask. We had been right. He was making up the numbers.

"You know, Buster. Vagrancy." Barney was practically begging.

"You boys got some money on you?" Buster inquired. "More'n five dollars each?"

"Sure do." I didn't want to commit how much in case this turned into a shakedown.

"Sorry, Edward," Buster said. "They got money. Cain't be no vagrants. Now get these cuffs off. Hurry up!"

Edward took off the cuffs. He whispered to us while he was doing it, "I don't ever want to see you two here in Ballinger again. If I do, I might just find me a bullet, ya know what I'm sayin'?"

"You'll need two bullets, Edward," Don said, rather calmly, "and I can tell for sure you'll *never* be able to come up with more than one."

Buster instructed Edward, beaten and severely disappointed, to take the green F-100 back to the office and, after ascertaining our destination, loaded us into the filthy squad car and stopped an Austex Chili truck. He told the driver to "get these here boys the hell out of town" and to take us all the way to Austin.

And so it was we got back to Austin that same night, right downtown, at the Austex plant, having avoided marching spiders, rain and hail, heartburn from a pretty bad chicken-fried steak, an overzealous and under-intelligent deputy, and, maybe even, a night in the Ballinger hoosegow. First stop: Hill's Café, for a real chicken fried steak.

A fairly typical quick trip for the two bus deliverers.

Hosanna!

Our last run for that summer came at the very tail end of August. It was to Center, Texas, a small town along the Louisiana border, deep in the piney woods.

We would leave on a Friday morning and try to get back Saturday, since Monday was Labor Day, and school reconvened on Tuesday for us. We would be in the eleventh grade.

When we went Thursday evening to pick up the paperwork

and buses, ol' Dave Trippett winked at us and said, "You guys do know, don't you, that at least half the women in that part of Texas, there along the Louisiana border, they're all nymphomaniacs. Have a safe trip." With that he turned on his heel and went back inside to his office.

Now, the two of us, virgins-apparent to the death, knew what he was talking about. We, like most sixteen-year-old boys, dreamed about such women. Twice nightly.

Right then, we determined to leave immediately, not in the morning as earlier planned. There was no logical rush, except an unspoken fear on our part, I guess, that all those women might repent before noon tomorrow.

Of course, we thought ol' Dave was probably just pulling our collective legs. But we couldn't be absolutely sure he wasn't telling the truth. So we gassed up.

And we lit out of Austin like our butts were on fire.

All these new buses had governors to keep the engines from over-revving during the break-in period. We pushed those two Chevys to their governors' limits. At railroad crossings we normally would have approached with our red lights flashing, then stopped, and opened the passenger entry door, before proceeding—we flew through those babies at 60 MPH-plus, never looking back.

As fate would have it, my bus began to overheat after about fifty miles. By then, darkness was approaching. We pulled off to the side of the road, turned on the amber caution flashers, and commenced our usual diagnostic procedure for an overheated radiator: idle the engine until the temperature goes down; carefully, with a thick rag on your palm, open the radiator cap to check the fluid level; pour in more water if it needs it; take off and see what happens.

Well, I idled. And I idled. Then I idled some more. The water temperature, according to the dashboard gauge, was too high, but not to the point of doing damage. And it wouldn't go down. So we shut the engine off and waited for it to cool.

By now, we had been struggling with the problem for about an hour and a half. Time was wasting. Every hour, we thought, a few more of those loose, Louisiana border women might be coming to Jesus.

It finally cooled to the point we could remove the radiator

BUS DRIVIN' GOURMETS PREFER HILL'S
Hill's Café's new building next to the Goodnight Motel on Austin's South Congress Avenue, home of the prototype chicken-fried steak. Those who cared enough to check it out agreed that Hill's served the best c-f steak in the universe, along with unbelievably tasty, yellow gravy. (Rendering courtesy Charlie Goodnight, Goodnight Properties.)

cap without replicating "Old Faithful." Sure enough, the radiator was full. Lack of coolant was not the problem.

Next step: Listen to the water pump and be sure it was functioning.

While trying to get my ear close enough to the water pump to hear if it might be rattling or squeaking, without having the radiator fan give me a nose-ectomy, suddenly I saw the problem. The belt driving both the water pump and the radiator fan was loose. Real loose.

To tighten it, we had to loosen a nut on a bracket holding the alternator, pry the alternator farther from the engine block, and then re-tighten the nut, thus taking up all the slack in the loose belt, making it tight again.

Simple enough. We had the tools for just such an occasion. I would loosen, Don would pry, and I would tighten. Done.

Except that the long rod we usually used for the "pry" part was not in the toolbox. It was nowhere to be found.

We tried by hand, but everything under the hood was still too hot to hang on to. Besides, we could never get it tight enough without leverage. Real leverage.

So we sat down and pondered alternate solutions while we had us a Pepsi. I had given up Grapettes a few months back. They were suddenly too sweet for me. Besides, they were getting harder to find than hens' teeth.

"The jack handle!" Don blurted out, all at once and quite unexpectedly, and began searching through both buses.

Neither had a jack.

More pondering. More time wasted. Probably more of those loose women finding salvation.

We were sitting beside a Farm-to-Market road in the middle of nowhere, staring through a barbed-wire fence into a freshly plowed, former cornfield.

Shazam! It hit us almost simultaneously.

"T-posts," I shouted out.

We took our locking pliers and wire cutters, and we ran, helter-skelter, to one of those fence posts. Cutting the little clamps that held the barbed wire to it, we freed the steel post from its moorings, pulled it up out of the dirt, raced back to my bus and, using the fencepost for a lever, quickly tightened the loose belt.

Although we couldn't, for lack of baling wire, re-attach the barbed wire to the post, we did put it back in place.

In spite of our former rush, we were suddenly tired. So we shut off both buses' lights and grabbed us a nap. All this rushing was goofy, anyway. Dave was kidding. Wasn't he?

After another four-hour delay with a leaking fuel pump on Don's bus, we rolled into Center late Friday afternoon. We tracked down the school superintendent at a preseason, intrasquad football scrimmage at the high school stadium.

"How were the buses coming over from Austin?" he asked us.

"Perfect. No problems," Don lied.

"Sure took you guys a while to get here. Been lookin' for you all day. Dave said he thought you left last evening," our friendly host offered.

"Changed plans. Decided to get some sleep first." Now I lied, picking up on his peculiar shorthand way of speaking.

"'Fraid the last Greyhound left about an hour ago. Need a place to stay?"

"No, thanks. We'll catch a ride pretty quickly," Don assured him.

So we walked back downtown, deciding along the way that, to minimize the likelihood we might just be eaten alive by mosquitoes, we could both get out of this place quicker if we split up. Don would hitchhike north, and I would hitchhike south. We would meet up in Austin Saturday evening.

We set up on opposite sides of the main street, which was also a major north-south U.S. highway.

Within thirty seconds, a state Highway Patrol car came through town, going north. He passed Don, made a U-turn, and pulled up right alongside me. His right front window was rolled all the way down, and lying across the sill was an enormous over-and-under shotgun.

I wasn't going to guess whether it was loaded.

He leaned across to make eye contact with me, and he asked, "Is that guy across the street with you?"

"Yes, sir," I replied. This was no Barney Fife.

"Call him over here." He was polite, but looked tense.

I did. Don walked on over and asked, "What's up?"

"Put your hands on top of the car, both of you!"

Where had we heard that before?

After a thorough pat-down that revealed no weapons, he decided not to handcuff us. Instead, he made us sit down on the curb. He asked us questions like: Why we were in Center? When had we arrived? Where were we going? Pretty routine.

He checked our IDs.

He looked very young, so I took a chance and said to him, "You may know my dad. He's in charge of the DPS training academy."

He did. Amazing.

He then explained to us that the first murder in Center since 1899, sixty years before, had occurred early in the afternoon. Eyewitnesses described the murderer as a tall, white male wearing a red Ban-Lon® shirt and wheat jeans.

I looked at Don. Don looked at me. We both had on red golf shirts and wheat jeans. Each of us was over six feet tall. Yikes!

A couple of phone calls to verify our story later, he loaded us in the black-and-white, pulled over a Texaco tanker, and asked him to take us to Port Arthur, from which we would catch a ride in a pickup pulling a luxurious horse trailer, all the way back to Austin.

We found that riding with horses was riding in style. At least compared to riding with sheep.

Tuesday afternoon, after school, when we took the return paperwork to Dave Trippett at Ward's, he asked if we had found any of the females he had told us about Thursday night.

"No, Dave, we didn't," Don said, "if they even exist. But we did break down twice, once in East Jesus and once in West Overshoe; we got eaten alive by mosquitoes beside U.S. 90 in Port Arthur; arrested for murder by the Highway Patrol in Center; and we rode back to Austin in a horse trailer that's nicer than your house.

"All in all, it was a pretty routine trip. You oughta try it sometime, Dave. Real work, that is."

Life's Lessons Learned:

- *The more you know about your little corner of the world, the better.*
- *Small-town life is far, far different from big city life.*

- *A good lunch ain't shucks to a new school bus. In some places, anyway.*
- *Mosquitoes can bite your ankles through your socks. And they will.*
- *Horses ride in better trailers than sheep. Or people.*
- *If you are ever a murder suspect, be sure the arresting officer knows your dad. It helps.*

CHAPTER 14

Looking for Love in All the Right Places

AUSTIN, 1960

My friend Don and I, approaching our senior year at Stephen F. Austin High School, went for broke, jobwise, that summer of 1960. We were determined to have spending money galore when school started.

Don's stepfather owned a small construction company, the kind of company that went around building sidewalks, parking lots and driveways, moving dirt and hauling gravel—that kind of construction.

So we latched onto that opportunity, and we didn't even have to start at the bottom. We started right out, because of our extensive experience driving big school buses, as dump truck drivers, one of the more sedentary, non-strenuous jobs at Young Construction. It paid $6 an hour, so I was edging ever closer to my first job's pay, $10 an hour for getting healed in a tent down by the Brazos River in Waco.

Jim, the stepdad, had a maintainer, a 'dozer, a front-end loader, various air hammers, and about a half-dozen pretty good dump trucks.

He also had a contract with Shell Oil to build aprons for several new gas stations and replace crumbling aprons at several more. The worst jobs at Young Construction Company involved breaking up the old concrete, either with an air hammer or by hand with a huge sledge. But Jim told us he would start us out as drivers.

None of the trucks was air-conditioned, but, heck, we couldn't have everything.

Each of the trucks had eight forward speeds, essentially two axles, a low and a high range each for gears one through four. He showed us how to use the little switch on the top of the gearshift to change from low to high range, and *vice versa*. When the truck was fully loaded, we would double-clutch our way through the gears: low-first, high-first, low-second, high-second, low-third, high-third, and—sometimes—even low and high in fourth gear, if we were cruising on a highway or major thoroughfare.

Don picked it up quickly, having natural coordination. I was a slow learner. On my first run, before I had traveled five complete miles, I somehow burned out the clutch on a big Ford F-850. Jim was irritated, but allowed as how it had been a long time since that clutch plate had been replaced. So he brought over his toolbox and a new clutch plate, and the two of us crawled under that behemoth and replaced the clutch.

While Jim and I were re-clutching the big Ford, Don cruised by on several runs hauling busted-up concrete, blowing his airhorn so that I jumped out of my skin and banged my head on the drive shaft. Every time. I could hear him laughing for a half-mile down the road.

With the right tools, it was a pretty easy job, but I had cost Young Construction two downtime hours and the price of a clutch plate. Thinking myself to be magnanimous, I apologized for the lost time and assured Jim he need not pay me for those two hours.

His response was succinct. "Don't worry. You're already docked."

Two hours on the job and I was in the hole $12.

The rest of that first day went pretty good. I hauled sixty or seventy tons of busted up concrete in eight runs and had me about $36 in daily pay coming for the effort.

At the end of each truck-driving day, the two of us just had time to race home, take a quick shower, and report for work at the old Varsity Theater where, three years later, we were still making a whopping seventy cents an hour. We did have better jobs, though. We were not just floor ushers anymore. No, sir. We had either doorman or concession status.

And we still had us those free passes to any movie in town.

I know what you're thinking. If we could make $48 a day, $240 a week driving trucks, why would we want to work another twenty-eight hours each week at the theater for a measly twenty or so incremental bucks? The answers may defy logic, but they made sense to us. Naturally.

First, we wanted to preserve our jobs and our advanced status as doormen or concessionaires for the fall when the Shell contract was complete and we went back to school. Then, too, we convinced ourselves that we would spend the theater earnings and save the truck driving wages.

Good plan.

Sometimes, though, as good plans go, things began to go awry. We were both so tired some mornings from working until midnight at the theater and, after that, shooting a couple of games of pool, that we began to fall asleep at the wheel. That's bad enough if you're driving a plain ol' car, but behind the wheel of an eight-ton dump truck, loaded with another twelve tons of debris or gravel, it could be deadly.

One morning Jim observed me cross the double center stripe of Burnet Road and end up in the parking lot of Southern Maid Donuts. I did my best to convince him that I was, indeed, just stopping off for a maple-covered, jelly-filled rootie-tootie and some chocolate milk. However, my left turn that took the better part of a block on the wrong side of the road in the face of screeching, scrambling, honking, oncoming traffic made that story hard to sell.

Jim told us we had to show up more awake. "You guys are gonna kill somebody fallin' asleep like that, and I don't want their blood on my trucks," he told us.

I wasn't sure if he was speaking metaphorically or literally. We guessed literally.

"He's not much up on metaphors," Don assured me.

The problem for me went away soon enough. After I took

out the clutches of a big GMC Boss and a Chevy, I was demoted from truck driver to concrete buster. The manual kind—with the big sledgehammer. Don kept driving trucks and made it through the summer. I told him he was able to keep driving only because of all the new clutches I had installed, but he said I just had poor hand-foot coordination.

That was the truth.

Because my original $1,300 in laundered heal-this-boy, lawn-mowing and Spudnut-selling money had been added to and had grown over the seven years since Ronnie Simmons was resurrected, both Don and I had a war chest for our senior year in high school, even though I gave up on the concrete-buster job after a couple of hot, agonizing weeks.

We both fancied ourselves BMOCs (Big Men on Campus) that year. Don was drum major of our 275-piece precision marching band. S.F. Austin, in those days, was a big, inner-city school.

And I was president of the student council for the fall term. Don, of course, was my vice president.

Now, neither of us was all that interested in politics, let alone simple *student government*. We had run for office and been elected by a landslide for one reason. And one reason only.

Girls.

You see, Miss Margaret Bradshaw, who was the spinster faculty sponsor of the student council, was also dean of women. And the student council president and vice president always had an assigned office space within *Valhalla*, which is what we called her second-floor office complex. The best and the worst of the 1,500 or so coeds on the campus would pass through her portals regularly.

If they didn't come by on their own, she would haul them in for measurement.

Measurement was performed by having the coed kneel on a small rubber floor mat. If her dress didn't touch the floor all the way around, home she would be sent by Mother Margaret Bradshaw to return "dressed decently." She was a tyrant about skirt length.

Of course, pants were verboten. You'd have to be totally a crazy-woman to challenge Margaret Bradshaw by wearing pants.

Culottes were all the rage in the real world. But they, too, were forbidden attire, according to St. Margaret.

One day about 200 girls showed up in culottes. Of course, it was a thinly disguised, not-so-secret plot to test Miss Bradshaw's resolve, the thinking being that she couldn't possibly round up all 200 girls and send them home.

Wrong.

She blistered up and down those old hallways like she was on roller skates. Four huge floors, a two-story annex, and the gym were purged of the culottes-wearing little hussies before the 10:00 bell. She was fast. She was thorough. She had a river of beauties flowing through the hallways of her little second-floor domain.

Don and I decided we wanted to swim in that river. Even to skinny-dip in that river. Or, maybe, some days, just to sit on the bank and watch it flow on by. *Woo-hah!*

So we ran for student council president and vice president on a frightfully progressive platform, including planting banana trees and having students take over the faculty parking lot. Let the teachers fight it out for places along the curb! We also promised two study halls for those who liked them, and none for those who didn't.

We made outrageous promises. Then, after we were elected, we promptly forgot most of them. We had learned a few things about politics, growing up in the shadow of the state capitol building in Austin.

But we had our office in the middle of Valhalla, right in the midst of Bradshaw's magic harem.

Hosanna!

Even better, we both had piled up so many credits that we each had three class periods a day with no class to attend. One hundred-fifty minutes of surreptitious gawking, and performing such sensitive acts as bringing glasses of ice water to those poor females in the nurse's station who were suffering from cramps.

Praise the Lord, and pass the potatoes! We were in heaven on earth.

Of course, we had to spend a little time on student government. Precious little. It mostly consisted of bringing Miss Bradshaw lists of outrageous student demands, to which she

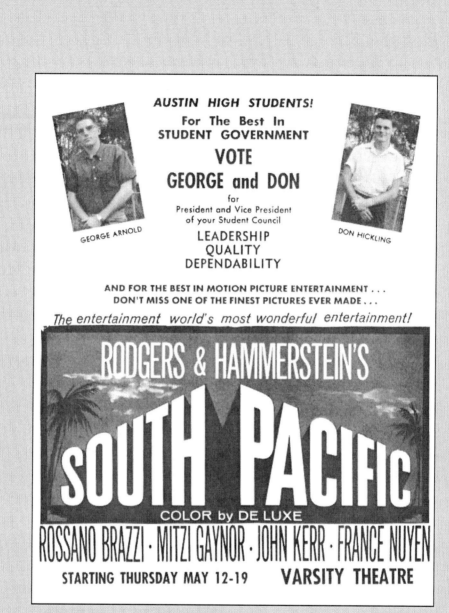

TAKE ANY ADVANTAGE YOU CAN GET

The good ol' Varsity Theater, our employer, made what was, undoubtedly, an illegal campaign contribution to our run for office, turning what otherwise would have been a solid victory into an obscene landslide.

BANANA SCAMA

Student Council President Arnold feeds Vice President Hickling a banana from tropical trees planted as one of our campaign promises. The whole banana-planting business was our own, private, little In-Betweener joke on the faculty and many of the more gullible students.

would invariably say, "No, no. No-no. Oh-no. You've got to be kidding!" Or "Just forget it!"

These official duties took up five or ten minutes every day.

Sometimes we would slip out to the field house during fifth period to watch the cheerleaders practice. They and their sponsor, being unaccustomed to having a peanut gallery, took a long time to figure out that we weren't just there as part of our student government duties. After about six weeks, somebody got wise (St. Margaret probably clued them in), and they started wearing their little opaque cheerleader bloomers under their skirts, instead of just their street clothes with Keds.

A week or so after we stopped showing up for their practices, one of the saltier among them sent us a note to our office in Valhalla. It said:

> "*Dear George and Don,*
> *You have to have a license to shoot squirrels in Texas.*
> *Love,*
> *Candy*"

We posted it on the student council bulletin board, where it stayed for several days until the unusual and persistent crowds tipped off St. Margaret, and she ripped it down and sent for Candy, "Immediately!"

They had themselves a discussion behind closed doors, I'll tell you. It was loud, and it was fierce. Nobody had ever, in our presence, stood-down Margaret Bradshaw before, but Candy did an admirable job of it.

As she left Valhalla, we met her in the hallway and proclaimed, in unison, "Hey, Candy, we got our licenses yesterday." We thought she might need a little humor after fifteen minutes of screaming back and forth with St. Margaret.

It worked.

She burst out laughing. She fell down against the wall laughing. And then she just sat there, on the floor, laughing hysterically. We had made her day. We were happy.

She was a good kid with a wicked sense of humor. That's all.

If you're starting to think that we had little interest in anything but girls, you are wrong. We just had plenty of time on our hands during the day to observe them. Or leer at them if we got the chance. And nobody was around to see us.

Each of us had had girlfriends before. We had "gone steady" with a couple of nice girls along the way, only to find that even the choicest would break your heart, given the slightest provocation.

We had sworn off monogamous relationships for our senior year, opting instead to sample as many of the best of the best as possible.

I even got up the nerve to ask the incomparably beautiful Laura Jane Martin to a sock hop after a football game. Laura went on to be elected "Valentine Queen" in our senior class. Unbelievably, she accepted my invitation and even seemed to be looking forward to it. The girl had class, and she was gorgeous, to boot. I was so petrified the whole evening that I never had the *huevos* to ask her out again.

Pretty girl–1, Rube–0.

Austin High School had a peculiar custom for seniors. Girls (or their parents, really) would throw elaborate parties on Saturday nights a couple of times a month, and the girls would invite the boys. It was truly Sadie Hawkins run amok.

I learned, quickly, what a girl must feel like sitting around and waiting to be asked to a dance or a movie. And hoping the one asking first wouldn't be Hopalong Bruce in his blue suede shoes with his Levi's hanging well below the top of his crack, like the Norge repairman.

Miss Bradshaw had no control over the way boys dressed.

I soon decided to refuse to answer the phone. Somebody else had to answer it and take a message for me—unless the caller was Don, Andy, Jack, or Kenny. My younger sister even cooperated in this heinous behavior. She said she didn't want me, her big brother, to be trapped by some lovely like Grieselda Fern or her equally attractive sister, Trudy.

I was the first to break our blood oath not to get entangled with just one girl. A sweet young thing by the name of Lee Lankford invited me to one of the parties in mid-June that she and some of her friends were throwing. To be honest, I didn't remember having ever seen her.

Before I returned her call, I whipped out my trusty reference

LOOKIN' GOOD

My first real true love, Lee Lankford, with me in tow, heads for yet another of those elaborate "senior parties."

(Photo courtesy Lee Lankford)

George Arnold • 183

copy of last year's yearbook and checked to be sure she didn't have two noses or an exposed breast in the middle of her forehead.

Turned out she was kinda cute, in the picture, at least. So I called her up and accepted her invitation with (mostly) feigned enthusiasm. I even suggested we should go for hamburgers one evening to get better acquainted before the big party. She accepted that invitation with equal enthusiasm, feigned or not, I don't know.

She trapped me. She cornered me. She had me in an exclusive straitjacket before I could say, "Want some fries with that burger?" She smiled at me with a smile like I had never seen before, or since, for that matter. It was gorgeous. Even spellbinding. I melted into a puddle, and she had to scrape me up off the floor at the local Holiday House so I could drive her home.

Immediately I just knew this was no ordinary girl, and our relationship was not going to be any ordinary relationship. She was completely unlike any of my former girlfriends. Or, rather, her effect on me was totally different. And devastating.

I thought maybe something was wrong with me all of a sudden. Instead of the urges I had experienced before to lip-lock a girl and see what I could grab onto, with Lee I found I just wanted to sit and stare at her, smell that scent she wore, and try to make her smile the smile that gave me the shivers.

Oh, sure, the hormonal activity was in high gear, all right. But it was completely different from anything I had ever felt. I found that just looking at her was enough to send me into a totally confused state I had never been to before. I actually noticed little things about her that I had never noticed on any girl: how shiny her hair always seemed to be; the transparent, light-blue color of her eyes and how they changed depending on what she was wearing; the fact that her skin was so clear and, on her neck, almost transparent; how her smell, like a bunch of wildflowers, actually made me salivate.

I had it bad. I had fallen so hard that it scared me, especially since I had never really fallen before. Ever.

The only person I could talk to about my fears was Ginna, Don's mom. She wasn't much more than a kid herself, and all us hooligans felt completely comfortable talking about anything with her.

So I dropped in on her and brought Lee along, just to introduce them. Then I took Lee home and raced back to try to find out if I was crazy or what, while Ginna's recollections of this amazing girl were still fresh on her mind.

I told her what was happening to me, straight on. I left out nothing because we could tell her anything. I finished up my graphic description by telling her that even my hormones had taken a sharp right turn. Was it possible that just a glimpse of that dazzling smile could be so devastatingly exciting? Even erotic?

The more I talked, the more I saw a twinkle growing in Ginna's eyes. When I ended my somewhat confused and desperate-sounding monologue with the questions, "Ginna, what the hell's wrong with me? Is this girl from outer space, or what?" she laughed right out loud, put her arm around me, gave me a hug and replied, "Nothing wrong with you. You're just head over heels in love for the first time. And you've got a *real* bad case of it."

Then she laughed again and told me, "She looks like an ordinary girl to me. Pretty, but no great beauty. But, obviously, you don't see anything ordinary about her. So, go with the flow. Do what you feel like doing. If that's just sitting and trying to make her laugh, she'll understand, if she has any sense. And I think she does. I saw the way she was looking at you, too. You're more than just a passing fancy to her. That's pretty obvious. Remember this, George, whatever happens, you'd be a great catch for any girl in her right mind."

Once again, Ginna had not only unscrambled a dilemma for me, but, as usual, also had made me feel better about myself.

So, go with the flow I did. Lee and I, we became a "thing." Every party, Don and Andy and Jack and Kenny had a different little beauty on their arms. But I had my one and only—and first—true love.

Sure enough, as almost always happens in high-school romances, she dumped me by Christmas. Or rather, her mother dumped me. I must admit I had not gone out of my way to ingratiate myself with her parents, especially her mother, who—immediately—did not seem to me to be a nice person. My Eddie Haskell persona had remained within when I was around her.

Her father was a medical researcher, a professor of microbiology at UT. Her mother fancied they were "really top drawer," if you know what I mean. Once she found out my father worked for the State and I lived on the east side of town, I was doomed. Never mind I was president of the student council. That I was a National Merit Scholar. That I had been elected president of both my sophomore and junior classes. That I was far smarter than the average bear; that Ginna said I was a special "catch" for any girl, and that the world truly was going to be my oyster.

As far as Mrs. Snootengruper was concerned, I was white trash. Lived on the wrong side of town, and totally unsuitable for her debutante-to-be daughter. In short, I was road-kill-in-training, just waiting for ol' mom to run me down like the demon she was.

I said I had not overworked endearing myself to her parents. Perhaps that was a tad-bit of an understatement.

One afternoon in early December, I had been to the dentist, where I had received a shot of codeine. Neither the dentist nor I had any reason to suspect that I had a severe allergy to that particular narcotic painkiller. I remember going to work at the Varsity Theater at 6:00 P.M., right on time. After that, my mind went blank.

Apparently I had left the theater for a half-hour or so, and dressed in my Russian-general-look-alike uniform, had driven to Lee's house and, when her father opened the door, smiling at me as he often did, I decked him. Punched him right in the face and sent him backward like a falling redwood. Mind you, I have no recollection of any of this. And no good excuse, or even remote reason, for having done it. Of her parents, he was the good guy—the nicer one. I actually really liked him. And I'm pretty sure he liked me, too.

In an hour or so, he and his lovely young daughter showed up at the Varsity Theater to inquire, ever so politely, why it was that I had tried to kill him.

By that time, I was pretty wild-eyed and beyond half-crazy from the effects of the codeine. Lee asked me repeatedly what was wrong with me. I didn't have a clue. Ol' dad, though, being a man of medicine, cut right to the chase.

"Have you been to the doctor or dentist today?" he asked.

I thought, "Wow! This ol' guy is a heck of a diagnostician."

"Dentist," I managed to utter.

He turned to his daughter and said but one word: "Codeine."

Wonder of wonders, he called my father from the theater and suggested that, as a biologist, he could recognize a very bad reaction to a painkiller, and that it would be a good idea for someone to come to get me and take me home. "He definitely should not be driving before tomorrow," the good doctor said.

I was still way spaced out when father and daughter turned to go home. I didn't even have the presence of mind to say I was sorry for knocking him silly.

Lee kept whispering to me, "Apologize to him."

I kept saying to her, "Later."

"Later" turned out to be the next afternoon. Lee would not let me out of her sight. After school was out, she insisted I accompany her to the ol' doc's office in the microbiology building at UT so I could "make amends."

I didn't look forward to it, but I did it because I was so stupid-faced crazy about her. And I did feel bad about what I had apparently done. I must say he was cool about it.

"Some people can't take narcotic painkillers," he said. "You were not yourself yesterday," he added, to be sure I remained calm. "I don't know who you were, but whoever he was, he packed a bodacious punch."

He actually laughed, swollen face, black eye, and all.

If that was not the final straw, in her mother's mind, it was next to the last. When I took Lee's Christmas present, a pink, table-model, clock radio, over to her house, the Witch of Agnese (my private, mathematical name for dear ol' mom) cornered me, for about the hundredth time in the past six months, like a cat might trap a rat. And she asked me straight-out, her index finger poking at my chest, "What fraternity are you going to try to pledge next summer?"

She had her *By-God* priorities, I'll tell you that, for sure.

My response cinched my fate.

Having had just about enough of her hateful badgering and little accusation sessions, I decided to fight back. Politely, of course. No need to behave like her.

I told her, just as straight-out, and poking at her with my

own index finger, that it was my opinion that fraternities were supercilious playgrounds for ne'er-do-wells, a complete waste of time and money. "I have no intention of playing that silly game," I said, right in her face. "I'm going there to get an education, not a hangover every night. So I won't be gracing the Pan Hellenic circuit."

I had my own *By-God* priorities, too.

Though she wasn't even at home, I could still visualize Lee's sparkling, gorgeous smile, and actually see her standing and clapping, silently and gleefully, behind her mother's back. As far as I was concerned at that moment, that apparition of her was real. And it was cheering me on! I guessed the real Lee, not at all socially pretentious like ol' mom, might still think she could somehow escape ol' mom's quest for her to pledge Delta Delta Delta.

That was the end.

The day after Christmas, ol' mom, on a slumming expedition, no doubt, brought back the brand new radio, still in its box, and announced to me, "Lee won't be seeing you anymore." Her hateful tirade, uncalled for and even somewhat on the side of mentally deranged, scarred me for life, I think.

I asked, "Does Lee know anything about this? Or is this a unilateral end-run by a pretentious, overzealous, conniving mom who actually believes her daughter will be a movie star soon?"

I thought that was a pretty good send-off for the old bat.

My mother, to her credit, added, "Your daughter will never find a finer boy than my son. Good luck in your (emphasis on *your*) search."

Of course, my mother, bless her heart, had not a clue what kind of son she had actually raised, me being able to cloud her mind, pull the wool over her eyes, and all.

So that was that. QED, as the geometry proof might say.

Although devastated, not so much because of being dumped, but because of being dumped for all the wrong reasons, and not even in person, but by proxy, I nevertheless resolved to make the best of a sad situation.

Getting over the excruciating pain of losing my first real love, the most important person in my life up to that point, was going to be difficult, if not impossible, for me.

Not even Ginna could make me feel better this time.

Don said, "I told you so, dumb-butt." We often spoke to one another like an early-day Beavis and Butthead. "Many girls don't have a clue how much you care about them, and lots of them have controlling mothers. You poor sucker; you just got a double dose."

When school re-opened after the holidays, in an effort to inject some artificial humor into my otherwise miserable life, I wore a tiny sign around my neck for two weeks. It said, simply, "I'm available." The sign, in fact, was Don's idea. And it worked.

The phone started ringing for those parties, again, and I started answering it myself. I never said "no." Not one time. Sure, some of them were "honkers," as we called the girls whom nature had dealt a cruel blow, but I figured Don was right. Again.

We resolved to have a good time, and to hell with women. Promise them anything, but don't tell them even one of your secrets. None. If you do, they'll bash you over the head with it someday when you least expect it.

Still, I could cry—a completely foreign emotion for me, previously—over almost nothing.

Life sucked, or so I thought.

And so, as our elected term ended, we cleaned out our little office in Valhalla for Dickie and Sally, our replacements for spring on the student council.

Dickie was a cool guy, so we let him in on our little caper with the river of women who passed through St. Margaret's portals.

He looked at us, sadly, and said, "You know Sally. She'll find a way to get between me and the sights, sounds, and smells you've enjoyed. I'll try, but I fear it's hopeless."

Yes. We knew Sally. Don knew her from the band. I knew her from the National Honor Society and Physics II. She was the smartest thing on two legs. Probably had an IQ approaching genius.

But there wasn't a molecule of good old Candy's evil sense of humor in her. So sad. She was all business.

We looked at Dickie. "Why in the world did you run with Sally?" Don asked.

"I ask myself that twenty times a day," he said, quickly claiming the smaller desk nearest the bank of the River Valhalla.

Life's Lessons Learned:

- *To paraphrase Wayne Gretzky, the Great One, skate to where the puck will be when you get there, not toward where it is now. In our case, that meant a prime perch in Valhalla.*
- *Listen to your best friends when they tell you you're making a mistake. They are likely right. You are probably just smitten.*
- *Conniving, social-climbing mothers have ruined many a young girl's life.*
- *Fraternities and sororities are probably a complete waste of time if you have any sense. Pledging Pi Phi doesn't enhance your brain or stiffen your backbone.*
- *If you have an unexpected reaction to a prescription drug, get somebody to tie you to a post with a thick rope. Real quick! Like Dum and Dee, the pesky little twins.*

CHAPTER 15

Queen for a . . . Night

AUSTIN, 1960

Nowhere was resistance to the old-fashioned ways of the past more prevalent than among the students at good ol' AHS. We tilled the soil of radical departure from what was expected. Planted the seeds. Heck, we even heaped on the fertilizer. Figuratively, of course. And only organic.

It was our goal in life, our holy quest, to question the sensibility of a lot of what the authority figures expected of us. To ask the quite simple, yet haunting (to authority figures, anyhow) questions, "Why do you keep doing this year after year? What's the point? Don't you think it's time to consider doing things differently?"

After all, weren't we moving from the pinnacle of the industrial revolution to the great electronic-information age? We could see it coming. Looked inevitable to us.

The *fat-and-happy, everything's-just-perfect-right-now* teachers and administrators were trying their best, and failing miserably, to grind us into submission. To convince us *their* way was not only the *right* way, but also the *only* way. Dumb as we were, we were still clever enough to figure out this little scam. And once we had it in our cross hairs, their efforts to mold us into their image were doomed. Kaput. Ancient history, so to speak.

It's not that we were rebellious just to be rebels. Not at all.

No, our rebellion, which we thought of as a way-overdue

dose of reality for our elders, was no little series of pranks. In our own way, without ever really thinking about it, we were actually being *serious*. Say what? Seriousness was not our thing, don't you know? And we would never have admitted to any level of it.

Ours was a straightforward attempt, by the students, to become the masters. To teach those trying their best to teach us that they, the authority figures, were missing life's boat. That their values were shallow and even insignificant. And that we not only questioned those values, but also rejected them. Outright and unequivocally.

Of course, the only way, in reality, to make the point was to avoid the point. Telling them straight-on that what they considered important was of no more significance than the flutter of butterfly wings in the passage of time … well, that would only strengthen their resolve to beat us into submission.

Typically, for the hooligans of the last days of the Eisenhower administration, a plan was needed. A secret plan. Insidious to the core. And totally effective. Before *they* ever sniffed it out.

Planning started late in the summer and evolved during the first days of classes in the fall. To work, the secret plan had to be relatively simple, but also contain a major, high-profile revolt. And, most important, it had to be kept an absolute secret even though it would involve the collective intrigue of more than 1,500 students—the entire complement of the junior and senior classes. It is a tribute to our resolve, single-minded determination and dedication, I believe, that the secret was kept until the trap was sprung. It was so good that even the Prunella-leaning types stayed in line. Not a snitch in a trainload of participants.

Amazing!

The plan began with a series of almost miniscule signs. Signals of discontent at being subjected to the same old party line, *ad infinitum*. Spontaneous, yet carried out in unison. Entire classrooms full of students were mobilized to react, to send little messages to the authority figures.

These little mini-pranks were phase one—*The Softening Up Era*—as we called it. They commenced the first day of classes and were scheduled, inflexibly and without exception, to end at the conclusion of the first three weeks of school, a full week before the annual homecoming football game. They would continue just long enough to create the need for a formal faculty response. And they would end just in time to foil the collective reaction the faculty would conjure up.

We knew it would take them a full three weeks to figure out how to respond. Always did. Always will. Another of life's irrefutable axioms. They would play right into our hands. As usual.

Now, these little pranks were, taken singularly, almost insignificant. Collectively, they applied just enough pressure to be diversionary tactics for what was coming in phase two: *The Big Bang*.

Hosanna!

The Softening Up Era's mini-pranks consisted of such tomfoolery as all thirty students in a classroom suddenly folding their hands on their desktops and twiddling their thumbs in time to some unheard music, complete with synchronized reversal of twiddling direction. Twiddle forward. Twiddle back. Give the desktop a hearty whack. Only with the left hand, of course.

It was symbolic.

We got pretty good at playing the silent rhythm section.

A couple of the English teachers, oddly both named Williams, wore hearing aids to enhance their perceptions of whispering in the back of the classroom, we guessed. In their classes, the mini-pranks *du jour* would inevitably involve mouthing silent responses to questions, thereby sending them into a frenzy of volume adjusting antics. Even the laughter that immediately followed was kept as silent as an early-day Laurel and Hardy flick.

In other actions, entire classes, upon dodging more of the same old nonsense tossed at us unbelievers, would stand, form a hands-to-hips single line, and proceed to do a thirty-second conga dance round and round the room. That one was sure to elicit a panic attack from the lecturer at hand.

These are just a few examples, mind you, of the brief, frequent and stealthy counterattacks mounted for those first three weeks of school. Pre-emptive strikes, leading up to *The Big Bang*.

For you to fully comprehend the genius of this whole plan, you have to understand a few things.

First, just imagine how hard it is to keep a plot secret when two-thirds of the 2,500 students are active participants. No president of the U.S. has been able to pull that one off. There's always a leak, somewhere—some individual seeking personal aggrandizement at the expense of the collective administrative whole. Believe me when I tell you, *We did it.* There was nary a leak, and about the time *The Softening Up Era* abruptly ended, the targets, namely the faculty propaganda spreaders, had just about figured out that something was up. When you think you're in a power position, you can be lulled easily into complacency.

And fooled.

Second thing you need to understand is that the predicted three-week reaction time was accurate. Creatures of habit can be read like a book. So to speak. So, on Monday morning of week four, just as expected, our beloved Principal Lipscomb Andrews lowered the boom. Threatened suspension. Expulsion. Even excommunication. If the antics didn't stop "this instant!"

Of course, they did. Stop, that is. Except the principal and the entire faculty had no idea they had actually stopped at 3:30 the previous Friday. Nothing further was planned, anyhow, making absolute compliance with the latest edict a piece of cake.

Are you starting to appreciate the subtlety Jack Clagett had introduced to the little gang of pranksters yet?

Let me continue to spell it out for you. Just in case you might, heaven forbid, be one of those self-satisfied, complacent elders. Or even a Church Lady.

Third, the principal and deans and teachers who had come in on the previous Saturday morning (thus sacrificing half of one of their measly 196 days off every year) to decide on a strategy to end the folderol, once and for all, actually believed they had done something to stop it. Really! Several of us made a point to congratulate Lippy and St. Margaret and Mr. King, dean of men, for their decisive stand. After all, the numerous random and disruptive shenanigans were hardly conducive to the process of learning we were so intent upon soaking up, don't you see?

They bought it. Hook, line, and sinker. Like a bigmouth bass slurping up a worm. Not one of them saw the hook to which that worm was attached. Because we wouldn't jerk their invisible little line until Friday—four days hence. Give them plenty of time to revel in their imagined victory. To glory in the misbelief of their triumph over anarchy. For four whole days.

Fourth, appreciate, please, that one of our merry band of heathens, Kenny Squier, stepped up and volunteered to lend,

TWO-WHEELED INFLAMMATORY PROBLEM

Kenny couldn't get girls to ride behind him on his little red, three-horsepower Allstate scooter. Seems the gas cap had a vent. You know, a tiny hole in the middle that allowed gasoline to slosh up and out, thus giving a girl a seat-of-pants soaking with potentially disastrous (so to speak) incendiary ramifications.

for the benefit of *The Big Bang,* his most prized possession in the entire universe, a possession more valued and sacred than his 1952 autographed Mickey Mantle baseball card: his shiny, red, three-horsepower Allstate motor scooter. The one with the kick-starter and the warped cylinder head that required a new gasket at least bi-weekly. The same scooter only he could roar down the interstate service road on, wind blowing his hair, bugs smashing relentlessly into his teeth, all the while singing "Round and Round," better than Perry Como had ever sung it, even in his dreams. Perry's dreams, that is.

I once asked him why he didn't just take the warped head to

a machine shop and have it milled and trued instead of continually replacing the head gasket. He said, "Why? I like to fix it." Go figure.

The whole matter eventually became moot, though, once he figured out that girls simply would not ride behind him on his little machine, and he mothballed it. Or, rather, put it on a pedestal in the family carport, draped it with a clear plastic cover ("so I can see it"), and only took it out occasionally. To "keep it fit."

It was still "fit," and he would bring it to the party. Good for him (I heard someone say).

The fifth, and final, factor requiring your understanding in order for you to achieve the proper level of appreciation for the insidious cleverness of our whole scheme to reject the old, tried and true, nonsensical values of our elders, was an incredible human being. A wonderful, malleable and fearless individualist.

Fat Max.

Max was a slippery sort, defying proper description. Even Max's name was misleading. He wasn't fat at all. And nobody knew if he had a last name, either. Didn't matter. Max was a big, strapping (hulking, even), and hairy member of the senior class whose attitude was pure gold. Well, fool's gold, at least. Max was likely either a genius (highly probable) or a moron (equally possible). Who knew? He marched to his own drummer, to paraphrase a trite old saying.

Max had no friends. And, yet, everybody loved him. He was a festering boil on the butt of education at our esteemed institution. Still, he was a faculty favorite.

As far as we knew, Fat Max was willing to try anything. Anywhere. Anytime. All you had to do was ask.

At various times in the recent past, he had blown the heads off thirty-odd parking meters some twit at city hall had ordered installed on the streets around the campus. With giant cherry bombs, fused in sequence so as to spray nickels and pennies in an ever-moving, cascading fountain that erupted around the block. Pop-pop. Pop-pop-pop. Pop. It was magnificent!

Thousands, literally, cheered him.

That little demonstration (the meters were never reinstalled—Hallelujah!) followed several days after a few hundred students, me included, saw Max lasso an Austin police officer off a three-wheel motorcycle on West Avenue, shouting all the while, "Hey! I want a drumstick! Stop! You're a lousy ice cream man." Of course, nobody had seen a thing when it came time to locate the perpetrator. Four hundred sixty-five students suddenly were struck blind. And deaf and dumb, too. If need be.

All the coaches wanted Fat Max to try out for athletics. He was obviously a jock. Physically, he was a specimen. Mentally, he was a chameleon. He had the perfect mentality to play football or chess and to be good at both. But he chose not to participate. Team things were not anywhere on his life's agenda. Any kind of activity that involved more than one person was too crowded for Fat Max. When he wanted to, he could make Howard Hughes seem like a flesh-pressing politician loose in Times Square on New Year's Eve. With a hundred television cameras focused on him.

But Max was not a loner. You know, the stereotypical, sociopath-serial killer type who starts out pulling one wing off a butterfly and moves on up to sacrificing black cats (the four-legged kind).

Max often rode to and from school with one of the more trustworthy female pranksters who popped into and out of our occasional Grapette-fed planning sessions. Her name was Peggy. Fat Max called her Peggy Sue. That wasn't her name. It was pretty close, though. Anyhow, she kept a full-sized barstool stowed behind the back seat of her Jeep CJ, just for Max. "The only way he'll ride in my Jeep is sitting on top of that barstool, perched up on the back seat. The top has to be down, of course."

Well, now you know Fat Max. As well as any of us ever did, leastways. It's no stretch to label Max with an oft-abused adjective: *unique*. Max *was* unique. He's the only *Homo sapien* I have ever encountered in my six decades on this earth who can truthfully be called by that label.

So it was quite natural, when it came time to flesh-out the tactical details of *The Big Bang* strategy, that Fat Max be brought into the circle of confidence and enlisted as the marquee star of what was about to happen.

When Kenny explained the role we were offering him, he instantly morphed from semi-comatose to hyper. He said, "Sure enough. I'd be honored."

Fat Max was ready.

Hallelujah!

With Fat Max now signed on and *The Softening Up Era* behind us, we were ready to set the timer on the *pièce de résistance* of outright revolt: *The Big Bang.*

I mentioned the homecoming football game that would be played in House Park, under the new mercury-vapor lights, on Friday night of the fourth week of school. That wasn't just an idle mention. Homecoming was key to proper, even magnificent, execution of *The Big Bang.*

You see, every year at about the third or fourth game of the fall, the Homecoming Queen was crowned. Right in the middle of the field, under the lights. And to the utter dismay of most of the student body who found the whole ritual a throwback to some tribal and sacrificial, symbolic and heathen practice from the days when our forerunners could still swing from treetop to treetop. And occasionally grab hold with their tails.

What was this nonsense all about, anyway? "Homecoming" was a misnomer, to be sure. Wasn't it? I mean, who would ever go back to their old high school in the first place? Nobody we knew. All we wanted to do was get the hell out. For good.

True to that suspicion, we could count the former students in attendance at "homecoming" on the fingers of one hand. We figured that probably was the sum of the homecomers' collective IQs, for sure.

So, we found ourselves questioning the wisdom of the past. One more time. If former students wouldn't be caught dead attending a "homecoming" game, why was it called "homecoming"? Made no sense to us. Simply a throwback to tradition?

"It's the way we've always done it." We could just hear the fat-and-happy answer.

How we hated that complacency. Total, mind-numbing cop-out. If not downright criminal.

Aside from the misnamed, nonexistent event, itself, there was the ever-present halftime ritual of crowning the Homecoming Queen. Like sacrificing a virgin, maybe? Only we doubted that anyone good-looking enough to win the title should also claim chastity. Not without having her nose grow to the point of gross disfigurement. Besides, even if there were to be a beautiful virgin, wouldn't she have the strength of character to reject the whole idea as, at the very least, demeaning?

We hoped so.

We were puzzled. Insulted. Indignant. And determined to make a statement that properly expressed our attitudes.

Enter Fat Max. Silently. And secretly.

You see, *The Big Bang* was conceived to have Max win the balloting for the sacrificial role of Homecoming Queen. By write-in. The "Queen's" chariot was to be the aforementioned three-horsepower Allstate, donated for the occasion by Kenny for visual and aural effect. And a quick exit.

What would the Jurassic-mentality administrators do about that? Would they dare reject a legitimate landslide winner? And, if they did, how would we get even? Just to make a point that should have been obvious to anybody other than comfortable reactionaries, anyway.

Well, once Fat Max said "Yes," the game was on.

Don and I, having access through a bit of snooping in Valhalla, office of St. Margaret Bradshaw, dean of women, could get into and study the rolls of each homeroom in each of the senior and junior classes. From those rolls, secretly accessed—kind of like early-day, manual hackers—we could, and did, quickly select a trustworthy individual in each of fifty-three morning start-up classrooms. Their names we put, individually, on three-by-five index cards until we had a stack of fifty-three cards, each containing the name of a known anti-Homecoming Queen advocate. These fifty-three name cards were then divided up and passed out to ten committee chairpersons, each with the admonishment to "write nothing down," but to contact your five or six names and ask them to quietly pass the word that the right thing to do would be to enter "Fat Max for Homecoming Queen" as a write-in candidate on their ballots. The ballots would be distributed, voted upon, and returned to the deans' offices for counting during the homeroom class first thing Thursday morning.

By Tuesday, there was nothing left to do but wait.

Oh, sure, Fat Max suddenly became an extrovert. Even came to school on Wednesday reeking of the unmistakable scent of Chanel No. 5. "Just to get into character," he explained. Nobody thought much about it, though. Max was given to abstract, even aberrant, behavior patterns of this type.

On a regular basis.

Don and I had a lot of visitors in our little office at Valhalla that week. The pace picked up about noon on Thursday when all the ballots had been cast and returned for counting. We didn't have any inside information at that point, since nothing much had happened. Apparently, the secret remained intact since no faculty huddles had been observed on the second-floor administrative area. Yet.

Foregoing our sometimes visit to watch the cheerleaders practice down at the field house during fifth and sixth periods, at the end of the day, Don and I holed-up in our office, just a thin partition away from where the vote counting would begin at 2:30. St. Margaret and a couple of teachers who had no end-of-day classes would count votes. You didn't think students would be trusted to do the counting, did you? Even after four days of placid, non-prankster inactivity?

The official candidates for Homecoming Queen were the usual suspects. The five or six best-looking babes in the senior class. Every one of them was at least a nine, and every one was pretty smart, too. That made running for, and accepting, such a demeaning crown even more of a mystery. We figured it probably meant a lot more to their mothers than to the babes themselves. Especially the mothers who attended S. F. Austin High School back in the dark ages, but who wouldn't show up for homecoming unless their own darling daughter turned out to be the symbolic, sacrificial virgin.

Well, the vote count began promptly at 2:35 on Thursday afternoon. Right on schedule. By 2:37, St. Margaret, Mrs. Bristol, and Mr. King had decided upon a plan of action, vote counting-wise. They would just put each ballot, individually, into one of five plastic tub-type containers—one for Janet, one for Sallie, one for Laura, one for Barbara, and one for Bette.

Simple enough, eh?

Little did they know they would need a sixth container.

The count began quietly enough. We could only hear muffled voices and a bit of levity from Mr. King. He had not yet had his obligatory humorectomy.

At exactly 2:44, all hell broke loose.

"Herman, I don't find this one bit humorous! How can you snicker like that?" It was St. Margaret, addressing Mr. King. Sounded like he was about to undergo the aforementioned but heretofore-unexecuted and completely-involuntary humorectomy.

"Here's another one! There's a whole shitload of them. This is NOT funny! Go get Lipscomb. Right now!" St. Margaret was coming unstrung. We couldn't recall ever having heard her use any eight-character, four-letter words before.

"I don't care. I'm stopping right here! Not counting one more!" Mrs. Bristol, the social studies teacher, chimed in with her take on the situation.

There ensued a lengthy and animated discussion which was joined, mid-expletive, by the principal himself. Shouting and table pounding had preceded his arrival, with Herman King holding out for a "fair" count, while St. Margaret and Lottie Bristol insisted that all the write-ins be summarily thrown out.

"You want the result of twenty-five hundred votes to be announced as 'seven to six to five to four to three?' That dog won't hunt, Margaret." Mr. King was standing up for the right answer, even though we guessed he probably didn't have a clue why he was doing it.

"Herman, we don't have to tell anybody what the actual vote count was. We just announce a winner and everybody else who's on the ballot, *legally and officially*, will be announced as her court. Just like every year."

There it was! St. Margaret was not above outright fraud and deception to avoid amending holy tradition—even in the slightest.

Among his other attributes, Lipscomb Andrews was a realist. Upon understanding the situation, sort of, he asked the key question: "Do any of the girls have enough votes that announcing her as Homecoming Queen will be anywhere near believable?"

Nobody knew. Yet.

With a tone of dismissal, he told the assembled precinct workers, "Finish counting. Give me an accurate count. But don't write anything down, for God's sake!"

Two things were clear: He was stalling for think time, not having a clue what he was going to do about the count, but hoping it would be manageable; and, he didn't yet take the constitutional provision for separation of church and state to mean he couldn't invoke the Almighty. Right inside the schoolhouse itself.

The counting resumed.

We couldn't hear anything but grumbling and growling, along with an occasional, "This is preposterous!" and "How the hell do you suppose they pulled this one off, right under our noses?"

Don and I immediately considered bailing out, knowing full well that the "they" in that question would most certainly include the two of us. And Jack and Kenny, for sure. Maybe even Andy. Of course, we were not known to consort with Fat Max. But then, neither was anyone else. Leastways not on any regular basis.

Dean King's snickering level continued to escalate as the counting proved what the counters feared most. This was a landslide. An undeniable mandate. Not even Franklin Roosevelt had won by these kinds of margins.

At about 3:20, we heard someone pick up the intercom phone, and Herman King (who still saw some humor in the situation) said, "Lipscomb, it's bad. Fat Max—does he have a last name?—got far more write-in votes than all the other five girls, combined." There was a pause. Then, "Lipscomb, there's no point. Janet got the second most votes, just looking at the piles of ballots. You have a problem, sir." He put the receiver back in its cradle and laughed out loud—a long and satisfying, to him, at least—guffaw that sent St. Margaret into higher orbit than Sputnik.

At the risk of discovery of our blatant eavesdropping, Don and I bolted for the hallway, did a ninety-degree left, away from Mr. Andrews' office, and ran smack into a wall of students, all waiting to hear, officially, what they already knew: *"I give you your 1960 Homecoming Queen of Stephen F. Austin High School (by an almost unanimous margin), Fat Max What's-his-face!!"*

We burrowed through the wall of bodies and headed for the street, just so as to be able to look innocent when the inevitable confrontation took place. Everyone, of course, wanted to know what happened. The only thing we knew, for sure, was that it was probably a good time to go immediately to Plan B.

Time to find Kenny. And Fat Max.

Next morning, our worst suspicions were confirmed. Over the loudspeaker system piped into each homeroom, Principal

Andrews announced the results: *"Your 1960 Homecoming Queen is Janet What's-her-name."*

A deathly silence, the ambient sounds of outer space, followed immediately. Unbroken. For what seemed an eternity. The powers-that-be had copped out, but the underwhelming, hushed reaction should have been fair warning to them.

It wasn't. They plodded on.

They would show us who was really in charge. Once and for all time. But they continued to underestimate us, swelled by their "victory" of Monday morning over *The Softening Up Era* pranks.

Had we cut them too much slack? Nah! They still didn't "get it."

So that was it. Not even lip service to the real winner, Fat Max.

Plan B was on. We were ready.

There would be righteous retribution. By 9:00 P.M. that very night, we would just see who really held the Royal Flush. And wore the cheap tiara.

The first half of the game that night was uneventful. With about eight minutes to go before halftime, Kenny and I slipped out of the stands, walking as though we were about to pee our pants, just to be sure the faculty spies didn't see us leaving the stands and suspect anything untoward.

Sure enough, there in the second stall of the men's room next to the east-side concession stand, we found Fat Max, his street clothes off and donning a stunning, white chiffon gown with a plunging neckline that exposed his massive, hairy chest all the way down to his navel. We taped it open with masking tape to assure total visibility.

Nothing deceptive about that cleavage.

Kenny pulled a red banner from his jacket pocket and draped it around Max's head and shoulders. It had gold lettering that read, "Homecoming Queen—AHS—1960."

"Where's your crown, Max?" Kenny had noticed it wasn't on his head. I hadn't. I was too mesmerized by the long, black, shiny wig. Max was almost pretty.

Almost.

"Rats! I forgot it." Max looked helpless for a second, but—ever inventive—he suddenly ripped the toilet paper holder from its anchor on the side of the stall and affixed it snugly atop the ridiculous wig. "There." He was satisfied.

Just as the first half ended and before the rush of the restroom invaders peaked, we sneaked out the north door and into the shadows behind the concession stand. There wasn't much room. A chain-link fence separated the stand's wall from the adjacent baseball diamond by a mere eighteen inches or so.

Kenny's shiny, red Allstate Queen's chariot-to-be sat in the shadows. "You know how to start it?" Kenny asked for the umpteenth time.

"I'm ready. Get the hell out of here, you two." Max had spoken.

Our big band and the Red Jackets were in full swing on the field as we slipped up the steps and took the first two seats on the front row, a spot that guaranteed us a quick getaway.

A quick getaway might be important. We noticed a cadre of local off-duty Austin PD gendarmes. Normally, there was just one. Hmmm. Paranoid precautions. A good call. We were impressed. But undeterred. Underestimation reigned.

One more time.

At the conclusion of the band's obligatory tribute to former students, none of whom were present, of course, the band and Red Jackets parted, creating a corridor for the queen and her court to enter the center of the field for the sacrificial ceremonies and the adoration that would surely follow. Just like last year. And the year before. And the year before that. We could see Janet and her court lining up for their triumphal march to the fifty-yard line.

The public address announcer, stepping on the end of a drumroll before the hushed crowd, made the big announcement.

"Students and faculty, visitors and former students, I give you your 1960 Stephen F. Austin High School Homecoming Queen: **F-A-A-A-A-T M-A-A-A-X!"**

In stark and completely appropriate contrast to that morning's silence, a deafening roar went up from the 2,000 students in the stands. The band members ripped off their silly plumed hats and threw them high into the air. Even the staid and normally stodgy Red Jackets completely lost their decorum, breaking ranks and waving their white-gloved hands in the air, wildly.

I turned to Kenny. He gave me a whoop and a thumbs up!

And another thumbs up! This time with both hands. Andy had "edited" the announcer's script and delivered it with the text to accompany the band's performance. Just like we expected, the announcer, a fellow student and band member, played it straight.

He read exactly what was in front of him.

As the roar died down, we heard the unmistakable and distinct pop-pop-pop-fzz, pop-pop-pop-fzz of Kenny's Allstate with another failing head gasket. Riding it, hell bent for glory, was our new Queen for a Night, Fat Max, long black tresses flying and blowing kisses with his right hand as he raced, full tilt, around the quarter-mile cinder track, steering with his left arm.

His victory lap. What a catharsis!

Everybody, except the outwitted, overestimating, defeated, and now skulking members of the faculty, quickly got into the spirit of common sense and reality. The adoration was on, big time, and Max was eating it up. After two trips around the track, throttle wide open, and to the never-ending roar of the crowd, the second round hampered by the aforementioned gendarmes who dived out of his path at the last possible second, Max made a ninety-degree turn at the fifty-yard line and slid to a stop in the center of the field. He flipped down the kickstand, dismounted the little red Allstate in a most unladylike vault, grabbed Janet, and gave her a huge kiss.

Janet reached up, removed her tiara, and placed it on Fat Max's head, tossing his toilet paper holder-crown aside.

It was a moment to be savored.

But not for long.

The off-duty, but fully uniformed cadre of APD officers was making its way, hastily, toward Fat Max and his Allstate chariot. Undoubtedly, the defeated faculty sore-losers were directing the invasion.

Quickly, the drum major's whistle blew and the band closed ranks tightly around Max, Janet, their courtesans, and the Allstate. Don was on the job. And they struck up "Loyal Forever," the old school's alma mater. That brought everything to a halt and everybody to a standstill. It wasn't "The Star-Spangled Banner," but it worked just as well.

As the last strains of the song wafted forth, Kenny and I heard the familiar rumble of the little Allstate cranking up. The band's ranks parted, and our Queen for a Night roared off, in a cloud of blue-white exhaust, into the darkness.

This time, nobody chased him.

Most of us just left. Right then. What could possibly happen in the second half of a football game that would top what had just taken place?

Nothing, we surmised.

And so, we retrieved Kenny's beloved Allstate, returned it to its museum-pedestal, covered it back up with the clear plastic sheeting, gathered on Andy's screened-in back porch, and re-lived a great night in our young lives.

Hosanna.

Oh, yes. I almost forgot. Janet whispered to me, confidentially, that she had voted for Fat Max. But she made me promise not to tell.

For at least forty years.

Life's Lessons Learned:

- *Straight-ahead confrontation is not nearly as effective as a cleverly persuasive plan. And sure not as much fun.*
- *It doesn't take a lot of effort to outsmart those who have already closed their minds to life's real possibilities.*
- *Only a near-perfect secret can ever be kept by 1,500 people. Or even ten, for that matter.*
- *It's cheaper to have the warped head of a three-horsepower Allstate engine milled and trued than it is to keep replacing head gaskets. Unless you just enjoy taking things apart.*

CHAPTER 16

Trouble in River City

AUSTIN, 1960

Somewhere along about the end of the 1950s, the ever-enlight-
ened citizenry of Austin resolved to build themselves a new dam
to create yet another lake in the string of lakes that already extended from Lake Buchanan, sixty or seventy miles to the northwest, all the way to Lake Austin, which ended at the Tom Miller
Dam on the west side of town.

All these lakes had been built by the federal Work Projects
Administration (WPA) in a long chain down the Colorado River
during the Great Depression, mostly just to create jobs.

The lagniappe was that they also provided water supply and
water recreation opportunities all the way from northeast of
Llano, in the Texas Hill Country, on down the river to Austin.
And flood control on the sometimes runaway Colorado.

With their advent also came the creation of the Lower
Colorado River Authority (LCRA) and the generation of considerable electricity using falling water to turn the turbines.

We all had "Mr. Sam" Rayburn, power-wielding Texas con-
gressman and Speaker of the House, to thank for the pork.

Pork or not, all in all, they were an economic boon, coming
and going.

The Austin city fathers saw an opportunity to extend and
build on that economic boon, right on through downtown. And

so they set about to build yet another dam. It was handily, and universally, approved, and Central Texas—Austin, in particular—was on its way to creating the seventh lake in the chain.

And a whole new water-sports industry.

With all the long-term creativity and imagination of last week's stale bologna sandwich, the new body of water, even before it existed, was dubbed "Town Lake."

Now, how clever is that name?

In a straw poll, the student body at Austin High School, where I and my little pack of incorrigible friends were starting our senior year, with Don and me at the helm of student government, voted to re-name the new body "Lake Bob."

"Bob" had defeated the two other nominees, "Bucky" and "Hortense," by a wide margin.

Well, don't laugh.

"Bob" was a better name than "Town." First, there must be 500 "Town Lakes" in the world. How mundane and ordinary. If this new body of water was going to generate the economic revolution the Chamber of Commerce touted for it, it needed a better name than "Town."

So far as our research could determine, there was not another Lake Bob anywhere on the face of the planet. It was a generic name, yet catchy. Simple, yet intriguing.

Who was this "Bob" character the lake was named for, anyway?

We had Lake Austin, Lake Travis, Lake Granite Shoals, Lake Buchanan, Lake Marble Falls, and Inks Lake, mostly named for pioneer heroes, contemporary political icons, or geologic formations.

With Lake Bob, anybody who had been christened either Robert or Bob, Roberta or Bobbie as any part of their name could claim the lake was named for them. Who would know better?

Yes, the re-naming could have been some fun. The world was starting to get too serious, we reasoned, so we petitioned the powers-that-be to relent, and to accede to our demands for "Lake Bob."

Of course, the twits at City Hall wanted to just blow us off, tell us to go jump into Lake Bob. Soon as it was full of water, anyhow.

We pointed out that we could get enough signatures on a pe-

HOUSE OF TWITS

Five innocent tongue-in-cheek pranksters turned Austin's City Hall into an armed fortress one evening in 1960 during a special hearing on re-naming the city's new lake.

(Photo PICA19125, Austin History Center, Austin Public Library)

tition to force a public hearing. They responded that we, not being twenty-one, technically weren't citizens yet.

Our signatures apparently meant nothing to them. Even legally speaking.

We responded with the fact that our school of 2,600 students was just one of a half dozen high schools in the city, and that we had already talked the matter over with both the editor of the *Daily Texan,* student newspaper at The University of Texas, which represented another 16,000 or so wild-eyed, liberal students, and with Ronnie Dugger, publisher of the way-out-liberal *Texas Observer.*

We told the green-visored, garter-sleeved minions at City Hall we might just have to make a federal case of it if they denied us a hearing.

That got their attention. They brought in the city attorney.

We re-stated our simple request for him, and we repeated, most politely and matter-of-factly, the breadth and width of populist support we were prepared, if necessary, to drum up for Lake "Bob."

I think we scared the bejeesus out of the guy.

There had been a few recent and isolated student protests of one thing or another, in other parts of the country. Elected and/or appointed officials, spurred on by J. Edgar Hoover's rampant paranoia and runaway imagination, not to mention his Saturday-night penchant for dressing up like the Andrews Sisters (which we didn't … mention, that is) were starting to live in fear of some kind of unbridled uprising, especially in places with large concentrations of those dratted students.

Like Austin.

So we got an item on the agenda for a city council meeting in about four weeks.

Meantime, we very deliberately, and with some style and flourish, stayed in daily contact with the city attorney's office, reporting on the hordes that potentially might show up at that meeting. We suggested to them, not too subtly, that there might just be a need for crowd control. And we assured them we could not be held responsible if some of the more outrageously zealous supporters of Lake "Bob" should get out of hand and decide to do something dramatic, like ransack downtown Austin. Just for example, you understand.

We completely rattled City Hall. They had no idea what to expect might happen when they brought up an issue they all considered stupid nonsense to begin with.

But, with the continuous, albeit polite, pressure we applied, they were afraid not to bring it up. Afraid of a little band of high school kids. Heh, heh.

Two dozen of Austin's finest were put on overtime and ordered to City Hall the evening of the hearing. The sheriff's department was on standby, should the police need extra help. And the Department of Public Safety was on alert, just in case a Texas Ranger might be needed to quell a riot.

The evening began with a bevy of those ugly, aqua-colored Austin Police cars cruising the perimeter, one behind the other. Lookouts were posted at the four corners of the roof of City Hall to alert the shock troops when they saw the first sign of the anticipated mob.

The city council was rushing through their agenda, trying, we thought, to get to the dreaded open hearing before some potential torch-bearing, drunken, half-crazed mob of 20,000, bent

MAKE WAY FOR "LAKE BOB"!

Or at least what should have been "Lake Bob." The old Colorado River bed through downtown Austin is dredged, widened, and prepared to receive runoff from upstream to become yet another lake in the chain stretching from Austin almost to San Saba.

(Photo PICA14505, Austin History Center, Austin Public Library)

BEAUTIFUL SHORELINE. STUPID NAME

Juvenile In-Betweeners questioned the lack of creativity (or even rudimentary thought) that went into the selection of "Town Lake" as the name for Austin's new landmark body of water, championing "Lake Bob" as a much more sensible alternative. We thought, "This dog (and its name) ain't gonna hunt."

on the destruction and embarrassment of the city, descended in all their fury.

Typical of their generation, the powers-that-be were more concerned that the city might be embarrassed, nationally, than that it might be burned to the ground. Go figure.

The constable who served as the official sergeant-at-arms provided continual updates to one side of the dais, and they were passed along, via whispers, to the other side. We wondered if the constable said "grits" to the councilman on the left, would it become "oatmeal" or "corn flakes" by the time it got to the last guy on the right?

When the gavel came down to open the public hearing on reconsideration of the name of the new lake, terror was written on the faces of the councilmen. In those days, since the populace, in general, was quite docile, anybody who intended to speak at public hearings was not required to register with the city clerk in advance.

In a classically daring understatement, we sent one, lone spokesperson to speak in favor of changing the name to "Bob."

His statement was equally understated. It went something like this: "We, the following residents of the City of Austin, hereby politely request that consideration be given to changing the name of the new lake to Lake Bob."

That was it.

The statement was signed by six people we had cornered—

at the last minute and at random—derelicts, winos, people with no fingerprints. But, by gum, all of them were over twenty-one.

We were making a point.

The mayor went berserk.

"Where is the mob you threatened us with?" he demanded of our spokesman. Mike, the spokesman, turned around and pointed to the four of us sitting, inconspicuously, in the third row.

"All of us are here, sir," he said politely.

"Five kids?" the mayor exploded. "We've practically called out the National Guard to fend off five well-behaved kids?" he thundered at the city attorney.

In a feeble attempt at self-defense, the city attorney sputtered, "They threatened me, Mr. Mayor. They said they could get all the high schools and university students down here to make demands, interrupt the meeting and even ransack the town."

The mayor looked at Mike. "Did you and your associates do these things?" he asked.

"No, sir," Mike responded, doing his best to look calm and unassuming, and not to laugh.

"We requested a hearing, sir. And we advised the city's attorney of some things that might potentially happen if that request were denied on some legal technicality, which is what he tried to do, at first. And we were convinced he would do that, if we turned our backs.

"We never said they would actually happen, sir. I believe he has overreacted to the fact that we called his office every day, just to keep in touch and be sure this whole public process wasn't about to run off in the ditch.

"His imagination must have gotten the best of him, sir."

Mike smiled at the city attorney, who looked as if he might like to kill all five of us, immediately and right there, in open court, in front of God, the press and a couple hundred other witnesses.

The mayor sat down, sipped some water, and tried to recompose himself. Various councilmen, depending on their political persuasion and their sense of humor, were either glowering or snickering, having realized they had been victimized by a phantom hoax of their own creation.

The mayor then said something I had never heard before, but have observed examples of a thousand times since. He said, turning his head side-to-side up and down the council table, then glaring at the city attorney, "Gentlemen, I believe we are all victims of child abuse, self-inflicted."

He called for a motion, a second, and a vote. Of course, we didn't get one councilman to support us. And so the name remained Town Lake.

Simple, mundane, stupid, insipid "Town Lake."

The whole magilla, which had inspired the call-up of every last available gendarme in the county, lasted no more than three or four minutes.

If a bunch of high school seniors had tried this little gambit in 1961 in Birmingham, let's say, they would probably have been attacked with cattle prods, severely beaten with lead-filled blackjacks, and would have ended up in jail on some trumped-up charges, been tried, convicted, and saved only by the Supreme Court and the U.S. Constitution.

Minutes before the executions.

But Austin was then, and remains today, a liberal bastion.

We just went on home, as we should have done. No harm. No foul.

Ours was a humorous prank, intended to make elected officials dance to our little tune and to knock some of the ever-increasing pomposity out of City Hall.

Needless to say, it was a rousing success. *"A good time was had by all,"* as they say. Except by the naïve, formerly pompous but now tight-assed and very, very embarrassed city attorney.

But other issues, entirely more serious than naming a lake "Bob," were lurking just over the horizon, about to pounce on River City and our beloved Varsity Theater, in particular.

Seems, unbeknownst to Don, Kenny and me, the Interstate Theater Circuit across Texas had observed a policy, since its founding by the Hoblitzelle family in Dallas some thirty years before, of not admitting blacks.

Having worked at our beloved Varsity Theater for almost four years and progressed from seventy cents an hour and all the popcorn we could eat to eighty-five cents an hour and who wants to eat any more of that greasy, rodent-dropping-infested popcorn, anyway? we had never been told of this policy. It just never came up.

Austin schools, unlike schools in most of the rest of the South, had begun quietly integrating in 1949, the year we all started to first grade. So we went to school—those who, unlike me, went all the way through school in Austin—with black kids from the get-go.

Austin High was probably 15 percent black in 1961. We all— Don, Kenny, Andy, Jack, and I—had black friends. They were in the band. They made our athletic teams better than they otherwise would have been, for sure. The whole thing was just no big deal to us.

We had never given a thought to the fact that our friends of color were not allowed to purchase tickets and enter the movie house where we worked, or any of the other Interstate movie houses in town that we frequented on free passes.

We were surprised, shocked even, when we were told. It was unsettling and quietly unnerving. How many times had we talked about movies with Garland Earls, a classmate and running back on the football team? Movies that he could not, by Interstate policy, go to see? How many others had we unintentionally, and completely innocently, violated in the same way?

Suddenly, we were not so proud to go to work. The formerly snappy uniforms that we wore had become crappy uniforms.

At first, we didn't know what to think about it. All the people we worked with were decent people. Well, almost all, anyway. Why would they try to keep some of our friends out of the Varsity?

I guess I should explain how the whole subject came up in the first place.

A group in Austin, led by the local SDS, if I remember correctly, had begun to line up, nightly, at our box office to buy tickets. Very quickly, they were joined by local ministers, local citizens who, like us, were dumbstruck by the policy, and—a week or so later—by hordes of ordinary university students.

Some of the university students were serious about changing the policy; others just needed a cause, and the Varsity was handy to the campus.

The objective of the "stand-in" was not really to directly

change the Interstate policy. Rather, the petitioners sought to interrupt the normal sale of tickets to those who were allowed to be admitted, thus creating an economic issue that would bring down the policy, for money's sake.

They knew where Interstate's heart lay—in box office and concession receipts.

After a couple of days of the stand-ins, the disruption began to work.

Interstate had a counterstrategy, and Charlie Roofe, our beloved city manager, came out to explain it to us.

As long-time, loyal, dependable, creative, and downright funny (to Charlie, at least) staff members, Don, Kenny, and I were to have the honor of being the *enforcers* of good ol' Interstate's unconscionable and outdated policy.

One of us was to insert himself, four or five would-be patrons deep, into the line, step in front of all blacks and anyone else who looked like they didn't really want to buy a ticket, but just wanted to register their disapproval of the policy and try to gum-up the ticket line. We were to repeat these words, from Interstate Circuit headquarters, on high, *verbatim:* *"It is the policy of Interstate Theaters not to admit Negroes."*

If that was my job, Don's would be to find and direct white (or brown, red, yellow, or magenta) patrons who really wanted to see the movie, in spite of Interstate's incomprehensible policy, to step around the line to the box office.

Kenny would then accompany the ticket purchasers to the lobby to be sure they felt safe and comfortable while patronizing a racist business.

What a plan! Genius was running rampant in Dallas.

So here we were—the *Interceptor and Denier,* the *By-passer,* and the *Seeing-eye-dog,* who led the blind.

That's what we called ourselves.

The three of us had never dealt with issues of conscience like this before. We hadn't had to. It was completely beyond our realm of experience and our scope of comprehension that any of our friends should be denied access to current entertainment because that person happened to be black.

Outrageous! How could anybody in his or her right mind contemplate such a ridiculous policy, even remotely?

Equally insane, why would the Interstate Circuit not take money from black people? As far as we knew, the color of commerce was green—as in greenbacks. Seemed to us that a dollar was a dollar, whether it came across the counter from a hand that was white, black, brown, yellow, red, or pea-green.

I remember Kenny said to Don and me one day, "What are we missing here? Something's going on that we just don't know about."

Don, already highly irritated, as we all were, at the rotten roles we had suddenly been forced into, lashed back, "Nothing going on here, Kenny, but pure hatred and fear. Mostly fear."

Strictly against company policy, we began to modify the official headquarters' statement. Soon it became, *"It is against Interstate Theaters' policy to admit Negroes. I'm sorry."* A day or two later, we added, *"I'm very sorry."* A day or two later, Don came up with the definitive statement, beginning with, *"This makes no sense to me, but ..."*

We found we could get through a shift in better spirits if we traded roles from time to time. So each of us took turns being *Enforcer and Denier, By-passer,* and *Seeing-eye dog.*

We talked it through amongst ourselves. Thoroughly. We discussed it within our little close-knit circle. We found that even we—spiritual, if not blood, brothers—had somewhat differing views.

"It's just a job that somebody has to do. Sure, we don't agree with it, but just grit your teeth, smile and be nice to everybody," Andy suggested.

Jack, always erudite and well reasoned in everything he said, advised, "Turn in your uniforms. Get out of that place. You're not making enough money to compromise your principles and be somebody else's stooge. Where's the guy who keeps this policy in effect? He's in Dallas, snug-as-a-bug. Why should he get his hands dirty with a corporate problem when he's got Larry, Curly, and Moe to do his dirty work for him?"

That was a good question. A very good question.

We didn't think it completely through before reacting, however.

While Don and Jack went to do some band chores, Kenny

and I shot downtown to the Paramount Theater to see Charlie Roofe.

"Charlie, we can't go on turning these people away for eighty-five cents an hour. We're not ushers, we're goons," I shot him straight between the eyes.

"How much do you think the job is worth?" Charlie asked us, sitting upright in his chair.

"A whole lot more than eighty-five cents an hour," Kenny replied.

"C'mon guys." Charlie, behind his big desk, leaned forward on his elbows and looked straight at us. "What's the bottom-line price of your everlasting souls?"

He had put a wooden stake through our hearts.

Head down, I said to him, "You're right, Charlie. It's not about money. I will give you and Jerry four weeks' notice for Don and me. We won't leave you in the lurch, but we can't keep doing this. Kenny can speak for himself."

"Me, too, Charlie. I didn't know some of our friends couldn't even buy tickets. I'll let them in free through the fire exit, or I'll quit. Four weeks."

"Accepted," Charlie said, smiling strangely.

We were shocked. We were his best employees, and he knew it.

It made Kenny and me sad to think that, not only had we been willing—eager, even—to sell ourselves out for another twenty-five or thirty cents an hour, but also that the big boss, our biggest fan for four years, kissed us off without even the hint of an argument.

It made us even sadder to have to go find Don and Jack and tell Don he had just quit his job of the last four years.

No more free popcorn. No more free movie passes. No more paycheck!

What had we done?

Don's reaction was more intelligent and thoughtful than our reaction to Charlie's rebuff.

"Something's going on," he said. "Charlie would have given us $2.50 an hour, at least, to stand out there and *Enforce/Deny, By-pass,* and *Guide dog.*" The terms had become so much a part of our everyday lexicon over the past three weeks that they rolled trippingly off his palate.

"Besides," Don continued, "Charlie loves us. Aside from movies, we're his only entertainment. Hide and watch, guys. And don't sign on for a new job yet. Something's up."

So saith St. Donald, the prophet.

Now, I had learned long ago not to dispute Don's predictions. My confidence had started three years earlier at a ninth-grade basketball game.

Don was a good basketball player. I was not. In fact, I was not even on the twelve-man squad. The UJH Eagles were playing the Fulmore Falcons, and we were playing in the Fulmore gym.

Don was one-on-one with their left guard in the first half, and the guy he was defending, or attempting to defend, was ripping the cords. He had sixteen points at halftime.

I was sitting right behind the bench, feeling bad for Don since he couldn't seem to stop this guy from scoring.

Just before the second half started, our coach asked Don, "Is there anything you can do with number 11? He's tearing us up. Can I give you some help?"

Don's reply was succinct: "Don't worry. I'll take care of number 11. I'll shut him down in less than two minutes."

A prediction.

It actually took twenty-three seconds.

We controlled the second-half tip-off, and Don, with an unusual enthusiasm, it seemed to me, popped in a basket from the top of the key. Swish.

Fulmore brought the ball down the court. Sure enough, the point guard stopped, looked, and passed the ball to ol' number 11.

Dribbling like a Globetrotter, he went right at Don, who was planted with his arms up, hands in the guy's face. Number 11 faked right, faked left, and then went straight up, just as he had the whole first half, to take a jump shot over Don's head.

This time, however, instead of jumping with him, Don stayed firmly fixed to the floor. As the opponent hit the top of his jump, fully extended and two feet off the floor, Don twisted ninety-degrees back and to his right, doubled up his fist, recoiled, and planted a roundhouse haymaker dead-center in the guy's solar plexus.

Ouch!

Well, ol' number 11 went down in agony. He writhed on the floor, moaning.

Don quietly walked over to our bench and put on his sweats and a towel just ahead of his formal ejection.

Number 11 was carried off the floor by his teammates, doubled up like a hairpin.

The referee came over to our coach to make Don's ejection official. On his way by, he leaned over to Don and asked, "Why did you do that?"

It wasn't a threatening tone he used. He just looked, and sounded, utterly amazed.

Don's response was equally amazing. "I have this problem. Sometimes I forget which game I'm playing. For just a moment, I thought I was boxing."

Ever since that day, I began to count on Don's predictions to come true.

One way or another.

Back to the Varsity Theater.

Two days after we all resigned, Charlie stopped by, on one of his rare visits, to tell us, a twinkle in his eye, that Interstate's policy would be suspended effective the following Monday. Seems anybody who had seventy-five cents would be able to buy a ticket and patronize any Interstate Theater, henceforth and forevermore.

Don smiled his "gotcha" grin at Kenny and me. Right. Again!

Still skeptical, I asked Charlie, "Will black people have to sit in the balcony or something?" I was remembering the back rows of the city buses in Waco, years before.

"Nope. Instant equality come noon Monday," was his response.

"Can we have our resignations back?" Kenny asked.

"What resignations?" Charlie looked at him and feigned a puzzled look.

"How about some more money then?" Don, ever the opportunist, seized the moment.

"Fifteen cents an hour, up to a dollar. Just don't threaten to quit. You know I can't run this company without you clowns around," Charlie concluded, turning to hurry back to his enclave at the Paramount.

It was a pretty good day. Not only did we get a fifteen-cent an hour raise, but also now all our friends could buy tickets and come to the Varsity to see movies. We vowed to let them in free for six months.

And we did. Through the 24th Street fire exit.

That Sunday's paper made a big deal of the policy change at Interstate Theaters. It quoted many of the people who had participated in the stand-ins, Interstate officials proclaiming a new day in access to entertainment, and it finished up with a short quote from the corporate moron in Dallas who had been hiding, for the past six weeks, behind Larry, Curly, and Moe.

He said, "We also want to recognize that many of our good employees have been uncomfortable with this policy. It is time we changed."

Well said, Butthead!

Life's Lessons Learned:

- *One of the most powerful words in the English language is "intimation." But it's not a fraction as powerful as "runaway imagination."*
- *A lot of our woes are brought on by self-inflicted child-abuse.*
- *Old policies are made to be changed, with a small and timely nudge in the right direction.*
- *Any establishment can try to pattern itself after a country club. Never work anywhere all your friends can't visit.*
- *In the game of life, do not let others exploit your weaknesses to their advantage. If they try it, simply change games without telling them. Until it's too late.*

CHAPTER 17

Running Flat-Out

AUSTIN, 1960/1961

Our wretched and depraved little gang was coming to the end of seeing one another every day as we entered the home stretch toward high school graduation. We were sad for that reason, but excited—even exhilarated—with what lay right before us.

Every last one of my small group of associates was going to at least try college. There was no Vietnam War, yet, although we did have to register for the draft, one by one, as we turned eighteen. That was no big deal, though, since nobody had been drafted for a long time ... not in our memories, at least.

Man, would that change in a New York minute.

Then there were the infernal SAT exams to get behind us and the college applications to complete and send in. Don, Jack, Kenny, Andy, and I had all opted to attend The University of Texas at Austin. We had, literally, lived most of our lives within its shadows. It didn't scare us a bit.

Besides, it was a cheap place to get a nationally recognized education, although I'm not sure we were actually clever enough to figure that out until later.

We did notice that all the "brains" were going to Stanford, Rice, Duke, Harvard, Yale, and UC Berkeley.

My really old girlfriend, Nancy, even announced she had been accepted at Oberlin College in Ohio. That figured, for sure. Nancy was a Quaker and a social liberal—two "firsts" in my experience.

Now, I graduated number six in a class of 479. I should have been able to go to one of those "big-time" schools. But I never applied anywhere except to UT. It was right at hand, tuition was $25 a semester, and I knew I was going to have to work and pay my own way.

Various UT entities actually seemed overjoyed at having me matriculate. I got some piece of "welcome aboard" propaganda in the mail, seems like every day.

Besides, all my buddies were going there. It would be just like another four years of high school, a few blocks away from where we had been going to school, already, for the past six years.

Only with less class time. That's what we thought, anyway, and it pretty much turned out to be right-on.

Of course, all the raging "type A" personalities were headed to Texas A&M University, archrival of UT. We thought they were nuts, once again (we had thought most of them nuts for years, anyway). In those days, girls were not allowed to attend A&M, and military classes and drill were mandatory.

Now, going to a school where there were no girls was stupid enough, slightly insane, maybe. But putting on those ridiculous jackboots and carrying around a swagger stick just reminded us of the old black-and-white movies we had seen starring the hyperactive, brainwashed, obedient little Brown Shirts in Nazi Germany in the 1930s.

Spooky, spooky, spooky!

No, thank you very much, we would stick with our Levi's, Haggar cotton slacks, and Hush Puppies. Our swagger sticks would be the baseball bats in the trunks of our cars in case we ever had the chance to gin up a quick game of flies and skinners.

The point is, we were pretty busy.

Besides going to school every day, even if some of us only had three real classes and continued to try to hang around Valhalla as much as St. Margaret would allow, we had our jobs at the good ol' Varsity Theater to attend to.

And the senior parties only became more numerous. And more and more elaborate.

The girls went through some kind of bizarre ritual that involved "teas."

"Well, la-di-dah for them," we thought. What a waste of time those silly tea parties must have been for most of those sweet little honeys. Only the strangest of them ever really got into the tea party scene seriously. Most of them just gritted their teeth, put on their little frocks and a pair of lacy-white gloves, and went through the motions as some kind of weird, incomprehensible homage to their mothers.

Like it was expected of them. And they had no option. None at all.

There was no doubt that our parents, the "Great Depression" generation, had absolutely no idea what was really going on in our heads. Like St. Margaret, they were mostly throwbacks to an era in which appearance and keeping up with the Joneses were terribly important.

With no exceptions—*nada, niente*—the eighteen-year-olds we knew in 1961 didn't much give a rat's-patootie about any of that silliness. We truly didn't think we had to impress anybody, and we had zero interest in trying. In fact, just thinking about it was disgusting to us.

Don, Kenny, and I had now been at the Varsity Theater for more than four years. We surely must have been making more than a dollar an hour by 1961, although there was no inflation to fight. A movie ticket was still seventy-five cents. But we hadn't paid to go to a movie since James Dean ran his Porsche into a telephone pole. And smashed his skull.

Creativity amongst the staff of the Varsity continued to get better and better, at least somewhat more sophisticated than making farting sounds and dropping Elgin Hot Gut onto prissy Church Ladies' prim little hats, complete with veils to cover up their hairline pimples.

But that creativity took on a forced escalation with the arrival of one George Flat, from Dallas, as the new assistant manager.

It was bad enough that somebody else got the job. Because any one of the three of us—Don, Kenny, or me—could run that, or any other theater, extremely well with our hands tied behind our backs and Margaret Bradshaw breathing down our necks.

In fact, each of us had actually managed the old Austin

Theater on South Congress Avenue for anywhere from a week to six weeks at a time. The career manager was having health problems. Whenever he wasn't able to get to work, one of the three of us had taken over.

We knew everything from concession reports to box office reports to payroll, and we could anticipate crowds and have the house ready all the time.

What did we need with a new assistant manager from Dallas? Especially George Flat?

This guy was not skilled in the people-managing business. It appeared to us that he was both a misfit and a counterfeit. You had to work hard to be that bad. Didn't you?

He came aboard like Lieutenant Fuzz. He actually held inspections, during which we would have to line up, and he would walk along like that other George—George Patton. And he would proceed to tell each of us what was wrong with us that day, the smug little piss ant.

He dressed straight out of *GQ*, and he told us that his father owned a big, fancy restaurant in Dallas. He not only acted like Lieutenant Fuzz, but he also never missed the chance to mention that he was rich.

Truthfully, the three of us were positively hostile toward him from the day he arrived. We believed that both our manager and, his boss, the city manager, knew and trusted us. If push came to shove, both of them would side with us, we were absolutely sure.

We wasted little time putting that theory to the test.

The day Lieutenant Fuzz called a meeting of the entire staff and told us we were never again to eat any popcorn without paying for it, and we wouldn't be allowed even to pay and eat while on duty, we immediately instituted "Operation Fuzz-flat."

The plan was a living organism whose only objective was to drive Mr. Flat either more insane or back to Dallas, or both.

We had lookouts posted at the marquee window who would warn us when he was approaching. Then one of us would commence to do something remarkably bizarre, like putting the trash can over his head and blundering around the lobby, banging into walls or the concession stand, like a pinball on steroids, imitating Carmen Miranda's singing.

Or riding the little broom we used to sweep up popcorn from the carpet while whinnying and saying things like, "Whoa, big fella."

George Flat would come storming in, red-faced, and immediately fire the culprit.

We tried to take turns being fired, so as to be equal amongst ourselves. Whoever was the designated firee-of-the-day would trudge upstairs, change into street clothes, and report to the office to say goodbye to our old friend, the manager.

Invariably, he (our manager, that is) would hire us back on the spot, especially when we claimed we had no idea what was on ol' George Flat's mind. "He just came in the lobby and fired me. I don't have a clue why. I was just sweeping up the popcorn."

Nor did George Flat approve of the way we changed the marquee.

He wanted us on ladders in the right-hand lane of Guadalupe Street. Instead, we preferred to simply hang over the side and change the letters and words from up above. Just like we had done for four years.

It was much safer that way. A ladder three feet from the curb on Guadalupe Street at 11:00 P.M. was a sure target for some frat-rat who was drunk and trying to navigate back to the frat house.

We appealed to George on the basis of safety. He was unrelenting.

We wondered, "What does this jackass care how we get the job done? We've been doing this very well for four years, only once misspelling a word."

We finally decided he was just trying to prove he had more power than us. *Ha!*

To make our point, we invited him out onto the marquee one Thursday night to see how much easier it was to change the letters from up above. "Here, George," Kenny said to him. "You just climb through this little window and drop down eighteen inches onto the floor of the marquee."

So unsuspecting George Flat did just that. He went through the window headfirst and dropped lightly onto the floor of the marquee. Nothing to it.

Except Kenny slammed the window, we locked it from inside, and we all went home, leaving him stranded outside, twenty feet above the sidewalk. Apparently sometime during the night, he broke the same window in order to get back inside.

But he was observed "breaking and entering" by one of Austin's finest, who hauled him in to the hoosegow, from which he was sprung the next morning by our manager, who had refused to get out of bed in the middle of the night to get him out of jail.

Turns out he wasn't really rich, either. On a trip to Dallas to see the annual UT-OU football game, we stopped by Chez Giorgio's Restaurant and Grille to pay our respects to the elder Mr. Flat.

He was a line cook.

True, it was a fancy restaurant, but he didn't own so much as the napkin concession. We took a picture of a couple of us with Father Flat, who seemed like a down-to-earth guy, not at all like his son. We left that photo right on ol' George's little metal desk.

He never acknowledged having seen it.

Don and I added, quite unexpectedly, an unplanned event to "Operation Fuzz-flat" one day in January. I mention it only so you will understand and, hopefully, believe that we were, in most respects, relatively normal teen-agers, and a lot like real brothers.

For one reason or another, I had spent the better part of the day doing my best to provoke Don. I worked hard at it, even though he asked me, repeatedly, to just back off and leave him alone.

HOME BASE

The ushers' dressing room, upstairs behind the balcony at the beautiful and venerable Varsity Theater, served for almost five years as the official headquarters, meeting place, and local lodge hall of la cosa nostra piccola, *In-Betweener pranksters of the first order.*

(Photo PICA06734, Austin History Center, Austin Public Library)

By the time we got to work at the Varsity a few minutes before 6:00 P.M., I had pushed him a tad-bit too far, if you know what I mean. We made it up the stairs to the ushers' dressing room behind the balcony, and we started to change into our uniforms.

However, one additional stupid remark from me was one stupid remark too many. I had crossed the line.

Don took a poke at me. I poked back. Then we started to wrestle on the wood floor, making one hell of a racket.

Don, being slightly bigger and stronger (besides being really mad at me), soon got the upper hand. As we thrashed and crashed our way around the room, at one point slamming into a row of wooden lockers so hard as to knock them fifteen degrees out of their normal vertical alignment, the noise of our brotherly disagreement began to rattle around the Varsity's big auditorium, kind of like a freight train in a phone booth.

Just as Don grabbed me in a hammer-lock and crashed the top of my head, down to below my ears, through the sheetrock in the wall separating the ushers' room from the projection booth, leaving me stuck and trying to decide if I wanted to keep those ears badly enough to not pull myself free, ol' George Flat opened the door, stuck in his head and said, "What the Sam Hill's going on in here?"

He often invoked the name of this Sam Hill character. We didn't know why.

Don immediately released me from his death grip, grabbed a big, push-type cleaning broom, and commenced to tap dance, making as much noise, with his heels and the top of the broom handle, on the wooden floor as possible.

I, bent at a ninety-degree angle, head stuck firmly in the wall at about waist height, and my posterior pointed straight at Lieutenant Fuzz, picked up on the cue, and began my best impression of clog-dancing-with-your-head-embedded-in-a-wall, also ratcheting up the decibels with leather heels on wood flooring.

This dancing fiasco was, I'm sure, even louder than the brawl that had preceded it.

George Flat repeated, "What's going on in here?"

Don answered for both of us, since I was preoccupied with saving myself from an ear-ectomy by trying my best to keep my stuck-in-the-wall head stationary whilst stomping out a hellishly noisy Latin beat with my heels.

"What's the matter with you, George?" Don asked him. "Can't you see? We're tap dancing!"

"Well, you're making way too much racket. Besides, you're supposed to be on the floor in two minutes."

The idiot was actually buying the tap-dancing tale. Unbelievable!

"We'll be down, don't you worry, Georgie-Boy," Don assured him. "But we certainly want to be prepared come Saturday morning, don't we now?"

Another of George Flat's hare-brained ideas had Don and me on the stage during intermission at the Saturday morning Kiddy Show, doing our own renditions of such childhood favorites as "Hector, the Garbage Collector," "Three Blind Mice," and various other nursery rhymes set to music. He never seemed to notice that we changed the lyrics to give each little ditty a sinister overtone so as to scare the popcorn out of the 600 or so little hellions we were babysitting.

The kids loved us, even if they didn't understand our modified librettos.

So, gullible ol' George Flat, with an admonition to "hurry up," closed the door and left.

Of course, I'm still stuck in the wall. A blatantly obvious, visual fact that apparently completely escaped Lieutenant Fuzz's normally eagle-eyed scrutiny.

Don finally got a hammer and gingerly chipped away the sheetrock around my head to the point I could pull it out without ripping off both ears.

By then, we were laughing so hard at George Flat's stupidity that neither of us could remember why we were fighting to begin with.

We still can't remember.

While my buddies and I made a fun little game out of upsetting Lieutenant Fuzz, our grandmotherly ticket-seller, Angie, really despised him. As a matter of fact, she made no effort to be even coolly polite to him, and we regularly heard her call him names, right to his face—names that we, worldly though we were, had never heard before.

One day in February, although we had not ever, in four years, experienced Angie's creative side, she cooked up her own version of "Operation Fuzz-flat." She needed help, so we conspired on the house intercom.

Other employees were not allowed to approach the box office. Seems Mr. Interstate trusted nobody when it came to the sanctity of his sequentially numbered tickets, even those of us who had proven our loyalty over four years.

Here's how our scam was to go.

When Lieutenant Fuzz came down to close the box office, several of us would be in position to strike. The box office was a stand-alone little kiosk, not much bigger than a phone booth. Lieutenant Fuzz's habit was to unlock the back door, slip inside, and pull the door closed, setting his impressive key ring, full of many more keys than there were locks at the theater, on a narrow shelf.

His job, at closing, was to bring the unsold tickets, the cash and the telephone, freed of its jack, upstairs into the office. There he would double-count the money, fill out the ticket and concession reports, and lock the cash in the safe for bank deposit the following morning.

Simple enough. Except for "Operation Angie-gets-even."

That night, as discussed and rehearsed on the intercom, when George unlocked the door and entered the box office, Angie bolted out right past him with the money and the rolls of tickets. Don quickly swabbed the inside doorknob with lots of lukewarm butter from the popcorn-buttering machine. I reached inside the little front window and scooped up Lieutenant Fuzz's incredible menagerie of keys, and we locked the turkey in the box office.

Angie accompanied Don and me as we took the money upstairs, calmly did the ticket, concessions and cash reports, made out the bank deposits, and put the money and rolls of tickets in the safe.

All the while, we ignored the insistent buzzing of the intercom. With only a telephone with no dial (his own clever idea to prevent Angie from making any outbound calls), his only forms of communication were the intercom or screaming out the little front opening where tickets and money changed hands regularly.

He kept trying to turn the inside knob, but—since it was covered with butter—he not only couldn't turn it, but it wouldn't have turned anyway after I locked it with his own keys.

I don't know how, or at what hour, he got out of that box office. He was still there, pounding and yelling when we closed the place down, turned out all the lights, locked the doors, and went home at 11:40 P.M.

Next evening, the city manager, Charlie Roofe, showed up. Now let me tell you that, in four years, we had seen him at the Varsity maybe twice. His *modus operandi* was to hang out downtown at the Paramount and State theaters, side-by-side houses on Congress Avenue. He rarely left the Paramount, in fact.

He called us into the office. Jerry, our manager, was there, but Lieutenant Fuzz was not.

His message was brief.

"I have transferred George Flat to full-time assistant manager at the Austin Theater. That will keep the little jerk out of your hair.

"We're not going to have an assistant here at the Varsity for the moment. So you guys need to pitch in and help Jerry. Thanks for doing a good job. See ya."

Yeah, sure. Right, Charlie. You bet! We're going to pitch in big-time for our dollar an hour.

But we did. Because we were free of Little George Flat, Lieutenant Fuzz. And we swore never again to darken the door of the Austin Theater, even if they were showing XXX naked high school girls of our own acquaintance on the big screen.

They didn't, as far as I know, and we didn't either. A very good long-term solution.

We took credit for the transfer of Lieutenant Fuzz. It was only right that we get some kudos, along with Angie, of course, for chasing him out of Dodge.

Our briefly anxiety-ridden lives now returned to normal with his transfer; we switched our creative juices back to having a good time, partying every chance we got.

Those senior parties were well chaperoned, let me tell you. Nothing untoward ever happened, except once.

We had all been invited to one of them at the Westwood Country Club. Now, on principle, none of us wanted anything to do with the inside of a country club. As far as we were concerned, country clubs were evil places from which emanated the kind of people we didn't like, couldn't trust, and mostly just hoped to avoid every chance we got.

Everyone but me had the courage of his convictions and declined the invitation, citing some hellishly creative excuse, such as, "My horse has eaten a bushel of corn cobs and foundered. I have to stay with her night and day." That actually happened to Don's horse, Blossom, but it had happened ten years before.

This was the time we first learned that Andy Scott, another friend who drifted into and out of our shenanigan-ridden lives, was Jewish. At least, I hadn't known that before, and it wouldn't have mattered if I had. His excuse for avoiding the country club party was straightforward. "Hey, I'm a Jew. Want to explain my presence to the board of stewards?"

So I, alone, defied my principles and better judgment, and I went to the party. The only real reason I went was I was invited by an especially good-looking little babe who, it was rumored, could get extra friendly, if she liked you. Know what I mean?

As you might expect, the evening was a disaster.

It was the only senior party I had been to at which liquor flowed freely. And some of the Aggie-bound type-A's, seeing that I was alone, so to speak, without my usual accompanying troops, anyway, decided I should be tossed into the club's pool, at the deep end.

Even the girl who invited me turned on me and joined the small mob.

Not wanting to prove their West-Austin, rich-ass assessment of me as "white-trash" correct, I attempted to reason with them. That didn't work.

So I claimed I couldn't swim. That was not only a lie, and a lot of people there knew it, but it was also a stupid mistake, like throwing gasoline on burning embers.

Relentlessly, they came at me.

With no other particular solution in mind, I bolted for the fence separating the pool from the parking lot. Although my position on the track team had been in weights—shot-putter and discus-thrower, I had seen the thin-clads practicing. And I had learned well from those observations. I hurdled that fence with two feet to spare, all the while pulling my car keys out of my pocket.

GETAWAY CAR

Only August Hartkopf's 1932 Ford (with a Corvette engine) was quicker than my somewhat "enhanced" '56 baby-blue Oldsmobile coupe. Mind you, quickness was a necessity for us pranksters. Only quick getaways allowed us to practice pranksterism yet another day.

My car, at the time, was really my mother's car, which I had discreetly modified, somewhat, to fit my particular lifestyle.

It was a 1956 Oldsmobile Super 88 coupe. It had a stock 260-cubic-inch Rocket 88 engine that Don and Kenny and I had quietly and secretly refined with aluminum pistons and new camshaft and valve assembly, along with two Holley four-barrel carburetors, "spinner" wheel covers, and heavy-duty shocks. The chrome valve and air cleaner covers and spinners were just for show.

It was baby blue, inside and outside, and I kept it absolutely pristine. In fact, I had eaten directly off the intake manifold to win bets more than once.

Nobody at our house ever realized what I had done to "enhance" its performance. Because nobody ever looked under the hood of that car but me, anyway.

About two weeks before, I had been stopped by a Highway Patrolman just north of Austin on a long straight stretch of Interstate 35. He said he clocked me with his radar doing 123 MPH going uphill.

I showed him my license and explained that the best cure for an intermittently sticking valve was some Casite upper cylinder lubricant poured into the gas tank, followed by almost redlining the engine for five or six miles.

I had good luck.

First, he absolutely agreed with my solution for a sticking valve. Second, he loved the cyclical *"thromp-thromp, thromp"* the modified camshaft gave the exhaust as it rumbled through twin glass-pack mufflers.

Best of all, he knew my father.

So he said, "Follow me." And he turned on his red lights and siren and proceeded to wind up his 1960, three-speed Ford Interceptor V-8.

He kept waving his arm for me to catch up. I did. At 110 MPH by my speedometer, I passed him and pulled away like he was dragging concrete.

My valve stopped sticking, just as I had known it would. I pulled into a rest stop to idle down the engine and wait for him.

Sure enough, he was impressed. He gave me his name and phone number and told me the next time I had a sticking valve to call him. He would escort me on U.S. 79 east of Taylor, a small town northeast of Austin, so I could get it unstuck in a safer, less congested place.

The night of the country club party, that car was a screaming machine. By the time I left the parking lot and hit the pavement, it was redlined at 5,500 RPM, and the speedometer was pushing 50.

Several of the crazed, future-Aggie idiots (no redundancy intended) who wanted to throw me into the pool tried to come after me. But they had little chance in their fathers' Chrysler New Yorkers, Cadillac Fleetwoods, and Buick Roadmasters.

I left them behind like they were towing thirty-two-foot

Airstreams, and I lit out for the bridge game I knew those with better sense were playing at Andy Scott's house.

My penance was, once again, to admit multiple cases of bad judgment.

Don, Jack, Andy Bailey, and Andy Scott all made me repeat several times, "I am a dumb-butt for ever going into a country club, but I somewhat redeemed myself for letting the little babe who was my date find her own way home."

Then we played us some serious bridge.

Life's Lessons Learned:

- *Nothing good ever came to me out of a country club. If you're ever invited to a party at one, even if by a well-known and notorious Louisiana-border nymphomaniac, decline. Politely, of course.*

- *If you are going to unstick your valves with Casite upper-cylinder lubricant and bursts of 125-MPH speed, be sure the policeman who stops you is a friend of the family.*

- *Never let anyone force you to carry a swagger stick. Unless it's a 36-inch, 36-ounce Adirondak. Or a Louisville Slugger.*

CHAPTER 18

Growing Up Simple

AUSTIN, 1961

As our schoolboy days began to dwindle and time for graduation approached, I began to think more and more about my bank account into which I had laundered that $900 in "heal-me" money and $400 in lawnmowing and Spudnut-selling funds eight years before.

I had added to it regularly until the balance was pushing $4,000. That was a pretty good chunk of change for an eighteen-year-old in 1961. It was probably close to the average annual salary of most people in Austin at the time.

I felt justified, after all these years, in wanting to spend some of it. To reward myself, so to speak, for sacrificing and saving all that dough. And, in the process, maybe, to regain some of my self-respect. Self-respect that had abandoned me when my first true love had dumped me.

But I didn't want to blow all of it. I had become accustomed to the semi-independence a sizable bank account provided.

My choice for self-reward was a brand new, just off the boat, 1961 Austin-Healey Sprite. It was British Racing Green (BRG), and it was built by the good craftsmen at Morris' Garage in England, home of the already-classic MG and even more stylish and higher-performing Austin-Healey. I had ordered it six months earlier, with the option to cancel the order up to delivery.

My dad drove me to Houston one Saturday morning early in May, where I plunked down $1,765 for the shiny new beauty. It was equipped with a Stromberg-Carlson AM radio, which I had negotiated for twenty extra dollars over the phone, and a heater.

The heater was free. And pretty much useless, as I later discovered.

Before we left the showroom of Overseas Motors on South Main, I had added bumper bars, front and rear, an optional tonneau cover for when the top was down, and side fender mirrors.

Grand total: $1,815. I still had more than $2,000 in the bank.

I think maybe that little car changed my life.

Let me give you an example or two of what I mean.

One of the rituals of graduation involved something called "senior picnic." In our year, 1961, the event was under the direction of our beloved dean of women, St. Margaret Bradshaw. It was to be held at Zilker Park, complete with swimming in the now-famous, forever-freezing Barton Springs.

If the weather were to be inclement, like a roaring thunderstorm or similar, the picnic would be moved to the old city coliseum, just behind the local Class AA Texas League baseball stadium where the Austin Pirates played.

As luck would have it, we had a half-inclement, half-fair-weather day.

It rained in the morning. So everyone was inside. Except Don and me. We were in my new, little green sports car, outside the building. By sighting and measuring with unaccustomed precision, for us at least, we had ascertained that the car, fully loaded with the both of us, was about four inches narrower than the southeast entrance to the old coliseum.

For some totally unknown and completely insane reason, we decided to drive through the indoor volleyball games. So, with Kenny manning the coliseum's southeast doors so they wouldn't scratch my new little baby, in we roared.

Once inside, we stopped. We used our blinkers, turned right and took a complete turn, a victory lap of sorts, around the outside wall of the coliseum's dirt floor, as if we had just won the Indianapolis 500, which we would listen to on the radio in a few days.

ON THE (RIGHT) ROAD, AGAIN

A brand-new, just off the boat from the friendly craftsmen at Morris' Garage in England, British Racing Green, 1961 Austin-Healey Sprite helped me regain some self-respect and a small measure of good humor following the unceremonious dumping I had suffered at the hands of my first true love. Kenny and I baited our hooks with Aqua Velva and went trolling, in style, for other sweet young honeys.

Miss Bradshaw was beside herself.

Four hundred about-to-be-graduated seniors, at least, were cheering us on while St. Margaret tried to run us down on foot. I kept watching her in the side fender mirrors until Don screamed that I was going to kill somebody if I didn't look where I was going.

We made one lap and, again using the blinkers, turned right, roared back outside once more, parked the car, zipped up the tonneau cover to keep the rain out, and strolled, nonchalantly, into the party, shaking off the raindrops that had drenched our hair and the tops of our shoulders.

St. Margaret was looking for us.

She came directly toward us like a bull at Pamplona. When she got a few feet away, she started to sputter. Nobody had ever driven through one of her senior picnics. She was almost tongue-tied, trying to figure out how to address a completely new, and totally unexpected, phenomenon.

It was our chance.

Don and I had, along with Andy Bailey, Kenny and Jack, become almost psychic when it came to reading one another's minds. We could act in unison, totally unrehearsed.

As St. Margaret began to sputter, and a crowd started to gather to see what punishment she could possibly mete out at this late date in our high school careers, we "seized the moment," as Mr. Price, our English IV teacher, had drummed into our heads to do.

Don grabbed Miss Bradshaw by the right arm, and I grabbed her by the left. Together, we picked her about a foot off the ground, which was no mean feat, because she was a hefty woman, to be sure.

With her sputtering, we each planted a noisy, juicy kiss on the cheek nearest us—Don on the right and me on the left.

Don immediately followed up with a brilliant red herring.

"Maggie," he said, smiling, "may we call you Maggie? We have decided, at long last, to reveal our secret. Haven't you figured out why we hang around your offices so much? We're both madly in love with you, and we want you to decide which of us will gain your favor before we put you down."

As if on cue, I continued, "That's right, my love. Or we could

GRABBIN' THE PRIZE

After twelve years of daily prank-filled public education at the hands of helpless (and sometimes hapless) teachers and administrators, graduation seemed insignificantly anticlimactic. The entire band of In-Betweener pranksters opted for higher education at The University of Texas at Austin. And why not? Big name school. Cheap tuition. And the best-looking women in the Western hemisphere. Hosanna!

all three run off to Pago-Pago and form a *ménage-à-trois*. Wouldn't that be fun, now?"

She started to laugh, then to guffaw. Then she commenced to squirm, and I noticed a stream coming down below her dress, splashing little spots of mud onto my already-wet shoes. She was peeing her pants! Right into a steaming puddle on the coliseum's dirt floor.

We had done it! We had joined Candy on the tiny list of those who had tamed "Maggie the Cat."

Hosanna!

When the rain stopped and the sun came out, just before noon, the picnic was moved back to its original site at Zilker Park. Don and I decided just to scope out the girls in Barton Springs and not to actually get into that shrinkage-inducing, ice-cold water.

Could life ever get better than this?

Maybe so.

As the day was wearing to an end, my former, but by no means forgotten, flame—Little Miss Lee—came strolling over to speak her first words to me in about five months.

"What you and Don did this morning was really funny. I liked it," she offered, as the first words she'd uttered to me since Christmas. "It reminded me of how funny you are sometimes, and how much I miss that."

She looked down, tossed her always shiny hair, blinked her extra-long lashes, and then continued, "Whose little green sports car is that?"

I couldn't resist, especially with Don starting to wave his arms like a runaway windmill behind her back. And to shake his head side-to-side and mouth, "No!"

"You remember last Christmas?" I asked her.

She looked hurt, as if I were going to bring up the hateful ol' Witch of Agnese's visit to my house, the return of the pink clock radio and the devastating, condescending "white trash" lecture from her I had been forced to listen to.

"Well, last October, I ordered this little British Racing Green Austin-Healey to give to you for Christmas. All the way from England."

Don dropped his outrageous pantomime and conjured up a smile of relief. He didn't know for sure exactly what was coming, but he knew it would be classic. And that it probably wouldn't get me back into trouble, Lee-wise.

"But, alas, it didn't come in time for Christmas," I continued. "Something about a back-order and not enough glymphpartzes to finish up and ship on schedule. Then your mom came over and brought back the new radio. She told me you weren't allowed to see me anymore. She said a lot of things I'd rather not repeat.

"So I thought to myself, 'Hey, self, you've got a barrel full o' money in the bank. Probably as much as the good professor and mother of Lee, anyway. So when the cute, little car comes, why not just keep it for yourself?'

"So that's what I did. It showed up in Houston last week. I couldn't give it to you because I'm not considered a good enough prospect by your manipulative mother."

Lee was starting to tear-up. I thought I had better back off . . . a little.

"But it is nice to see you, again," I said, smiling directly at her.

"You know," she started to speak haltingly, trying to smile that billion-dollar smile that she had used so often to wind me around her little finger (or any other appendage that was handy).

"You know," she started over. "All that was my mother's doing. I had nothing to do with it. I wanted to go on seeing you, put your little radio by my bedside to remind me of you. You know you are special to me."

There was that smile, again, in all its spellbinding radiance. Instantly, my stomach lunged upward and grabbed me by the throat. I felt my knees buckling, and I started to melt. So I looked to Don for support.

He was . . . well, I'm not right sure what he was doing, but he was agitating like a monkey in a banana store.

I took a deep breath, and I got back my grip.

"What are you going to do about it?" I asked her.

"About what?" She smiled an even bigger smile than I had ever seen on her face before. She knew she was pretty, but still fairly ordinary looking unless she was smiling.

But, smiling, she was gorgeous.

"You said you wanted to see me. What are you going to do about that?" I asked a fairly simple question.

Don relaxed. By now, he had already figured out, more or less, where my twisted mind was leading this conversation … and where it was all headed. And he could see I was in pretty good control, all things considered.

"What do you want me to do?" she responded.

"If you want to see me, something's going to have to change. Unless there's been some kind of a miracle, I remain *persona non grata* amongst your parent-types," I concluded.

"Just my mother," she said. "My father thinks you are something special. And so do I."

"So, what are you going to do about it?" I repeated.

"I'll be living in a sorority house in a couple of weeks. You can call me there and we can go out again."

This time she was sure she had the answer, and her dazzling pearly-whites broke all radiance records. Pepsodent would have called in camera crews, on the spot, if they had seen her.

I swallowed, hard. Twice.

"No, Lee, I can't do that. That would be too dishonest, even for me, going behind your mother's back."

"She would never know. I'm afraid she's going to try to arrange a marriage for me with some foreigner. Or maybe even a New Yorker."

She actually looked frightened. Like a big-eyed doe, frozen by your headlights at night.

"My question stands, Lee. What are you going to do about it? Are you going to let your mother run your life, or are you going to tell her it's time she backed off and let you run your own life?" I was speaking harsh words, but gently. And softly. I wanted to challenge her, but I had no wish to be cruel.

"I don't know. I'm so confused."

She was going to try her poor-little-confused-girl gambit. I wouldn't bite. I had sworn never to fall for that trick again.

Instead, I took the initiative.

"Tell you what," I offered. "I'd really like to see you, too. I've missed you more than you could ever believe. Hop in my new little green sports car, there, and I'll drive you home. We'll tell your mom to piss off. We're going to be inseparable once again."

I thought Don was going to gag. Or maybe even throw up on my shoes.

She looked at me. She looked at my new little BRG Austin-Healey. She tossed her always-shiny hair. And then looked back at me with real tears in her eyes.

"I can't fight my mother in the open," she said. "I can't even fight her with you holding my hand, although that's the nicest, most gentlemanly offer I have ever heard. But I still want to see you. Without her knowing it, which you won't do. I'm so confused."

I believed she really was, but she seemed to still lack the will to fight her mother and to help herself.

"I want to be with you," she sounded almost mournful, "but I can't. What am I going to do?"

Tears were rolling. Mascara was running. Makeup base was dripping down onto her fetchingly scanty little designer playsuit.

She repeated, almost forlornly, "What am I going to do?"

Now there are precious few times in your life when the gods take hold of you and cause you to be rational, realistic, and honest with yourself and everybody else.

Maybe even a tad flamboyant.

At that moment, I was so seized. A stranger's voice was coming out of me. It was saying out loud, matter-of-factly, with sincerity and not a trace of a smirk, "Frankly, my dear, I don't give a damn."

Don Hickling and Rhett Butler climbed into that new, shiny, British Racing Green Austin-Healey, fired her up, backed her out, and drove slowly away, like Shane riding into the sunset.

Don looked up. "You know what?" he said, smiling his most gracious and satisfied grin, "You just grew up!"

I replied, tears welling up in my eyes and a huge lump in my throat, "Thanks. It was simple."

Life's Lessons Learned:

- *Good humor and love, even feigned in exaggeration, will get you out of more scrapes than honesty or money. Or even a good lawyer.*
- *Give the beautiful leopard a chance to change her spots. If she doesn't, or can't, stay the heck away from her. Or you may end up as road-kill.*
- *Growing up takes a while. But, in the end, it's pretty simple.*

Epilogue

FREDERICKSBURG, 2002

In spite of our early and nonstop penchant for mischief, each member of the little group of *In-Betweeners,* who took no prisoners while growing up in Austin during the 1950s, seems to have turned out okay.

At least, so far, anyway.

DON HICKLING interrupted his college years with a tour in the U.S. Navy as an electronics technician. He returned to The University of Texas at Austin and earned his B.S. degree in electrical engineering. For the past thirty years, he has lived in the Gulf Coast areas of Texas and Louisiana, working in supervisory and management positions for Texaco, Bentley-Nevada, and Houston Industries. Currently, he is semi-retired, teaching algebra in a suburban Houston high school and adult religion classes at his church. He and his wife, Mary, have two grown children and two grandchildren.

JACK CLAGETT finished his degree at UT and immediately was drafted. After a stint in the U.S. Army, where he did not go to Vietnam only because his brother, Billy, was already serving there, he returned to Austin. Jack (Felix) and Don (Oscar)—the *real* Odd Couple—were roommates during Don's last two years of college. Jack has remained in Austin all these years and recently retired as head of information systems for the Texas Parks and Wildlife Department. He takes on an occasional consulting

ICE DOWN THE GRAPETTES

Forty years after high school, our little group of creative pranksters still gets together to plot yet more ongoing mischief. Left to right, in 2001—Susan Clagett, Jack Clagett, Mary Arnold, Don Hickling, Mary Hickling, George Arnold, Martha Bailey, Andy Bailey.

project. He is treasurer of his church in Austin. His wife, Susan, is a career administrator at The University of Texas at Austin. They have no children.

ANDY BAILEY also went into the U.S. Navy, where he was trained as an air traffic controller, a job he took back with him to the Dallas/Fort Worth regional FAA center in civilian life, only to be fired by Ronald Reagan in the great ATC purge of the early 1980s. He then worked for the Internal Revenue Service. He and his wife, Martha, have five grown children. Andy lost his battle with cancer in June 2002.

KENNY SQUIER, after college, remained in the movie exhibition business with Santikos Theatres in San Antonio, originators of the multi-screen movie house concept. He later became an entrepreneur, founding, managing, and selling several businesses in the Austin area. Currently, he is a management recruiter and cooking up another potential business venture. He and his wife, Judy, have five children and four grandchildren.

JIM ARNOLD, my older brother and would-be murderer, finished his college degree at The University of Texas at Austin and went into the navy as an officer-aviator. He recently retired as a senior captain following thirty-plus years with United Airlines, flying everything from the DC-6 to 747s. He and his wife, Barbara (daughter of Mr. Colonel Sinclair, the geometry teacher) have two grown daughters and five grandchildren.

MARY SHAW, my younger sister, has been married to a good guy from (gasp) Oklahoma for about thirty-five years. He is now retired from the electric utility generation business, and she's running a suburban branch bank for, I think, Giganty Cass Bancorp. They have two grown sons and three grandchildren. She is still pretty funny. But she no longer smells like Johnson's baby powder.

My father, **JAMES R. ARNOLD,** died of complications following completely unnecessary elective surgery in 1991, at the age of seventy-seven. His tendency to perfectionism did him in.

My mother, **MARY V. ARNOLD,** is in her mid-eighties. She is a retired nurse, having started her career in health care at the age of fifty. I have had a lot of fun needling her in this book. After first becoming indignant and denying anything and everything in the manuscript, she has become a good sport and even admits

WAIT FOR US!

Kenny and Judy Squier, 2001. Kenny's the one with the goatee. Judy's the good-looking one without a cap.

she might have actually tried to enroll me at the Deaf School. She still has wool-covered eyes when it comes to the kind of sons she raised. And, like her whole generation, she's mostly preoccupied with "what the neighbors will think," even though she doesn't know most of them. It is her fervent hope that Billy Graham never reads this book.

Go figure.

In a worldwide search that began in Buenos Aires, Argentina, we found **LEE LANKFORD** in, of all places, Houston, where she is a very successful practicing artist and teacher of languages. She has a daughter and a son, both grown, is married, and seems to be reasonably happy.

After forty years, I'm still trying to convince myself that I don't much give a damn.

Special Thanks

I wish to express special thanks to a group of very special people who read my manuscript and responded with suggestions, corrections, and great ideas for making the book better. I am indebted to each of them.

Members of the Great Depression Generation:
Richard Brown, Dallas, retired public relations executive
Jeanette Smith, Dallas, author; retired public relations practitioner
Bill Aston, Dallas, retired utility company chief executive
Wayne Massey, Fredericksburg, retired Marine officer/home builder
Jack Matthews, Fredericksburg, retired U.S. attorney
Jim Arnold, St. Petersburg, retired airline captain
Barbara Arnold, St. Petersburg, sailor; yacht racer

Baby Boomers:
Marilyn Pippin, Dallas, public relations executive
Bert Miller, Jr., Houston, certified financial planner
Barbara Ivancich, Seattle, accounting supervisor
Deborah Arnold, Cincinnati, elementary schoolteacher
Steve Dodd, Phoenix, real estate broker

Generation X'ers:
Christopher Shaw, Dallas, telecommunications consultant

Margery Arnold, Ph.D., Boston, psychologist
Lara Nieto, Albuquerque, public relations practitioner

In-Betweeners:
Michelle Waring, Seattle, accounting systems supervisor
Nancy Golden, Fredericksburg, small business owner
Sam Golden, Fredericksburg, rancher; retired CEO
Camey Stewart, Fredericksburg, rancher
Marion Woodfield, Seattle, assistant controller
Sherry McDonnell, Houston, public relations practitioner
Mick Cummins, San Francisco, retired advertising executive
Mary Arnold, Fredericksburg, rancher/horse breeder

Principal In-Betweeners:
Don Hickling, Houston, retired engineer/algebra teacher
Jack Clagett, Austin, retired computer systems executive
Andy Bailey, Dallas, Internal Revenue Service agent
Kenny Squier, Austin, management recruiter; entrepreneur
Lee Lankford, Houston, artist; language and writing teacher

These special people have been of immense help to me. Any mistakes in the book that are not deliberate are mine, alone. Of course, if you find a mistake, I'll tell you it was deliberate.
That's the *In-Betweener* way.

—GEORGE ARNOLD
2002

About the Author

George Arnold was born in Missouri but grew up in Texas. He attended public schools in Uvalde (very briefly), San Antonio, Waco, and Austin. He was eight years old in 1950 and eighteen years old in 1960. As one of the *In-Betweeners,* he grew up, simply, in the simple 1950s.

He holds bachelor of journalism and master of arts in communication degrees, with honors, from the School of Communication at The University of Texas at Austin.

His thirty-two-year career was spent entirely in the marketing/advertising/public relations business. From 1977 through 1998, he was president of one of the more creative advertising and public relations firms in Dallas, from which he retired at the end of 1998.

He and Mary, his wife of almost forty years, have four grown children and two granddaughters. They live on a small ranch just outside Fredericksburg in the Texas Hill Country, where they raise registered Half-Arabian horses, coastal Bermuda grass hay, BB English red bantams, cats, dogs, geese, and invisible goats.